THE RELATIONSHIP EDGE

THE KEY TO STRATEGIC INFLUENCE AND SELLING SUCCESS

THIRD EDITION

Jerry Acuff
with **Wally Wood**

WILEY

John Wiley & Sons, Inc.

Published by John Wiley & Sons, Inc., Hoboken, New Jersey.
Published simultaneously in Canada.

For general information on our other products and services or for technical support,
please contact our Customer Care Department within the United States at
(800) 762-2974, outside the United States at (317) 572-3993 or fax (317) 572-4002.

Wiley also publishes its books in a variety of electronic formats. Some content that
appears in print may not be available in electronic books. For more information about
Wiley products, visit our web site at www.wiley.com.

ISBN 978-0-470-91547-9 (paper); ISBN 978-1-118-01653-4 (ebk);
ISBN 978-1-118-01654-1 (ebk); ISBN 978-1-118-01655-8 (ebk)

Printed in the United States of America.

SKY10032984_020122

CONTENTS

PREFACE

This book originally came about because a group vice president at Pfizer asked me to give some thought to ways sales representatives could spend more time with their customers.

In the pharmaceutical industry, salespeople typically spend only two to three minutes actually talking to a doctor. What can you say in that time? "HiI'mJerryAcuffandIwanttotellyouallaboutournew drug...." It's not very effective. I thought there had to be some way that sales representatives could spend more quality time with prospects, customers, and colleagues.

Thinking about Pfizer's challenge on the plane home, I thought about the unpublished book that my friend Peter Ciano and I wrote. We called it *What Momma Never Taught You* and we included short chapters on life's great truths—including "If They Like You, You Have a Shot."

Our premise in that chapter was that the quality and richness of our relationships determine in many ways the quality and richness of our lives, both professionally and personally. The more great relationships we have, the more fulfilled we are. Strong relationships are not the only measure of success and happiness, but they certainly help determine our success and happiness.

That caused me to think about the kinds of relationships you could have with another human being. It seems to me there are six possibilities, from people who do not even know your name to those who value a close, personal relationship with you. It was obvious that as you move through these six relationship levels, you have fewer and fewer relationships at the higher levels. Hence, a Relationship Pyramid is formed, with big numbers at the bottom and small numbers at the top.

I told the Pfizer executive what I believed: If you enhance the relationship, customers will give you more time. Of course, if you offer something unique and interesting to customers, they will also give you more time. The problem with the second strategy is that as soon as you've given them something unique and interesting, you're back looking for something else unique and interesting. I wouldn't reject that strategy, but I wouldn't rely on it. On the other hand, if you are at the top of someone's Relationship Pyramid, he or she will spend time with you because they value the relationship.

I assumed that somebody had already answered the question of how to actually build a strong, positive relationship; perhaps in Dale Carnegie's *How to Win Friends and Influence People*; Les Giblin's *How to Have Confidence and Power in Dealing with People*; Nicholas Boothman's *How to Make People Like You in 90 Seconds or Less*; or Leil Lowndes's *How to Be a People Magnet*.

I studied these and every other book that seemed to promise an answer. The books are full of good, solid advice. They all say you have to be other-focused. They all say you have to learn what your customers want. They all say you have to do things for customers. Their suggestions are, for the most part, unimpeachable.

But they do not offer a specific, concrete relationship-building process, so I created one and you now hold a description of it with suggestions on how to make the most of it.

The process is, as you will see, one that virtually anyone can use. You need not be gregarious, outgoing, and extraverted to be great at building relationships. You do not have to be a salesperson, a manager, or even, for that matter, in business.

You *do* have to believe that relationships are important. You do have to learn what interests other people. And if you do the inexpensive, unexpected, and thoughtful acts that show your professionalism, integrity, caring, and knowledge, you will be successful.

Companies did not teach relationship-building in the past because the ideas were neither actionable nor measurable. The process I describe here is both actionable and measurable. It's not perfect, and it does not work with everyone (but then, what does?), and you don't have any idea how long it will take with any given individual. So it should come as no surprise that building a positive relationship is like every other people skill—dating and parenting, as two other examples.

This is the third edition of *The Relationship Edge*. The process I developed has hardly changed, but the technology and the social media available have changed dramatically. Sites like LinkedIn, Twitter, Facebook, YouTube, and dozens of others mean that you have opportunities to identify and connect with people in ways that simply were not possible when this book was first published.

Because relationship-building is a process with specific, concrete steps, almost everyone can learn it. If you consciously practice the strategies this book teaches, you will find yourself at the top of the Relationship Pyramid with many more people than you are today. And once there, I trust you will find—as I have—a richer, happier, and more enjoyable life.

ACKNOWLEDGMENTS

Writing a book, I have discovered, is the personification of team effort. It may begin with ideas and concepts, but it will never become a reality without the unselfish help and support of many, many people. With that in mind, I want to record for posterity many of the people who made this book possible.

First, I must acknowledge Wally Wood for working with me over all these months to take my ideas (and many of his) and write them in a way that makes me very proud. Wally will always be at the top of my Relationship Pyramid. Second, I must thank Wally's wife, Marian Wood, for her support and contributions to the book and her willingness to do whatever we needed to make the book better. Mary Maki had the arduous task of trying to decipher my English in order to create the transcripts that Wally and I worked from. The people at John Wiley & Sons did what publishers do. Shannon Vargo, though, has helped shape this book and my thinking about the ideas in this book and I am grateful for her honesty, insight, and guidance. She is at the top of my Pyramid.

Many people agreed to be interviewed and have their stories told, and it is their stories that make the concepts come alive. To everyone we write about, thank you for being a very important part of this book.

Since this book is the result of all my experiences and learnings over the years, I must take this opportunity to thank and acknowledge those whose guidance, support, and relationships with me have shaped who I am and what I believe.

My father, Gerald Sr., and my brothers and sisters (Jan, Jude, Joanne, and Tracey) have been a source of support and love and learning that have enriched me beyond words. My children, Laura and Ryan, inspire me and humble me and I am honored to be their Dad. My wife, Maryann, is the nicest person I ever met and an incredible life partner. Her love, support, and advice in many ways made this book possible and as an editor, mother, and partner she may be without equal. Joan and Mike Molocznik deserve special mention for all they have done to help my family, my business, and me. All in-laws should be modeled after Joanie and Mike, and their son and my brother-in-law Michael is the best.

There are a number of people who touched my life in ways they may not even know, realize, or understand, but without them I am not who or what I am today. Bud Garrett, my junior high school coach, is the greatest builder of people I met in the first 25 years of my life. Jim Crutchfield, Gene Vezina, and Don Cutcliff were my first three bosses—the best trio of business leaders and motivators a person could ever work for. For 14 years, I learned at their feet, and all three know how to bring out greatness in others. Their lasting influence on me is immeasurable. My first sales district, The Generals (John Fuqua, Frank Tortorici, Bonita Crowe, Van Walker, Vikki Thomas, Danny Craven, Pat Kelly, Brenda Scott, David Snow, Mike Northington, Wyatt Wilson, Chris Free, Joey Smelser, Debra Hulett, Sarah Tant, and Ed Cannon). Working with these people over eight years was the best working experience of my life and I will always be a General. A special note must be written about John Fuqua, my first hire. He has been my close friend for 23 years and he taught me more about building business relationships than any other single person. He is what this book is about and it is why he is such an extraordinary salesperson and sales manager.

I also want to thank a few of my clients, who have not only helped me learn and grow but who have impacted me professionally and personally. David Snow, Mike Tilton, Jesus Leal, Gary Casto, Mike Weber, Clarissa Etter-Smith, Dave Bonnell, Frank Amato,

ACKNOWLEDGMENTS

Lori Tierney, and Joe Canning are at the top of my Relationship Pyramid and their leadership wisdom inspires me. To Peter Ciano, my great friend, thank you for your friendship and for writing with me *What Mamma Never Taught You*. The chapter in that unpublished book is what started all of this. To Mark Cohen, my best friend of 25 years, I owe so much. He naturally builds relationships as well as anyone on the planet. He and Lynne have been so supportive and helpful and have encouraged me at all the right times. Mark is integrity personified, and anyone who knows him knows that Mark is the quintessential gentleman.

The final acknowledgment goes to my alma mater, the Virginia Military Institute (VMI). It was a great experience to attend a school with great teachers, John G. Barrett, especially, and great people (my roommates, Tommy Lawson, Mike Strickland, Mark Palmer, and Ken Coleman). It was there I met "Rooster" (Jim Westbrook) and "Aragon" (Dick Randolph)—two cadets who would become lifelong friends as my roommates have. It was there that I learned the power of friendship, relationships, learning, and striving. It was at VMI that I learned "You may be whatever you resolve to be." If you resolve to be an author and you are blessed by God to have great family, friends, business associates, and teachers, you can do just that.

I thank you all.

CHAPTER 1

RELATIONSHIPS ARE EVERYTHING

We all would like an edge in life, a quality or factor that makes us superior in performance, in ability, in achievement. Strong, positive relationships with other people—associates, superiors, customers, family members, and casual acquaintances—give us that edge. When I ask seminar groups, "How important are relationships in your business?" most answer, "Relationships are everything" or "Nothing is more important." It's hardly news that your relationships—positive or negative—affect your business and personal life profoundly.

What *is* news these days, however, is that the way we establish, build, and maintain relationships is being affected in a big way by social media—LinkedIn, Facebook, Twitter, and scores of other sites.

True, you cannot put up a LinkedIn or Facebook profile and expect positive relationships to follow automatically. You have to do a lot more work. On the other hand, if you expect to increase and improve your business relationships, you cannot ignore social media or underestimate the importance of technology and the role it will play in relationship development from now on. Your presence on the Web doesn't have to be major (although that wouldn't hurt), but you have to be there. In today's world you need these three things: a process to build a positive relationship, a meaningful presence on the

Web, and a mastery of how best to use technology to build, maintain, and leverage relationships.

And not just any relationship. The whole idea of the Relationship Edge process is to help you connect with people with whom you don't naturally connect. You don't need this process to build relationships with people you naturally connect with because the process happens instantaneously and without effort. But when you don't naturally connect with somebody—a prospect, a customer, a colleague, a manager—that's when you need a process in order to increase the likelihood that you *will* connect.

Based on my experience and very informal research, many of us are able to connect naturally with something like 25 out of 100 people. If you use this process, you may be able to increase that to 40 or 50 out of 100, a huge success. The real value in the Relationship Edge process is having a systematic way to engage with people with whom we don't naturally connect—people we meet for the first time, people we don't know well, and people we haven't connected with in the past. Because nothing is more important than positive relationships in your business life (or personal life, for that matter), and having a solid process you can count on to establish, build, and maintain relationships is invaluable.

BREATHE AIR INTO RELATIONSHIPS

Before I talk about the process you can use to build a relationship with virtually anyone, however, I should define what I mean by a valuable business relationship. I contend it's those that have lots of AIR—Access, Impact, and Results.

By "Access" I mean that when you have a valuable business relationship with people, they will take your calls, they will answer your messages, they will see you because they believe there's a value in doing so. They believe time spent with you will not be wasted. They believe you offer more than idle chatter. You are a source of news, information, ideas, suggestions, possibilities, options, contacts, insights, skills, abilities, experiences, or all of the above. At the same time, they see you as an exceptional listener; you pay attention to what they say, ask questions, and demonstrate that you've heard and understand them. They may not respond to you or see you immediately because of the urgent pressures or realities in their lives, but they *will* see you.

Of course, many people will see you, in either a business or in a selling situation, but at their convenience. They will see anybody else as well for the reasons I just listed, but they do not regard you as special and you may have to wait until it suits their schedule, which may be in a week or in a month. You do not, by my definition, have Access. When you say you have Access to somebody, it means that if you need him (or her), you are 100 percent certain you can reach him in a reasonable time.

"Impact" means you have an opportunity to affect those people you reach and influence their actions. When you have a valuable business relationship with people, you believe—based on their behavior and your past experience—that they are going to listen to what you say, and that what you say can, and often will, influence their actions. Not every time, but whenever it makes sense to them and the action is one that will benefit them.

But even when the transaction is more abstract—you bring new information, no money changes hands—there can be value. The information helps your client do a better job, stay abreast of industry trends, be alert to new possibilities.. . .something

And what do you get out of it? An improved relationship and an opportunity to return in the future.

Finally, "Results" is the most important part of the acronym. Many people say to me, "I have a great relationship with so-and-so." But when I probe, I discover that what they have is a good rapport. They have a pleasant friendship. They don't have a valuable *business* relationship.

When we have valuable business relationships with people, they are doing things proactively to help us succeed. (Note, by the way, that this applies to our relationship with team members, colleagues, and employees; I am not talking in this book about only salespeople and customers.) The results from those activities should be materially greater than what you get from people with whom you don't have a valuable business relationship. Moreover, they should be measurable.

For example, I once called on a Birmingham physician who did not treat the kind of patients who needed the pharmaceutical I was selling. I could not, therefore, use sales results with this doctor as a barometer of success because he wasn't prescribing what I sold. What I *could* use, however, was how he proactively helped me succeed. He introduced me to almost every physician in Birmingham who was important for me to meet, who *did* treat patients who needed our medication but who would not ordinarily spend time seeing pharmaceutical salespeople. That was a measurable result of my success with him and proof that he valued a relationship with me.

All salespeople have examples of customers with whom they've built relationships, customers who buy their product or service because they find value in the relationship. But there can be valuable business relationships where the results are not as easily measured as units or dollars.

I am going to assume throughout this book that most customers have options among products and services. These may not be exact equivalents in features, benefits, and price, but they are close enough that a salesperson's knowledge, empathy, and assistance can highlight the differences between one offering and another to the benefit of one he or she is selling.

I often hear sales executives say, "Well, my sales rep has a great relationship with this customer, but they're not using any of our stuff." Or "They're not using much of our stuff."

I always say, "Then the rep doesn't have a valuable business relationship."

Time after time, when I force salespeople to look at their relationships through this prism, they replace "I have great relationships with 50, 60, 70 percent of my customers" with "I have great relationships with maybe 10 or 15 percent."

The point here is that if you don't know your destination, you don't know when you've arrived. You need to know what you're looking for in a valuable business relationship. Because if you think you have a great relationship with people but it lacks Access, Impact, and Results, it's not a relationship they truly value. Without AIR, things you do with them and for them are probably not going to be very effective.

LEARN TO BUILD RELATIONSHIPS

Relationships are the basic unit of every business—positive relationships with customers, employees, and suppliers. A business grows as it adds positive relationships, improves its network of relationships, and then enhances the quality of those relationships. Without positive relationships, a business will not grow. Obviously some businesses (management consultants, accountants, lawyers) depend more heavily on personal relationships with their customers than others (discount chains, self-serve gas stations, and direct marketing firms). Nonetheless, relationships with other people are critical to every business. (Ask Walmart's management whether relationships with employees and suppliers are important.)

As an individual, you grow in your career as you expand and improve your network of relationships with co-workers, managers, customers, and prospects. If you are a project manager or work in a cross-functional team, you probably have much responsibility but little authority. You can do your job well only through your relationships with others in the organization. If those relationships are strong and positive, you can be effective. If those relationships are indifferent or, worse, negative, you can't get anything done.

If you have superior relationships with key business contacts—customers, co-workers, and managers—you will, almost automatically, be more successful in your business life, assuming you know how to nurture and leverage those relationships. Certainly the converse is true: When you have poor relationships with customers, co-workers, and managers, your business life suffers (not to mention your personal life).

The key words here are *consciously*, *systematically*, and *routinely*. Building business relationships that last is a skill anyone can learn. It requires a process you can master, since you already know instinctively what the process requires. Adopt the simple steps this book will teach you, and your business and personal relationships will improve.

I've seen it happen hundreds of times with people I have managed and counseled.

The three steps in the process, which I'll describe in the chapters ahead, are:

1. *Have the right mind-set.* You must think that relationships are important. You must believe you are someone with whom other people would want to have a relationship. Why? Because you have experience, training, skills, abilities, knowledge, other relationships (or all six) they value. You must also think well of others and learn to think as much as you can from the other person's point of view.

2. *Ask the right questions.* You must also ask them in the right way for the right reasons. In a later chapter, you will find specific questions and the principles behind them. The goal is to discover common ground—mutual friends, interests, or concerns. Or if there is no obvious common ground and the other person cares passionately for something about which you know little, the goal is to learn from him or her.

3. *Do the right thing.* Demonstrate your professionalism, integrity, caring, and knowledge, and, when appropriate, do inexpensive, unexpected, and thoughtful acts based on what you've learned about the other person. This process may be simple in outline, but it takes weeks or even months of thought and care to apply it properly.

Why bother to improve your relationships? The cold, hard truth is that the quality of our personal and professional relationships in many ways determines the quality of our lives. Not in every way, of course, but in many. The more high-quality personal and professional relationships we have, the more easily we will sell our products, our ideas, ourselves—and the more rewarding, fulfilling, and successful our lives tend to be. The ability to build and maintain high-quality business relationships has no down side and an up side that knows no limits. Take Mike Accardi, a friend of mine from high school.

PAYBACK TIME IN MEMPHIS

Mike has been a commissioned salesman for Wurzburg, Inc., a pack-aging supply distributor in Memphis, Tennessee, for many years. Although he is now very successful, it was not always that way. Two months after he started working for the company, the Accardi family's kitchen blender broke. "We were dirt poor," says Mike. "We couldn't afford a new blender, so I told my wife, I go out to this area of town every Tuesday where there's a Sunbeam/Oster repair shop."

The older gentleman at the shop said he could repair the blender, and Mike explained that because he was in the area every Tuesday he'd pick it up on his next run. The following Tuesday, the blender was ready and the bill was $2.50. Mike could not believe the repair cost so little, but the man said it was no big deal. Mike recalls saying, "Sir, you don't understand how big a deal it is to me to have this repaired. I can pay you the $2.50, and I appreciate it. But I tell you what, I don't know if you do any packaging or shipping out of here, but let me return the favor. If you ever need anything, call me and I'll see that you don't pay list price."

Mike began stopping by the shop the second Tuesday of every month just to say hello and visit for a bit. Mike knew that the business would never be a major customer, but he enjoyed building the relationship. Over the next two years, the man ordered perhaps a case of tape, two cases of padded envelopes, and a few bundles of 25 boxes. One Tuesday the man asked, "Do you have a few minutes today?" Mike said, "Sure. I come here to give you my time. I have as much time as you need."

"Let's get in your car. I want to show you something." They drove to the northern part of the city as Mike asked, "Where are we going?"

"Don't worry about it, I want to show you something." They pulled into the parking lot of what was to become a million-square-foot building. Mike asked, "What is this?"

"This is payback."

"What are you talking about?"

"For two years, you're the only salesperson that's treated me like I was worth anything. Now it's payback. Sunbeam's headquarters in

Chicago is closing, and they're moving everything here. So get your business cards and come with me." He took Mike to every department, and said, "This is Mike Accardi. You buy all your packaging supplies from him."

Until Sunbeam left Memphis 12 years later, Mike had enough orders to deliver a 40-foot trailer of packaging supplies every week. Mike's customers were so loyal to him that when his competitors asked to speak to someone about Sunbeam's packaging needs, the Sunbeam people would give them Mike's card. When a competitor asked, "What's this?" Mike's customers would say, "You want to talk to whoever handles our packaging."

The salespeople would then say something like, "No, no, you don't understand. That's our competitor."

And Mike's customers would respond with something like, "No, *you* don't understand. That's who handles our packaging. If you have an idea, give it to him and he'll bring it to us."

When Sunbeam left Memphis, the department heads, assistants, and janitors found new jobs, but Mike maintained the relationships he'd built. Although in the metropolitan area accounts generally go to the salesperson who develops the business, former Sunbeam executives would call Mike's company to say, "Tell Accardi to come see me at this new business." On occasion, this has meant strained relations with Mike's friends in his own company. Other salespeople have lost accounts because a customer insisted, "I'm not going to deal with anybody other than Mike Accardi."

RELATIONSHIPS CAN TRUMP PRICE

Not only can the Relationship Edge help you build your career, it can help you keep the business you now have. Take Bob Holman's experience.

Bob is president of Donaldson, Holman & West, PC, a firm of certified public accountants in Birmingham, Alabama. Several years ago, one of the firm's staff accountants left to join the local branch of a larger, international CPA firm. Following normal procedure, the firm's management asked their new employee about the substantial, profitable DH&W clients with whom she had worked with an eye toward soliciting their business. Armed with the information, the former employee and her new employer visited one large DH&W client and reportedly said in effect, "As an international organization, we can give you the same or better service than you've been getting, *and* for the next three years we'll provide that service at 75 percent of what you are paying now. We will give you that as a guarantee. And of course you will have the same person working on your account who already knows your business."

The client immediately responded with something like, "Thank you very much. That's very enticing. However, we have a good relationship with our current CPA firm and money is not an issue. Service is important, and we're getting the service we want, so we're not interested in changing."

Bob says that in the world of accounting and the way accountants often seem to compete on price, "It really rang the bell for me how important the relationship is."

I asked Bob what he thought his client had been talking about, since every CPA—and certainly a large, international firm—offers "service."

"I think it was a combination of things," he says. "We were not only doing traditional services for them—tax and audit services—but they were relying on us more or less as a consultant to them in various areas. I don't want to say that we were going so far as to be on their management team; we were not. But it was very seldom they made a large decision or sometimes even minor decisions without consulting us. We did not socialize with the management there a lot, but they knew we were available, knew we were interested in what they were doing and how they were doing it. We spoke almost every week. They knew we were interested in them personally and knew their families, knew where their kids were in school, and we talked about those things." In other words, Donaldson, Holman & West were not only professional accountants, they had the Relationship Edge.

Finally, while building strong business relationships is not the same as making friends—the point here is to improve your professional life, not your personal—it can lead to building true, long-lasting friendships.

John Fuqua, an area sales manager in Birmingham for the pharmaceutical company Aventis, told me that building relationships has helped him not only monetarily, but "the fun part of selling anything is when the customer becomes your friend. I have been asked to do a number of things at a personal level I would not have been asked to do if I hadn't been a friend as well as being a person who happens to sell something customers like and recommend. I've been in weddings. I've been a pallbearer at funerals. I've been asked to do talks at their children's schools. It's a great feeling to know I can pick up the phone and reach someone even though they are busy people." Which illustrates Access in addition to John's friendship.

FOUR FUNDAMENTAL SELLING TRUTHS

Selling is part of life. I use "selling" here and throughout this book in its broadest possible sense. "Selling" includes not only convincing a prospect or customer to buy your firm's product or service, but also persuading a manager that your idea is valuable. It includes everything from influencing a client to adopt a new service policy to bringing a co-worker around to your viewpoint. Whether you call it selling, persuasion, convincing, or teaching, really successful people in almost any endeavor rely on it to achieve their goals (which I also talk about in this book).

Consider these four fundamental truths about selling.

1. *Without meaningful dialogue there is no selling.* There may be buying, but there is no selling. Selling requires a significant exchange between two parties that is rooted in the truth. The buyer has needs, wants, desires. The seller has a solution—a product, a service, an idea, a suggestion. The buyer and seller must communicate so they both understand the need (which, initially, may not even be clear to the buyer) and how the product meets that need. Good relationships facilitate meaningful dialogue.

2. *Where trust and rapport are strong, selling pressure will always seem weak.*[1] If buyers believe the seller has their best interests at heart (always understanding there is something in the exchange for the seller), they listen to the seller's suggestions and ideas with an open mind. Good relationships build trust and rapport.

3. *Where trust and rapport are weak, any selling pressure will appear strong.* This perception of pressure, which tends to grow out of distrust, will have a negative effect on sales. A buyer who believes the seller cares only for his or her own interests will be skeptical, even hostile. Poor rapport can mean that instead of two colleagues trying to solve a mutual problem, it will be a cynical seller trying to selfishly foist something onto a gullible buyer. Even if the seller's solution is appropriate and worthy, it becomes impossible to convince a hostile or indifferent buyer. Good relationships minimize the negativity in a selling situation.

4. *The more you learn from customers, clients, and co-workers, the more likely you are to have positive personal relationships with them.* The better the personal relationship, the greater the trust and rapport between people.

Think of your own experiences. Have you ever walked away from a sales situation—a car dealership or an appliance showroom—because you just did not trust the salesperson? Conversely, have you ever bought something because a friend recommended it? It felt nothing like sales pressure (your friend was not working for the seller and earned no commission), but she persuaded you. She sold you.

Have you ever recommended something to a friend—a book, a movie, a gadget—because you knew your friend's tastes and interests and, therefore, had a good idea of what to suggest? Having learned over time to trust your recommendations, your friend picked up the book, went to the movie, bought the gadget. You sold her.

Your goal is to have strong, positive personal relationships with the key people in your business life because they can help you be more effective in selling or persuading. These key people may be customers, clients, co-workers, managers, suppliers, or someone else.

Because your situation is unique, of course, you will have to decide who those key figures are. And while it's not possible to have a strong relationship—one that requires the investment in time and concentration this book prescribes—with every single person in your business life, knowing and applying what you learn here can be the difference between extraordinary success and something much less.

MEANINGFUL DIALOGUE COMES WITH TRUST

In a solid personal relationship, trust and rapport are strong. And where trust and rapport are present, you can have *meaningful dialogue*. And what do I mean by meaningful dialogue?

In a meaningful dialogue both parties speak the truth. The participants talk about what is real, important, and factual. Relationships and companies are too often ruined because people can't get at the truth. It's been written that customers reveal only 20 percent of what they are thinking in a normal sales interaction. They may not actively lie, but they evade, shade, and spin. However, the more truth customers or colleagues are comfortable sharing with you about their problems and concerns, the more likely you and they will be able to solve their problems—if a solution exists.

If potential customers will not share with you the problems they face in their business lives, how can you possibly help solve them? If they will not tell you what they honestly think about your company, your products, and your service, what is the likelihood you can do business with them? (The answer: Very little.)

I find that too many salespeople do not even address this issue. Indeed, some sales executives say in effect, "You're out there to sell, not to make friends." Their salespeople do not make it a priority to build personal relationships or to establish a dialogue. Rather, they use what little time they have to tell prospects about their product or service and then leave. They give a monologue and feel they've accomplished their goal if they can make it to the pitch's end without interruption. At best, they only try to guess what prospects truly need.

If the salesperson knows enough about the industry, the prospect's business, and the competitive situation, the guess may be close to the reality. But it's still a guess and may be wildly wrong. Even if the guess is correct, if prospects don't recognize their need, they're not going to buy. Without a meaningful dialogue, prospects themselves may not understand the issues.

If you can't get customers to engage in a meaningful dialogue, to tell you the things that are really bothering them, there is little likelihood you will ever move them to your point of view. If you do not have a strong positive relationship, why should someone spend any more time than necessary listening to you? You will always be dealing with smoke and fog because you will not be able to uncover the truth. You end up giving a meaningless (to them) speech rather than having a meaningful conversation.

Accordingly, you want to strive for a better business relationship because it encourages meaningful dialogue. When you have a good relationship, the other person listens to you differently. He or she shares more openly. In a good relationship (think about your own good relationships, business or personal), when the other person talks, you pay attention. You are not immediately skeptical, looking for the hidden agenda, expecting a trick.

Similarly, you expect colleagues with whom you have a positive relationship to listen to you because they know they can trust what you say. They will give you the time to hear you out (usually). They expect you to tell the truth and want you to challenge them when you don't agree with or understand something they say—just as they feel free to question whatever you say.

Good business relationships will not do your selling or persuading for you. You still must explain the features and benefits, the service requirements, the contractual obligations, the time line, all the myriad details of the product or service or idea you're trying to sell. But a good relationship will allow you to get a fair hearing with a meaningful dialogue for your ideas, plans, and proposals. People who like, respect, and trust you want to hear what you have to say. Ultimately, they buy more or accept more because they listen differently—better, perhaps, or more profoundly—than when they are indifferent or hostile.

At the same time, because you're building a long-term relationship, you don't sell them something you know they cannot use or is inappropriate for their situation. You don't sell them something inappropriate even if your company has put an extra commission on the product to move it. You don't sell them something inappropriate even if you are one sale short of winning the "Salesman of the Quarter" plaque. Not even if this project will be the difference between making a profit for the year and breaking even.

You don't knowingly do something inappropriate unless you want to chip away at or destroy the trust and respect you've been able to build. You don't do it because it isn't right for the other person. It takes time and effort to reach the top of the Relationship Pyramid and you don't want to slide back down through one selfish or thoughtless act.

What, you ask, is a Relationship Pyramid? Good question. It's the subject of the next chapter.

CHAPTER 2

CLIMB THE RELATIONSHIP PYRAMID

The Relationship Pyramid, which illustrates the relationships you can have with another human being, has six levels (see Figure 2.1). The relationships form a Pyramid because a great many people, literally billions, form the base—the people who do not even know your name—and relatively few are at the peak—the people who truly value a relationship with you.

I'll talk in a moment about the levels and how you move from one to the next, but I should make it clear immediately that these levels are not always as precisely divided as the illustration makes them appear. While there's a clear demarcation between the bottom level and the first (someone either knows your name or doesn't), the five positive levels tend to shade into one another. The line between the people who like you and the people who are friendly with you, for example, is more like a gray area than a sharp division.

Another key point: Getting to the top of the Relationship Pyramid is a long-term proposition. Moving to the top of the Pyramid does not happen overnight. The only way to get people to respect you overnight is either you have some specialized and extraordinary knowledge that they respect when they first meet you or you do something so cataclysmic (such as pulling them from a burning building) it causes them to look at you differently. In day-to-day dealings,

Figure 2.1
The Relationship Pyramid

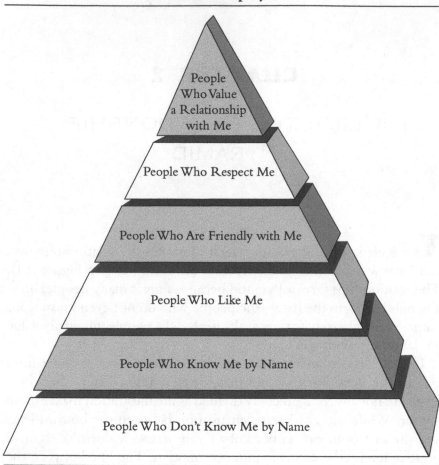

People Who Value a Relationship with Me

People Who Respect Me

People Who Are Friendly with Me

People Who Like Me

People Who Know Me by Name

People Who Don't Know Me by Name

you have to put in the time and effort to get someone to respect you or to value a relationship with you.

Finally, it is a lot easier to come down the Pyramid than to go up, which is another way of saying that it's a lot easier to lose someone's trust and respect than to earn it. It can take months to reach the top, but you can destroy someone's trust and respect overnight. If you say "We'll have it to you by next Friday," you'd better have it there by next Friday. If not, you risk losing some trust.

Interestingly, often you don't have to give next Friday as the deadline anyway. You could say Friday after next; the client does not care. But if you set your own deadline and then miss it, the client *will* care. If you can't do something when you say you'll do it, don't say you will. Whenever your actions are disconnected from your words (or your intentions), you lose respect. Once you have positive relationships, cherish them because you can ruin them very, very quickly.

If do you have a good relationship and are high on the Pyramid, you may be granted a greater degree of forgiveness when something *does* go wrong, as things almost inevitably do. Friends are more willing to forgive mistakes because they see them as anomalies, not patterns. For example, if someone doesn't know you well and you do not return a call, the person you've slighted may assume that is your pattern of behavior. If you have a good relationship with someone, however, and do not return a call, the person understands that is not your typical behavior and looks for another explanation. When you have a good relationship, you get more forgiveness.

Which suggests another important point: Many times you can dramatically improve your relationship by the way you handle adversity. You have said the product will be delivered on Friday, but through no fault of yours (there's a fire at the plant, a wildcat strike, the truck breaks down) you learn on Wednesday it will not make the deadline. The way you handle the situation to inform the customer promptly and make alternate arrangements can dramatically change the nature of your relationship for the better.

THE RELATIONSHIP PYRAMID LEVELS

At the bottom level are *the people who don't know you by name*. If you meet these people outside of the work environment, they may not recognize you, or may recognize you but will not know your name.

People who know you by name make up the level above the base. These people call you by name every time you see them in the office setting. Also, if you meet people you know at this basic level outside the work environment, they know who you are and remember your name.

People who like you. At this level, you've begun to have a positive relationship. You feel, based on some evidence, that these people are comfortable when you are around. They smile and acknowledge you when you arrive but don't spend much time in personal conversation. Talk focuses on business.

People who are friendly with you. At this level, you know and discuss routinely what is of special interest to the other person—hobbies, sports, books, movies, concerns. You have identified common interests and are beginning to share more personal information with each other on an ongoing basis.

People who respect you. This is based on what they say and how they treat you, not just how you feel about them. When you reach this level on the Pyramid, people see you differently than they see others in your position. For example, if you are in sales, they regard you as more than a "typical" sales person. If you are co-workers, they think of you as a true associate and collaborator. They view you as a person of integrity. They come to you for advice within your defined area of expertise, knowing that you will help if you can.

People who value a relationship with you. These are the relatively few people who come to you for advice or help in solving problems that are not necessarily within your defined area of expertise. When you are at the top of someone's Pyramid, your relationship has lots of AIR – Access, Impact, Results. These people will take your calls, listen to what you say, and act on it. They will gladly introduce you to a colleague with a recommendation. You share a level of mutual trust. You share knowledge and feel safe with each other. People who value a relationship with you believe it's in *their* best interest to have a relationship with you and will proactively help you succeed.

Advance to the Next Level

Moving from the bottom level—people who don't know you by name—is the easiest level to advance from and one of the most important. Everything starts to change when they know and remember who you are. If you call prospects, clients, co-workers by name every time you see them, they will (in most cases) become uncomfortable in not knowing your name and ultimately will reciprocate by learning it.

You can prompt the learning by offering a mnemonic trick that will help them remember. On meeting someone for the first time, writer Wally Wood introduces himself by saying, "I'm Wally Wood from Hollywood." People are more likely to remember that than a simple "Wally Wood." It also often leads to the question, "Are you really from Hollywood?" He's not, but it becomes a conversation starter. The point is: Make it easy for people to remember who you are.

In business, you ought to know someone's name immediately because it's on the office door, engraved on a nameplate on the desk, and, sometimes, printed on the nametag the person wears. The other person also ought to know yours, especially when you're wearing a visitor's tag and after you've exchanged cards. Nevertheless, the first step in building a business relationship is to have somebody not just look at your name but remember it. Always start by using the other person's name immediately. Here are some hints to help you remember the names of people you meet.

- Repeat the name when you meet the person.
- Think of this name as something important to remember (it usually is). If you tell yourself it's important to remember a name, you are more prone to focus and commit it to memory.
- When someone gives her (or his) name, try to think of something about that name that will help you remember it. You might verbalize the connection when meeting the person: "My best friend in grammar school was named Sue." Or you have an aunt named Sue who traveled all over the country. If you can't think of someone you know with a similar name, try to commit something to memory about the name: Richard—remembering this will help make you rich. Steven—even Steven—even you can remember the name Steven.
- If the name is unusual, ask how to spell it and write it down.

- Use the name in a sentence. "Sue, thank you so much for helping me understand." As soon as possible after the meeting, write down the person's name, what you talked about, and any distinguishing features that will help you remember that person the next time you meet: Glasses, mannerisms (does this person say "you know" often), accent.

- Record anything that distinguishes this person from others you may have met in the office.

To get people to remember your name, you need to share something about yourself. Perhaps the best way to do this is to first learn something personal about the other person. Express your interest in them—learn about who they are. Make the most of your time in their environment. When not actively engaged in talking with someone, be a detective. Look around the area to see if you can note any identifying signs. These may be pictures, art work or trophies, degrees or other certificates. If you see something interesting, think of a way to ask a sincere, meaningful question to gain further insight. If the person's work environment gives you no hint, or if you are in an impersonal conference room, ask one of the Link 20 questions I list in a chapter ahead, starting with "What do you do when you're not working?"

On to Level 2—People Who Know You by Name

When people call you by name, it makes you feel appreciated. The same is true for them. Calling someone by name distinguishes that person from other people. Knowing each other's names, however, is just the first step. Now you need to learn more about them. Start asking some of the Link 20 questions. Learn about the other people—especially what is going on in their day-to-day lives so when you see them next, you can ask about their kids, their pets, or their challenges. The goal here is to show them that they are important to you, which, of course, they are.

Level 3—People Who Like You

Generally, people tend to like people who take an interest in them. If you've asked someone a few of the Link 20 questions (and genuinely listened to the answers), it shows you're interested. Continue to show that interest.

Use the questions to learn more about them, perhaps things that few other people know—an interest in antique quilts, a collection of classic tin toys, private lessons on the dobro—and use this to build a bond.

Another alternative is to find out what is most challenging for them right now to see if you can offer some information that may be helpful—even if it's outside of your area of expertise. Perhaps you can relate a story of an experience you had or someone you know who went through a similar situation and dealt with it successfully.

The key is to build upon the knowledge you have developed about that person and to continue to think of ways you can provide value—either through your professional or personal connections. One good way to demonstrate your interest in another person is to ask simple follow-up questions the next time you see them. "How did your son's game turn out?" "Did your daughter get admitted to her first-choice college?"

Level 4—People Who Are Friendly with You

People who are friendly with you will start seeing you as a person outside of your professional role. You will find that you have common interests and can share conversations about those interests. They may chat about the football game or what you did last weekend or where they went on vacation. At this level you are establishing and sharing common interests and concerns, and you now can routinely talk about those concerns.

You may want to research and study information that relates to the other person's interest or concern and consider bringing it with you the next time you see that person. ("I thought you'd be interested in this CD of Mike Auldridge playing blues on dobro.") It's important to make sure that whatever you might bring into an office complies with company rules and industry guidelines. For example, if a person is interested in hiking, you may want to bring in some information about hiking groups or hiking trails in the area—an unexpected, inexpensive, and thoughtful act.

One thing to keep in mind is that you are developing business relationships, not friendships. When friendships do start to develop, keep in mind that this relationship has business as its foundation. Therefore, when you meet this person and start talking about personal things, plan ahead of time a way to segue to the business discussion so that you meet your business objectives.

Level 5—People Who Respect You

When you have reached this level, you have set yourself apart from almost everyone else. I'll be talking in detail later about respect and how to gain it, but for now I mean by "respect" what the dictionary defines as "esteem for or a sense of the worth or excellence of a person, a personal quality, or ability." If someone has a high opinion of your integrity, your knowledge, your courage, or all three, he or she respects you by definition.

Respect normally has to be earned. The exception is the respect you give someone due to their position. But that is respect of the title, not of the person. I am talking about personal respect. To earn someone's respect:

- Be genuinely interested in the other person.
- Fulfill commitments—do what you say when you say you will.
- Know when to contribute and when to be quiet. Contribute when you have something substantive to add to the discussion; by being quiet and listening, you are also contributing.
- Control your emotions—do not react in anger or sarcasm.
- Be honest in word and deed.
- Be objective. Avoid sounding biased.

- Routinely do your work competently and on time.
- Be courteous to everyone; each person is important. Demonstrate this by showing your respect for everyone you meet.
- Show trustworthiness—be dependable and circumspect in repeating things.
- Seek to understand the other's point of view by learning how to listen; listening is how you show respect to whoever is talking. The only way you will truly learn about another person is from the source. You don't learn if you are the one doing the talking. If you listen well, you can be positioned to learn of the new trends or changes that may be in the future.
- Be other-focused. Concentrate on what people are asking of you and what they want you to do to help them.
- Do something unselfish.

I know that this list sounds a little like the Boy Scout Oath, and I know that what I'm suggesting is neither original nor unique. But I offer it as a reminder that can help you continue to earn others' respect.

Level 6—People Who Value a Relationship with You

The last level contains the people who value a relationship with you, because they believe it is in their best interest to have one. (*You* may believe it's in their best interest to have a relationship with you, but if they don't agree, it doesn't count.) They trust you, think you can help them, and are confident you will not abuse their trust. Even better, the feeling is mutual; just as you help people at the top of the Pyramid, they will help you.

You deserve congratulations when you reach this level. When you arrive at this level with people, you know they value and seek your counsel. They see you as someone who has their best interests at heart. You frequently exhibit reciprocity in the relationship.

People who value a relationship with you know that you each contribute and provide for each other. As you do something for the others—provide information, favors, advice, and the like—they acknowledge your value in the relationship with similar things. I am not talking about a quid pro quo, but doing things for each other based on mutual affection. This type of relationship outlives business needs and can last a lifetime.

I tell people that very often their perception of the business relationship is not the other person's perception. You may think you are friendly with someone when they merely like you. You may think you have a valuable business relationship when they are only being friendly. If you assume yourself to be higher on the Relationship Pyramid with them, they are likely to see the actions you take with them personally as not appropriate. What I suggest is that when you are considering where you are on someone's Pyramid, guess low. View the relationship through the customer's eyes.

Often you think the relationship is one thing, but that's not what the other person thinks it is. It's why salespeople frequently say they have a great relationship with prospects but they don't get any business from them. They don't have a great relationship with them. They really aren't at the top of the prospects' Pyramids although they are friendly. I suggest you guess low as the place where you stand on someone's Pyramid, because you are more likely to develop a proper plan of action if you guess low than if you guess high.

Most business relationships are at the Know-Me-by-Name/Like-Me/Friendly-with-Me levels. These are all about likeability. Using the questions and techniques in this book, you can get almost anybody to like you reasonably quickly. The best and fastest way to get people to like you is to encourage them to talk about themselves and the things they treasure. The Link 20 questions in Chapter 4 are designed to get people to talk about themselves and about the things that are important to them.

Just to be liked is not enough, however. When you reach the top two levels in the Relationship Pyramid, the Respect-Me/Value-a-Relationship-with-Me levels, you have relationships that can help you reach even your stretch goals. But how do you get people to respect you and how do you get people to value a relationship with you?

While I'll be answering these questions in far more detail in the chapters ahead, for now I should say the answers are a function of your knowledge, your integrity, and your actions.

YOU NEED KNOWLEDGE, INTEGRITY, ACTIONS

Clients, prospects, and co-workers will not respect you if they think you are an idiot. They expect you to know your product, your service, or your idea intimately. They expect you to be able to answer their questions and help them solve their problems. This expertise is the price of entry; if you don't have it, a great relationship will not be an adequate substitute—assuming it's possible to build such a relationship without such expertise . . . and it's probably not. You need the expertise to build the relationship. In addition, you should also have some specialized knowledge that makes you a more interesting person. This knowledge can be about wine, or running a Boy Scout troop, or the Civil War, or convertible debentures, or it can be about religion, photography, cooking, football, or old television shows. It can be about anything that appeals to you.

People respect someone who has specialized knowledge (which need not be encyclopedic, just more than a passing acquaintance). Ask yourself: What specialized knowledge do I have? It may be of college basketball or Italian culture or quilting. Then, are you leveraging that specialized knowledge by allowing people to know you have it? Doing that successfully involves a technique I describe in a later chapter. (It's not by casually remarking during a conversational lull, "Did you know the Double Wedding Ring pattern is one of the most difficult quilts to make?")

I am not going to spend a lot of time talking about your integrity. If you don't have it, I'm not sure a book is going to help you get it. If you do have it, you don't need me to tell you how to get it.

My experience has taught me that most people have integrity. They want to do what is right. They are sometimes tempted to compromise their integrity when they feel pressures to perform, when there is a conflict between what they believe is right (honest, truthful, decent) and what they are convinced the organization wants. These pressures may be external—a sales quota, a management threat, a deteriorating business situation—or they may be internal. Whatever the cause, any professional who allows a temporary situation to override their sense of what is right risks permanent career damage. (Mark Hurd, the former CEO of Hewlett-Packard, is, at this writing, only the most recent, highly publicized example of a professional who apparently allowed a situation to override his sense of what was right.) At some level, most of us know when we have done something wrong: the warnings of our conscience help us keep our self-respect. A friend says, "I would rather be an honest failure than a successful cheat."

Last, you reach the top two levels of The Relationship Pyramid not with words but through your actions—what you do, how you do it, and how consistently and predictably you do it. Not only do you act consistently, but you must act in a way that makes other people exclaim (if only to themselves), "Wow! That impresses me."

The action may be something small. Anne Cobuzzi, portfolio planning liaison at the pharmaceutical company AstraZeneca in Wilmington, Delaware, talks about a small thing that had a big impact on her relationship with a co-worker in Sweden: "Building relationships overseas has been very challenging, but I think I do well globally because I become friends with my colleagues first, before we really get into a work relationship. One of the women I've come to know and work with in the Swedish office went to her hometown over the holidays and sent me a little wreath with a red ribbon and a note that said, 'I wanted you to have this. It's very indicative of my small town.' She sent it as a holiday gift. It was from someone I have a very good working relationship with, but I didn't expect her to do anything like that. To think she went all the way back to her hometown, which is several hours from the office where she works, and to think of me while she was with her family, was like ... WOW! It made a real impact."

More often than not, salespeople don't impress their customers because they do exactly what prospects and customers expect them to do. That is, they dash into the office and, in 30 seconds or less, bellow about how great their stuff is, with the implied point: "You're a functional idiot if you don't buy my product or come over to my way of thinking!"

Mouthing a sales pitch, no matter how professionally crafted, does not build credibility. It does not build respect. Even if what you are selling is truly superb and prospects who do not buy are short-sighted idiots, implying they are does not build your relationship. True, at some point you have to talk about what you want to sell, but there is a right way to make your presentation that I describe later in this book.

KEY POINTS ABOUT THE PYRAMID

As you read on, you should keep a number of key points about the Relationship Pyramid in mind. As I said earlier, it's a lot easier to come down a Pyramid than it is to go up.

Movement up the Relationship Pyramid is not always sequential. But if you are at the bottom and want to reach the top you must go through the steps. Someone has to know you by name; has to like you; has to be friendly with you; and has to respect you before you are going to get to the top of the Pyramid. But someone might be friendly without knowing your name. Also, while unusual, it is possible to have a productive business relationship with someone you don't particularly like, although the reverse is not true. Someone who does not like you will not value a relationship with you, so you cannot skip that step. Also, you may move up two steps almost at once.

Unfortunately, the process this book discusses will not work with everyone. Some people simply don't want a relationship with you. Their attitude may be irrational, given how friendly, courteous, kind, obedient, thrifty, brave, clean, and reverent you are—but it's a fact of life. You remind them of a hated elementary school teacher, a high school bully, an ex-wife, conditions over which you have no control. If you follow the process in this book, however, you will be able to build a strong, positive relationship with most people, and when you come across someone who will not respond to the questions in the following chapters, all you can do is move on to someone who will.

So, to sum up:

- Good relationships help us achieve abundant success in our business lives.
- Few of us know how to consciously and systematically build and maintain positive relationships.
- Without meaningful dialogue there is no selling or persuading—not of products, not of services, not of ideas. Meaningful dialogue is a sharing of truths.
- The more you know about someone, the more likely you are to have a solid personal relationship with him or her.

The goal of this book is to teach you how to consciously, systematically, and routinely move from the bottom of the Relationship Pyramid to the peak with your key business contacts so you can experience the success you deserve.

With all this as background, let's talk in detail about how exactly to build a relationship leveraging social technology to the point where customers and colleagues value a relationship with you and you are at the top of their Relationship Pyramids.

CHAPTER 3

HOW TO BUILD A RELATIONSHIP

As I said at the beginning, building a strong business relationship, moving up the Relationship Pyramid, is a process that you can learn. Actually, it's one you've already practiced. It's not magic, it's not chemistry, it's not luck. Because it's a process, you can master it and you can replicate it. If you need to build a relationship, you are holding the instructions for building one and have no excuse for not doing so.

On the other hand, as I said, the process will not work with every person every time. The failure in such a situation is not the process, but the other person's personality, or the circumstances, or an issue over which you have no control.

Nevertheless, everyone who has a close friend, a loving spouse, or a loyal colleague has gone through the relationship building process. Unknowingly, perhaps, but he or she has succeeded in taking the three steps the process requires.

Taking the steps unknowingly, the way most people build relationships, is the difference between unconscious competence and conscious competence. Most people are unconsciously competent at building good relationships. They do the right thing without deliberation with some people, and it turns out well.

If you understand the process, however, you are consciously competent, a good place to be. The relationship-building process does not merely happen. You know how to do it and you can do it when it counts, when you have to build a relationship with someone with whom you do not naturally connect.

Winning relationships result when two human beings make a positive connection, and, again, strong relationships seldom happen overnight. It takes time to gain trust, to obtain information, and to demonstrate your integrity. Rarely do we completely trust someone on first meeting (which is wise, given that not everyone is trustworthy). We have to get to know them and they have to get to know us. We have to demonstrate our integrity by acting with integrity—by doing what we say we'll do—over time. Each small act of responsibility, truth, or trustworthiness demonstrates our integrity. These small (or large) acts take time. How much time it takes to build a strong relationship varies with the situation and the personalities involved, but it cannot be rushed.

The three steps in building a positive business relationship involve:

1. What you think—your mind-set
2. What you ask—the information you gather
3. What you do—the actions you take

No structure can stand tall without a solid foundation, and the Relationship Pyramid's foundation in Figure 3.1 shows genuine care and concern for others, what you think of others, and what you think of yourself.

WHAT YOU THINK IS STEP 1

Not surprisingly, you must first believe in the value of building business relationships. If you don't think your relationships make a difference to your business or personal success, why make the effort (and it *is* an effort) to learn how to build good ones?

If you don't think your relationships make a difference, you are in a minority. Lance Perkins, an executive account manager for General Electric Medical Systems, sells enterprise-wide solutions to hospital executives. These solutions range from managing assets to increasing

Figure 3.1
No Structure Can Stand Tall without a Solid Foundation

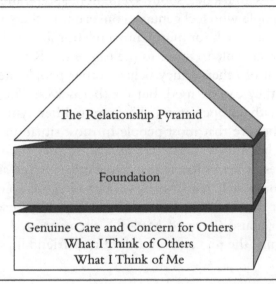

The Relationship Pyramid

Foundation

Genuine Care and Concern for Others
What I Think of Others
What I Think of Me

productivity, and Perkins deals mainly with chief executives and chief financial executives at hospitals. The hospitals are generally large; General Electric is gigantic. One might believe a strong relationship is irrelevant between a salesperson representing GE and a large hospital; isn't the corporation's name and reputation enough?

No, it's not. Perkins tells me, "We sell multimillion-dollar deals. Executives are not going to invest that kind of money in an individual they don't trust, they don't like, and they don't feel good about. So having rapport with those executives is key. In today's business life, people look in terms of partnerships. We are going to be working as partners. When you think about partnerships, what is implicit is an open dialogue, a trust, and that trust and dialogue are built on the foundation of rapport."

I believe most people do feel a genuine care and concern for others. Those who don't feel a genuine concern for others tend to regard other people as a means to self-centered ends. They use people. They do not care about building long-term relationships. Or if, at some level they care, they cannot imagine doing what is necessary to

31

create and maintain a relationship. Their lives are strewn with failed relationships—with friends, spouses, children, and business associates. In contrast, people who feel genuine concern for others are not users; they try to put as much (or more) into a relationship as they take out.

People who are able to move to the top of the Relationship Pyramid think well of others. They believe other people are important, not for how they can be used, but for themselves. They meet each new person with an open mind. They are neither cynical nor credulous. They believe that most people in most situations are honest, truthful, and helpful, while at the same time they know the world contains snakes. It seems to me that two dangers in life are to believe everyone is completely trustworthy . . . or to believe no one can ever be trusted. In the first case, you routinely expose yourself to financial and other abuse (Bernard Madoff's clients trusted him). In the second, you miss the joys and rewards of true friendship.

Think Well of Yourself

To build any successful relationship, you must think well of yourself. This is not a self-help psychology text, but to build a winning relationship you must believe you are someone with whom other people would want to have a relationship. This may be why very famous people sometimes have difficulty getting dates. Noncelebrities assume those important stars would not go out with them and they don't ask.

If you decide you can't have a relationship with a certain high-powered executive, then guess what? You can't. If you don't care for yourself or if you believe you are unlikable, it's difficult for other people to like you. The belief becomes a self-fulfilling prophecy, a variation on Groucho Marx's famous remark: "I wouldn't want to have a relationship with the kind of person who would have a relationship with me."

Many people think well of themselves, but are shy, and that may be because their brains process the world differently than people do who are more outgoing. According to a recent study conducted by researchers at Stony Brook University in New York, and Southwest

University and the Chinese Academy of Sciences, both in China, about 20 percent of people are born with a personality trait called "sensory perception sensitivity" that can manifest itself as the tendency to be shy or introverted.

The results, which were published in the journal *Social Cognitive and Affective Neuroscience*, suggest that these individuals pay more attention to detail and have more activity in certain regions of their brains when trying to process visual information than those who are not classified as highly sensitive. Individuals with this trait prefer to take longer to make decisions, are more conscientious, need more time to themselves to reflect, and are more easily bored with small talk.[1] So being shy is not all bad.

But if you are shy, you may think you'll have difficulty building strong relationships. People have told me in my seminars, "I'm shy. People aren't interested in me. I don't know what to say to someone."

One way to overcome your natural shyness is to force yourself to talk to strangers. Talk to people standing in line at the bank or waiting to get into a busy restaurant or the person standing alone at a reception or party. It does not have to be profound. "What do you think of this weather?" or "Nice day, isn't it?" is a start. A shyness clinic in California actually suggested getting on elevators just for the ride and snaring unsuspecting strangers for a 30-second conversation.

In my experience, most people have never been taught how to have a genuine interest in other people. However, a genuine interest in other people—what they say, what they think, and what they know—is a good start toward overcoming shyness. We all (many of us, anyway) do have and will show a genuine interest in people outside of our work—the people we meet socially. We will ask someone at a party what they do when they're not working, where they went to school, what their vacation plans are.

But for some reason, we have decided that bringing to work a genuine interest in people conflicts in some way with business concerns. Companies and people are not very good at drawing the line between what they must do to accomplish business objectives and how they deal with more personal issues. When you're totally focused on making the sales call, or giving the presentation, or finishing the project, it's difficult to focus at the same time on what someone else did this weekend.

I think most people have a natural curiosity and a genuine concern for others, but they are not overly comfortable bringing it to the office. The tragedy of 9/11 or the January 2010 Haiti earthquake should have taught us there is an incredible latent concern for people other than ourselves. Total strangers gave billions of dollars because they were interested in, and cared about, other people. The challenge is to take what is in your heart, that natural interest in helping others, and bring it to work.

This is not to say there is no difference between your family/social and your business lives. It *is* to say that many people in business are more brusque, impassive, and detached than necessary.

For example, salespeople are correctly interested in selling their product or service; that's what they're paid to do. But most believe the way to sell is to tell prospects about the features, about the benefits, about the service, about the pricing, about the company, about the ... but you get the idea. They're not supposed to waste time talking about vacations, hobbies, and children.

And this applies not only to salespeople. Colleagues who want to promote their ideas, consultants who want to promote their services, and those who want to persuade someone else of anything tend to focus on *their* ideas, *their* services, and *their* plans.

In truth, those who persuade most effectively understand the primary topic is not—should not be—about what they have to offer. It's about the prospect, colleague, or client. The focus is on what others think, want, or need. The great paradox of selling is that the less you care about the sale, the more you sell. The more that people like and trust you, the more likely they will take your ideas into account. If you can learn to balance a genuine interest and curiosity in other people with your desire for business success, you can be wildly successful.

Make Self-Fulfilling Prophecies Positive

Perhaps the best way to overcome the suspicion (or fear) that you are unlikable is to act as if you expect to be liked. If there's going to be a self-fulfilling prophecy, make it a positive one. Conduct yourself as if you expect to be liked, and you'll be amazed at how many people will act as if they like you. As an example of what I'm talking about, consider Van Walker, a sales representative I met in 1981.

The first day I worked with Van, it was clear he was brilliant. A member of Mensa, he never finished his degree in astrophysics because college bored him. He was naturally thoughtful, quiet, and introverted, yet when we called on a customer, he tried to crack jokes and pat people on the back. His behavior was the antithesis of what his real personality seemed to be, but apparently he thought that to be a salesperson you had to be a bluff, back-slapping, hail-fellow-well-met.

We were riding back to the office at the end of the day when he asked me, "What do you think?"

"My suggestion is that you get another job."

He said, "What?"

"Van, you must be the most miserable person on the planet. How can anybody with your personality get out of the car and become a completely different human being when you're in front of a customer?"

He thought for a moment. "I don't think they'll like me if I'm me."

"I think you are a hundred percent wrong. What do you think these people we're selling to really look for? They're looking for someone who is sincere, someone who is genuine, someone who is intelligent, and someone who can help them solve their problems. You don't have to be a Jay Leno to do that. You can just be Van."

He thought about it for a mile or so. "Do you really think they'll like me?"

"I know they'll like you. In the first place, most of them are intelligent people and they respect other intelligent people. Most of them are shy; they respect someone who is shy. You're just like them." It occurred to me he was trying to be like his previous boss, who was a bluff, hearty fellow. "Don't be like your old boss," I told him, "be like Van."

He said, "I feel like a hundred-pound weight is being lifted off my shoulders. I've been miserable trying to be somebody else."

I said, "Just be you."

By the end of the year, Van was number four in sales of 550 salespeople in the company. I promoted him and the new account reported Van was the best representative they'd ever had. I promoted him again and gave him responsibility for one of the most important accounts in the country with the same result—the best representative they'd ever had. All because Van stopped being some corn pone, snake oil salesman and began being himself.

Think Well of Others (Even the Jerks)

You must also think well of others even when they are not, on the surface, likable. This is not always easy, given the fact there are some real jerks in the world. When I was a district manager for a pharmaceutical company, I competed with Dick McDonald, then a district manager in Detroit. I never really liked Dick. In fact, I didn't like being around him because I thought we were completely different people. We had different likes, different dislikes. In addition, we competed. We were both district managers, both wanted to have the top district, both wanted to be promoted, and I felt the natural competition you feel with peers that exists in any business—but perhaps I felt it more than was healthy.

One day my boss was telling me something about Dick McDonald and I remarked, "I don't like Dick McDonald."

He said, "Well, that's an interesting point of view." He thought about it for a minute, then said, "Here's what I want you to do. You go to Detroit and spend a day with Dick McDonald. I want you to come back and write me a report about why you like Dick McDonald."

"That's impossible."

He said, "I don't care if it's impossible, you're going to do it."

Reluctantly, I called McDonald and, under the guise of coming to Detroit to learn his ideas on what we might do to sell certain national accounts, I arranged to spend a day with him.

Once with him, I discovered McDonald was more like me than not, a guy who had strong family values (like me), who had a genuine love for his associates (like me), and who also had a unique sense of humor. I learned I had not fully appreciated his humor. I learned he is a stand-up guy with lots of character and integrity. It is difficult to see integrity when you see someone only from the outside (and even more difficult when you think you're looking at a jerk). When I began to see how McDonald functioned and how he dealt with his people, I saw someone with great personal influence. I looked at his track record and saw not only had he been successful personally, but he'd promoted many people and many went on to become successful leaders. Because my boss forced me to look objectively at McDonald and try to remove my bias, I began to see McDonald for what he really was, not what I erroneously imagined him to be.

At the end of the day, I did like Dick McDonald, and he hadn't changed one bit. I went to Detroit knowing I had no choice but to find something about him I liked. When I took that perspective, I was able to learn things about him I not only liked, but also admired. McDonald was no longer a jerk in my mind. After the day we spent together, I felt more comfortable collaborating with Dick on corporate projects, and I was more open to his ideas when we worked together. When I left the company, Dick was one of the few colleagues with whom I maintained a close relationship, a relationship that continues to this day (even after he reads this book).

Indeed, not long ago, I was in Detroit giving a seminar for a division of the company for which McDonald now works and I told this story. One of the representatives in the seminar had worked for McDonald, and during the morning break and without my knowledge, she called him to say I was in town.

Thirty minutes before lunch, McDonald walked in the room and hugged me. "This used to be my boss," he told the group, "and now he's my good friend, and I wanted to come say hello." I could not have scripted it better.

Over cocktails that night, I told McDonald this story for the first time, adding that when I wrote my book I would tell it there. To which he said, "I always liked you."

I said, "Well, I can't say the same. I wasn't as open-minded as you."

Implement the Process Completely

Relationships that are not what you want them to be can usually be traced to a failure to implement the three-step process completely. In almost every case of a failed (or failing) relationship, you can ask yourself: Is it failing because I don't think correctly about the other person? Because I don't think well of myself? Because I haven't asked the right questions? (I talk about the questions in the next chapter.) Because I haven't done what is necessary to show the relationship is important to me? Failure to do one or more of those things will hold back a relationship in almost every case.

Too often the relationships that aren't what we want them to be are so because we don't know the other person well enough yet. Generally, the better you know someone, the better you like him or her. My antipathy toward Dick McDonald was a function of not knowing him. I was making superficial judgments about him based on very sketchy information. Because I was forced to be objective, I began to learn who he was, and my attitude adjusted. McDonald didn't change; I changed. Once I knew something about him, my belief changed to the view that McDonald was somebody I could and should like, trust, admire, and respect.

Often we assume what the relationship must be without testing our assumptions. (And sometimes our assumptions are based on unconscious stereotypes of successful businesswomen ... or of Jewish doctors ... or of Republican executives ... you get the idea.) Nor do we know how to consciously build the relationship over time. One good way to do that, the one this book describes, is to ask the right questions in the right way for the right reasons.

The right reason is not so you can sell more. The right reason is so you understand enough about the person that you can build a meaningful relationship. If you have a positive relationship—that is, the person listens to you differently than to a mere acquaintance or to another salesperson—ultimately he or she will buy more if you have a reasonable value premise.

This is a key point. Good relationships will never help you sell lousy products (or not for long). If you do not believe in what you are selling, you should quit reading and start looking for another job. Lousy products or services will corrupt any relationships you build. If a change in management or corporate direction meant I had to sell something in which I did not believe, I would find another job rather than damage or destroy my solid business relationships. Good relationships are too valuable to throw away for any short-term gain.

The next chapters give you the questions to ask and the principles behind them. The goal is to discover common ground, mutual friends, interests, or concerns. Or, if you truly have no common ground (unusual, but it can happen), the goal is to discover what the other person cares passionately about and learn from him or her. Most people are delighted to teach you something about their passion.

Ewell Hopkins is director of client relations for Sapient Corporation, a publicly traded provider of business and technology consulting services based in Cambridge, Massachusetts. Ewell says that if you can get into a person's workplace, whether a cubicle or a mahogany office on the penthouse floor, anything personal is fair game. If the item were too private and the client did not want you to know about it, he or she wouldn't have it showing. "A man won't have a picture of his wife and his mistress next to each other," says Hopkins. "If there are two pictures, you can talk about them."

Ewell believes that when you go into someone's office, you should routinely scan for examples of interests. Is there a picture of a fly fisherman on the wall? A NASCAR model in the corner? Golf clubs leaning against the wall? Crayoned pictures by a first grader? Each may be an example of an individual's passion, whether recreation, family, church, or something else.

"When you see it, you acknowledge it," says Ewell. But don't be obvious: "Oh, I see you have a picture of fly fishing up there. Is that something you really enjoy doing?" And don't try to pass yourself off as a fly fishing expert if you're not. When you're caught as a phony, it does not help build your integrity.

You *can* say something like, "Hey, it's always important to find a personal outlet. You have to find a way to unwind. I do [whatever it is you do]. Is that what fly fishing is to you?"

The prospect may say, "You're absolutely right; it's the only thing that keeps me sane." Or, "I live for it." Or, "I really don't like it. My wife gave me that damn picture. . . ."

Ewell has found, as I have, that people do not usually stay on personal subjects for long. "I always start the meeting there," he says, "and they will let you know when they want to move on. If they want to stay on the subject for an hour or five minutes, they'll let you know."

Not long ago, a sales representative I was coaching and I were in a doctor's outer office where pictures of two mosques hung on one wall. After we talked with the doctor, I asked him if he would mind my asking a personal question. He said, no, so I said, "I couldn't help but see the beautiful pictures of the mosques outside. I am quite sure one of them is Mecca, but I'm not familiar with the other one."

He told me it was Medina. I learned Saudi Arabia has two landmark mosques, Mecca and Medina. The doctor then told me the history of these mosques and about being Muslim. Before we left, he gave me a copy of the Koran and booklets showing the ties between Islam and Christianity. The doctor had said he had no more time for us, but he talked for 20 minutes about the link between Christianity and Islam. Again, when you can encourage people to talk about something in which they're interested, they will talk for a long time.

The doctor might well have answered my question with, "That's Medina," and let it go at that. But unless you ask, you'll never know other people's passions. You'll never learn what they treasure.

LEARN STRATEGIES, NOT TACTICS

This book does not teach tactics designed to get you to some definite place—a commitment, a signed order, a sale—in a particular time frame. It is not: Ask this question, get that answer, use it in this way. Get to "Yes" as directly and quickly as possible.

Ideally, the book teaches strategies you can use to improve the quality of your life and the time you spend in business (or in any kind of relationship for that matter).

Harvey Mackay, in his book *Swim with the Sharks without Being Eaten Alive*, describes a 66-question customer profile designed to help salespeople know their customers and prospects. The profile is also a tool companies can use to retain a salesperson's accounts when the salesperson leaves. "It gets their successor up and running with a decided timing edge, a much shorter learning curve than would be necessary if the salesperson had to start from scratch."[2]

There is nothing wrong with the Mackay 66. Indeed, those who are familiar with Mackay's book will realize some of the questions in the next chapter are variations on them. The difference between the Mackay customer profile and what I'm suggesting is in intent. Mackay's goal is to sell more envelopes. Mine is to build winning business relationships.

Actually, Mackay's practices are perhaps closer to mine than might first be apparent. Mackay says he once called on a Fortune 500 company in New York and noticed on the prospect's wall "a picture of the company president awarding the buyer a certificate for writing a position paper on unemployment. A week later, I sent him a book on unemployment. The orders have never stopped coming." Sending a book on unemployment to someone who cares passionately about unemployment is the sort of, unexpected, inexpensive, and thoughtful act that helps you move up the Relationship Pyramid. It's the kind of action I'll talk about in detail.

Because these are strategies, they are not designed to produce a specific benefit in a specific time. Some things work; some things don't. Sometimes customers or colleagues want to talk forever about what's on the wall, and sometimes they have nothing to say about it.

Sometimes, when you do something nice for someone, the person does something incredibly nice for you in return. Sometimes you send a book on unemployment and you receive an order for envelopes. But sometimes you do 10 nice things, and nothing whatever happens. That's human nature, but in this situation you're not keeping score.

You do not ask the question or do something nice because you expect a quid pro quo (Latin for "You scratch my back, I'll scratch yours"). You ask questions and you do nice things because it makes your job more fun, it sets you apart from other people, and it ultimately gives you an opportunity to have the other person listen to you differently. You do not ask about this picture or that model ship because the other person will like you better. You do not do an unexpected, inexpensive, and unselfish act because they will order your product. They may, but that's secondary. Your primary reason is to move up the Relationship Pyramid and gain a Relationship Edge.

Nevertheless, you can assume the things customers and colleagues surround themselves with are things that interest them. They are clues, but you still must ask the question. Does the model sailboat mean you like to sail? Yes? Do you have a boat? Yes? Tell me about your boat. The goal, always, is to learn what the other person treasures.

Do the Right Thing

In the third step in the process of building a positive relationship, you must do the right thing to avoid undermining the goodwill you have built. The information you gather should not simply sit in your personal information manager—you must use it regularly to take actions that will build the relationship over time. This takes weeks or even months. It cannot be hurried. You need to learn the process, gather information, act on it, and move up to the next level of the Relationship Pyramid for profitable long-term business relationships.

If you dispense with any part of this process, relationships will not develop. If your mind-set is not positive, if you do not gather enough information, and if you do not do unexpected, inexpensive, and thoughtful acts to demonstrate the relationship's importance to you, it will not happen.

To move up the Relationship Pyramid, you must set yourself apart from every other person your prospect, client, or colleague comes in contact with. Otherwise, you remain at the bottom of the Pyramid; they know your name, but that's about all. Moreover, how would someone know you are different . . . and worth having a relationship with? You have to say something or act in such a way that distinguishes you from every other salesperson or colleague the person meets.

At one time, I became a district manager for a company that sold pharmaceuticals exclusively to hospitals. I wanted to see all

132 hospitals in my district, and I went with the representatives to visit them. We would go to the director of pharmacy and I would say, "My objective is to never counter you. I am never going to go around you to try to sell to your doctors directly. I have no clue how you feel about our drug. If you and I disagree—and we very well could—I will do everything in my power to change your mind, but I will not put you at odds with your doctors. If I cannot convince you, I lose the battle. I will not go behind your back."

How smart was that? I was telling the pharmacist that even if he was mistaken about our drug's capabilities and I could not persuade him otherwise, I would not try to convince the hospital's doctors to override his decision. I was saying—without saying it—that my relationship with him was more important than selling our drug.

In one light, it was not very smart. But how many district managers ever told hospital pharmacists they would not go around them? None. All my competitors were doing whatever they could to sell their products. And if that meant being adversarial toward the director of pharmacy, tough cookies.

The second thing I told the pharmacist was, "I want to be known as the company that gives something back. If you want a speaker on the disease our product addresses, call me. Call me even if you want a speaker on a condition for which we don't have a medication, because that way you know the speaker won't be parroting a company line."

One of my representatives once called to ask for $500, almost 10 percent of my event budget at the time, to sponsor a speaker on euthanasia at a hospice. The oncologist involved was not a big customer, so I asked the representative what he thought. The doctor had the potential to be a much bigger customer; but then again, maybe not. The representative said, "I think it's a good idea." I authorized the money.

Two weeks after the event, the doctor himself called me to thank us for the $500. I said we were glad to do it.

He said, "I asked 14 companies before I came to you. Fourteen companies told me no."

I said, "First, I'm embarrassed that we were number fifteen. I wish you had asked us sooner." But 14 other companies felt there was no value in helping this doctor so they turned him down. I felt it was the right thing to do, even if it did not have any direct and immediate value to my company.

He told me, "I would love to use your drug if there were a paper that said that oncologists should use it. But for now ..."

Four months later, an article in the *New England Journal of Medicine* discussed a similar drug for infected cancer patients. It was a competitor's drug, but I sent the paper to the doctor with a note, "This is not exactly what you are looking for, but if you believe that these drugs have a class effect...." He called to say, "That's all I need to see," and from that moment he became one of our best customers.

The point is, how are you going to differentiate yourself? What are you going to do that makes prospects, clients, and colleagues know you are different from everybody else? Or are you simply going to be like everybody else?

Do Unexpected, Inexpensive, Thoughtful Acts

Prospects and customers with whom you do not have a good relationship expect you to do self-serving things. When you do unexpected, unselfish things, you gain respect, credibility, and trust because it demonstrates with actions that you care.

As you think about how customers and colleagues feel about you, think about things you can do that are unexpected, thoughtful, and, ideally, inexpensive. The more of those things you can do, the more you are likely to gain or develop a relationship.

Zig Ziglar, in his book *See You at the Top*, says you get everything in life you want if you simply help enough other people get what they want.[3] That's true, but it's difficult to practice because, when a situation arises, our impulse is to think in terms of our own business needs—I could have spent the $500 on somebody who would talk about our product. Why waste it helping someone who's not even a customer?

You do these unselfish acts because if you plant enough seeds, some will sprout—and you never know which ones or when they'll be important.

A rep I know was calling on a doctor new to the area someplace in New York State. She asked some of the Link 20 questions: How did you wind up here? Do you like living here? The doctor said in passing that his daughter had just been diagnosed with a rare disease and one his challenges was to find a specialist who could treat it. "There's nobody around here, so I guess I'm going to have to look in one of the big cities."

The rep called her colleague, the hospital rep in the city, and said in effect, "This doctor has a child with this disease. Can you find out who is the specialist in it?" The hospital rep happened to know the specialist and had a relationship with him. The hospital rep called the specialist, who said he would be glad to see the patient. The very next day the rep returned to the doctor and said, "I found the specialist your daughter needs to see. This is his name and contact information and he's expecting your call." The doctor said, "I've been in practice fifteen years, and nobody has ever done anything that nice for me."

My whole point is that the rep performed an unexpected, inexpensive, thoughtful act, but she could not have done it if she hadn't been listening for things that she could do to add value to the relationship.

Your goal is to listen closely to other people because, as you move up the Pyramid, they listen to you differently. If you can get people to listen to you differently, they will share more of what you need to learn so that you can accomplish whatever you want to achieve and have more fun in your job.

People Using Competitive Products Are Not Enemies

I have noticed that salespeople tend to regard customers who use a competitive product as enemies and adversaries. But how likely are we to have a good relationship with someone we disdain, dislike, or find annoying? Someone who is so blind as to be swayed by competitive offers?

When you look at prospects who are loyal to your competitors, the first thing you have to change is how you think about them. If you don't change that, the likelihood you will ever bring them around to your point of view is not good. Few salespeople deal with the prospects with whom they do not have a good relationship the same way they deal with their good customers. They treat them more like antagonists than associates.

When you anticipate that prospects or colleagues will not respond positively to you, you don't act toward them the same way you do toward those with whom you have good relationships. When a relationship is not what you would like it to be, therefore, ask yourself: Am I treating this person the same way I treat those with whom I have a good relationship? The answer is almost always no.

We have to understand that customers made their choices in most cases for sound, ethical, personal reasons. Their decisions are not about you; they are about them. If they have not decided to use your product (or adopt your idea or embrace your plan), it is usually your failure to help them see that what you offer would personally benefit them and their organizations more than what they currently use. It is not their recalcitrance or their stubbornness.

If, in fact, the competitor's product or service is actually better for particular customers in a particular situation (and I suppose that can happen), it would be wrong for you and probably a waste of your time and theirs to try to convince them otherwise. But rejections like, "We find your competitor's product meets our needs adequately," or "We've done business with your competitor for years," or "We're not ready to make a decision at this time" often mask real reasons. Without a good relationship and consequently meaningful dialogue, it is difficult or impossible to glimpse behind the mask.

In an ideal world, you take information about a competitor's true advantage back to your company, and the company improves the product, service, packaging, price, terms, or whatever. In an ideal world, companies are sensitive to what salespeople learn in the field and act on the information; they use the salespeople as a source of invaluable competitive intelligence to improve their own offering. In an ideal world, salespeople do not spend time trying to persuade the unpersuadable.

Social technology may be nudging us toward this ideal world. A free tool like Yammer makes it easy for a salesperson—or anyone else in the company—to post information about prospects, problems, objections, ideas. The only people who can read the post are those with a company e-mail address, so the information stays within the family. Deloitte, the international accounting firm, says it uses Yammer for knowledge sharing. "It first started as a bit of an in-house social chat room. But it wasn't long before the imperatives of doing business seeped into the conversation and the team started to pose questions and solve problems. It has proved to be a great way to seek input, test ideas, and gather feedback quickly."[4] It's a way for a salesperson on one side of the country—or world—to share with salespeople, marketing people, product designers, service reps, even senior management on the other side of the country.

Another way to say all this is that if you are going to be in sales, you should be spending your time where your product or service is the best for the customer. Once there, your job is to get prospects to listen to you in such a way that they begin to understand that while what you're offering may not be right for everything or everybody, there are certain places where this product or this company is in their best interest. But the only way you can possibly do that is to understand their interests.

You can have a product that is virtually the same as a competitor's or you can have a product that costs more money, but it still would be in the prospect's best interest to do business with you because the decision would be based on value, not on price. If you can show prospects ancillary things your company does to add value, you ought to get the business. You need to understand clearly where your product or service is undeniably the best choice. That does not make the job of persuading any easier, but it makes it possible.

If we truly want to learn what customers want and need in a broad context, we need to ask questions. What are the two or three key initiatives in your organization? Tell me about the things your CEO stands for. What is management doing to drive this business? If you looked at this business in a perfect world, what would be different a year from now or two years from now?

As you begin to understand those things, you can begin to think about ways you can help customers and prospects that you never thought about before. You may help them solve another problem that seems tangential to what you are selling, for example: "Do you know anyone who understands state government procurement procedures?" Solving that problem may help you move up the Relationship Pyramid.

Building a Relationship Takes Time

Relationships are built over time, and time is one of the most important elements of relationship building. The time you spend with another person is key. If you really want a good relationship with someone, put yourself in a position where you can spend time together. The more time you can give, the more likely you are to learn something about the person's interests, cares, and concerns. In turn, the other person will learn something about you.

A barrier to building relationships is that people are cautious until they feel safe with you. How long does it take to make people feel safe with you? The only answer is: It depends. The more time people have with you and the more predictable your behavior and personality become, the more likely they are to feel comfortable. The more comfortable they are, the more they feel they can share. The more they share, the deeper the relationship.

Lance Perkins at General Electric Medical Systems has read Albert Mehrabian's and Anthony Robbins' theories on communication and he has confirmed that a large component of the communication process is nonverbal—body language. Another large component is tonality—how you say something.

Putting theory into practice, Perkins tries to establish rapport by mirroring a prospect's behavior. "You try to take the same stance the other person takes. If he is leaning back in his chair, you lean back in the chair. If he speaks slowly and you tend to speak fast, you need to bring your tempo down to the same level. You try to match your tonality to theirs. You're sending the signal to them that they tend to pick up unconsciously, that 'Hey, this person is a lot like me.' They tend to like you, because people who are like each other, tend to like each other."

Perkins has found that top salespeople try to enter the other person's world by building rapport, by matching and marrying their body language and their tonality, and by using the same type of words that the other person uses—really entering that person's world and speaking his or her language. The executives he deals with "understand the world through the language of finance. They want to know what a return on asset is, what liquidation rates are, what the profit margin is. When I communicate with them I speak that language, which automatically builds a bond."

He confirms again that a key component to building trust is delivering what you commit to deliver, even if your commitment is no more than "I'll get back to you on that. I'll give you a call tomorrow at 1:00." But people often don't do what they say they'll do, and that can damage the trust and ruin the relationship.

Perkins also agrees that you don't try to put relationship building on steroids by trying to establish rapport overnight. "You don't want to be obsequious or to come on too strong," he says. "Just dance at the customer's pace and know that it is a long-term process. Someone is not going to trust you necessarily just because of two meetings. It may require meetings over the course of months, if not a year."

People have the idea that in this high-speed world, we have to speed it up. We have to do everything faster. But relationships are not things you can put in the fast lane. Relationships develop naturally at their own pace and are more likely to develop if you want them to develop.

Sharing food improves the process. Robert B. Cialdini points out in his book, *Influence: Science and Practice*, that it is a White House tradition "to try to sway the votes of balking legislators over a meal. It can be a picnic lunch, a sumptuous breakfast, or an elegant dinner; but when an important bill is up for grabs, out comes the silverware."[5]

Cialdini cites psychologist Gregory Razran's research of the 1930s. Razran "found that his subjects became fonder of the people and things they experienced while they were eating." In one experiment, "subjects were presented with some political statements they had rated once before. At the end of the experiment, after all the political statements had been presented, Razran found that only certain of them had gained in approval—those that had been shown while food was being eaten. These changes in liking seem to have occurred unconsciously, since the subjects could not remember which of the statements they had seen while the food was being served."

There is something about eating with someone that is different from meeting in an office or conference room. When you eat with somebody, it almost automatically takes the relationship to another level on the Relationship Pyramid. You feel differently about the encounter. If you tell somebody, "I had a meeting with Tom Griffin," a high-level corporate executive, the connotation is different from saying, "I had lunch with Tom Griffin." The two sentences carry dramatically different meanings.

Someone understands that when you say, "I had lunch with Tom Griffin," Griffin wouldn't eat lunch with you unless you have a certain level of relationship. Almost anybody might meet with you (once), but not everyone will eat with you; therefore, eating is a wonderful activity in which to forge relationships.

I teach the people I coach to have a meal with the customers and colleagues they identify as key to their business success. Whenever you can break bread with someone, it improves the likelihood you can develop the relationship. When you eat, the talk should be about topics other than business. People will tell you things about themselves when you eat in the natural course of the conversation. You can develop a completely different relationship over a meal, especially if you focus on the other person and the meal, not your interests.

If you want a relationship with someone, you can usually build one, but it will take time.

Decide Who's Key, Then Do Something

In 1983, I sat in an audience with 139 other people and first heard Danny Cox speak at a seminar. Cox is a professional speaker, has a Council of Peers Award for Excellence (the highest honor a speaker can earn), and is in the Speaker's Hall of Fame.

He had been an Air Force fighter pilot, where he'd become "a sonic boom salesman." He and other pilots flew their planes at supersonic speeds, and residents in the area did not like the noise. Cox had to go to Rotary Club and town meetings to convince unhappy groups that the noise, although uncomfortable for the residents, was a good thing for the country. He developed his speaking talent and is now probably one of the 20 best speakers in the world.

I liked what he had to say at the seminar, so I introduced myself to him at the end and began to develop a relationship with him. We stayed in touch and ultimately became friends. I have suggested him for speaking engagements with clients where I thought he was a perfect match, and he has recommended me to potential clients. He asked me to provide a quote for his book (*Leadership When the Heat's On*, McGraw-Hill Trade, 2002).

Recently, a friend talked to me about his becoming a speaker. I called Danny and said, "This guy lives close to you. Would you spend a day with him?" He said yes, so Danny and I spent a day with my friend trying to help him learn how to get into the speaking business. Today, I can assure you I am the only person from that 1983 seminar who has a relationship with Danny Cox. Any one of the other 139 people in the group could have had one, and the reason I have one is because I made a decision: I wanted to get to know this guy.

Therefore, take a minute before you read on to decide whom you want to have a winning relationship with. Who are the eight or ten people most important to your business success today? If you had a better relationship with these people, it would improve the quality of your personal and professional life. They may be prospects, customers, clients, colleagues, associates, superiors, or the clerk in the travel department who arranges your flights. Write down their names, and as you continue reading, think back to them, what you need to know about them, and what you can do to move up the Relationship Pyramid with them.

In summary, the building blocks of strong relationships are:

- Believe others are important.
- Focus on others.
- Appreciate and understand people's differences and their points of view.

- Make people feel important.
- Seek common ground by learning about people.
- Listen because you want to hear.

Remember that building a business relationship is a process. When you ask yourself why you don't have a good relationship with your key contacts or colleagues, the answer is probably your mind-set, the information you gather, or the actions you take—or neglect to take.

You expect to have a poor relationship, so it *is* a poor relationship.

Or, you have a positive attitude, but you don't know anything about the other person. You may assume, guess, or suspect, but you don't really know.

Or, you do know what the other person treasures; she is a passionate gardener, he loves to cook—to take only two possible examples—but you've never clipped an article or bought a book on gardening or cooking, sent her a plant or him an ingredient. You've never acted on that knowledge in an unexpected, inexpensive, and unselfish way.

But how do you learn what someone treasures?

I thought you'd never ask.

CHAPTER 4

ASK THE TWENTY QUESTIONS

Once you have identified the people most important to your business success, you need to identify where exactly you think you are on the Relationship Pyramid with each. Then, if you are not at the top of their Pyramid, begin to learn what they treasure.

What do you think about him or her? What do you think he or she thinks of you? Does he or she even know your name? (If not, you know where to start.) With most of the key people in your life, you're probably somewhere in the middle of the Pyramid. They know your name, they like you, and maybe they're friendly with you.

Your goal is to be at the top with them all and to have them respect and value a relationship with you. These are the relationships that offer the most AIR: Access, Impact, and Results. But how do you move up the Pyramid to the top two levels (Figure 4.1)?

You start by systematically learning things about these people that you don't already know. You ask the right questions in the right way to learn what they treasure. You do this not as a cold-blooded, calculated tactic to worm your way into their confidence, but as a way to make a genuine connection with another human being who you hope will end up liking and trusting you. The 20 questions in this chapter are starting points. You will almost never move a relationship to the top of the Pyramid until you know something about the other person and he or she knows something about you and how you conduct yourself. Once you do begin to learn, you have the beginnings of

Figure 4.1
The Relationship Pyramid

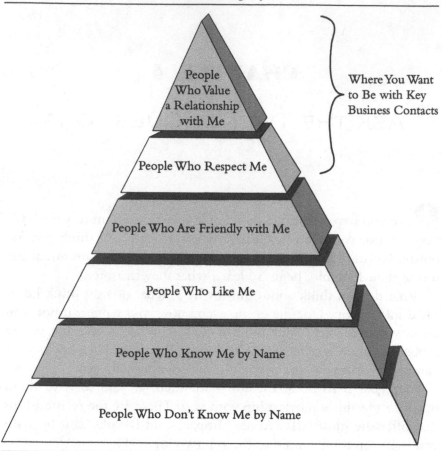

People Who Value a Relationship with Me

Where You Want to Be with Key Business Contacts

People Who Respect Me

People Who Are Friendly with Me

People Who Like Me

People Who Know Me by Name

People Who Don't Know Me by Name

a human connection and the possibility of meaningful dialogue that can ultimately benefit you both.

Until you know what and whom the other person treasures—and act on the information in a way that demonstrates that you care—you're at a relationship impasse. People are friendly enough, but you can't get much done. They don't share their real concerns with you. They don't listen to you the way someone who knows and trusts you listens. Remember that without a meaningful dialogue, there is no selling or persuasion.

Building a winning relationship—moving up the Relationship Pyramid—does require a bit of rigor and planning, but it's not impossible, and it's definitely worth the effort. Most of us do a better job of planning a vacation than we do of planning how to build the relationships that will make our businesses more successful and our lives more meaningful.

START WITH A SELF-CHECK

It should be clear that when I talk about relationship building and selling, I am talking about situations that require a relationship. If a prospect walks into a Honda dealership with *Consumer Reports* magazine in one hand and a pocketbook full of money in the other, she does not want a relationship. She is buying a car; the salesperson is not selling her one. There's a difference. It's a transaction, not a relationship. The salesperson may learn something about the customer—a skillful salesperson will pick up a great deal—but seldom is this a long-term, close, positive relationship. The Relationship Edge helps most in ongoing sales situations or, as with GE Medical Services, complex sales.

Ewell Hopkins from Sapient says that if he wants to build a business relationship: "I want to get to know this person. I want to understand how they tick. I want to understand their drivers. I want to understand how I can add value in their business or personal lives."

To do that, you need to begin with a self-check. You have to acknowledge that you are prepared to invest time and attention in the relationship. As Ewell puts it, "If you're in there to sell something today and be out tomorrow, I don't think relationship building is an approach to take because it's going to take too much work and you're not going to see the benefit in the short term. If you have something to sell really quick and you want to move on, be honest with yourself. Don't go in talking about wanting a relationship. You've got something and you want to figure out if they need it. Customers will appreciate that frankness."

If you are trying to build business relationships, make sure you have your organization's support because, in the short term, it may be more expensive than the quick in-and-out, and it's going to be time-consuming. If your company does not support you and if your management does not value the edge that positive business relationships give you—and unfortunately such managements exist—you have a problem this book cannot solve.

Business relationships by their nature are more difficult to initiate than personal relationships. When you meet people in private life, you usually have some common ground. You have a similar interest, a similar political affiliation, a similar religious belief. You usually start with some common context: You live in the same neighborhood, go to the same church, or have been invited to the same party and know the hosts.

When you first meet people professionally, you may have no clue if there is some common ground. You are meeting this person for a purely mechanical, business reason. You may have no clue as to the company values the person represents. You don't know if you would meet the individual in another setting. Would you live in the same neighborhood? Send your kids to the same school? Pray in the same house of worship? Rather, you often walk into a relationship cold and have to break through all the uncertainty to find the human element that brings you together although, as we'll see in a moment, you seldom have to walk into a relationship cold.

SHARING CREATES THE RELATIONSHIP

What do you know about the people who are key to your business success?

You know their names. You probably know their job titles and something about their responsibilities. You know their physical characteristics; she wears glasses, he's bald. But what do you know that is particularly important (and unique) to them, their interests, concerns, hopes, aspirations, dreams? Back to my original question, what do they treasure?

This is not what you guess is important . . . what you assume . . . what you think . . . what you've heard. What do you know in fact because they themselves have told you?

When I ask this question in seminars, the participants inevitably conclude, "We don't know very much about them." They don't know where their closest associates—let alone their clients and prospects—went to school, where they love to go on vacation, or what they would like to do more of if time permitted.

Someone in a seminar once asked, "What if you can answer all of the questions? Does that mean you have a good relationship?"

Not necessarily, but it's a good start. Remember, the process has three parts: Have the right mind-set. Ask the right questions. And do the right thing in inexpensive, unexpected, and thoughtful actions.

You want information from the person directly. Just because you read in a news story or a trade magazine that a man is an avid golfer or a woman is an ardent skier does not mean that he loves golf or she loves skiing. The information you learn through outside investigation may help you frame a question, but it is not the answer to the question. For one thing, the information may be wrong or outdated. Similarly, the information in company files, from lunchroom gossip, or from the last salesperson on the account is doubtful.

On the other hand, social media like LinkedIn, Twitter, Facebook, YouTube, and blogs can give you a wealth of information about someone. Indeed, they are the place to start whenever you are meeting someone new. In a chapter ahead, I'll talk about ways you can use these tools to build relationships; for now, let me point out that they can help introduce you to someone.

For example, someone's LinkedIn profile may tell you he is a graduate of Virginia Military Institute, was a scholarship football player, and, by clicking to his linked website, you can learn that he was born in Memphis, Tennessee, his first job was mowing lawns, and his favorite weekend activity is family outings. Someone else's profile will tell you that he is a graduate of City College of New York, is married, is interested in Japanese, Italian, marketing, sales, and criminal justice.

Following someone on Twitter will give you brief flashes into what they are doing, thinking, or following. Over time, short messages like the following tweets can give you major insights into an individual: "Think social media will replace e-mail and direct mail? Not so fast!" "Not including mobile in a marketing plan is a risk: new post about behavior-driven marketing." "Fascinating to see GE's Crotonville in action, in evolution. Learning and teaching at a mecca of leadership development."

Facebook may or may not have much information available to you; it depends on how much people want to share and whom they want to share it with. Similarly with YouTube; it depends on what a person wants to share. It is embarrassingly easy and cheap to create a perfectly adequate video, and reportedly people post more than 24 hours worth of video to YouTube every minute. Sales trainer Jeffrey Gitomer has more than 260 brief videos on his own YouTube channel, "buygitomer." Gitomer is sharing a great deal.

What you learn on social media, however, is only the beginning. The information means something only when the other person personally shares it with you. That sharing process, not the knowledge, creates a relationship's power. The other person's willingness to tell you—to want to tell you—about himself or herself makes the relationship real. It is the feelings, the emotions that come when someone talks to you about himself or herself. It is the mental progression a person takes that says, "I like me better and I feel better about myself when I am with you, talking with you."

So, learning what is important to people is key; learning it from them is crucial. You absolutely must get people to talk to you about themselves. When they share information with you personally, a dynamic starts and accelerates the relationship-building process.

This is why the raw facts about someone's favorite vacation or high school experience are less important than the telling about it. The act of telling is vital. When I observe people talking about themselves in seminars, I see three things: They are smiling . . . they are engaged . . . and they are interactive. Use the Link 20 questions to engender those positive emotions. The dynamic that takes place when two people converse meaningfully is infinitely more important than simply learning that someone went to Virginia Military Institute.

LEARN WHAT SOMEONE TREASURES

You are seeking two things: What does the other person treasure? In addition, what does he or she want/need to know from us? We have to learn not only what is important to other people personally, but also what they treasure professionally and what they need from us professionally. What do they require to do their jobs? What is important for them to accomplish?

The two are closely connected. If you know what and who people treasure—and you act on that information to show you know and care—they are much more likely to tell you what they need professionally.

True, in some situations you can learn what people need professionally through careful and persistent questioning. You do not need to build a strong relationship in every situation. If you are knowledgeable about the industry, the competition, and the business context, your questions may extract enough information to tell you what you need to know. But this is going about it the hard way. When other people respect and value you, you don't need careful and persistent questioning. They'll volunteer the information with a little prompting.

Whatever you are trying to accomplish, whether you are an accountant, a consultant, a project manager, or a salesperson, in essence you are trying to solve someone else's problems. You cannot begin to solve someone's business problems unless you understand his or her problems, the ramifications of those problems, and the issues surrounding those problems.

The only way to reach this understanding is to have people tell you truly what is going on in their business lives. To learn what is going on, you must find a way to engender meaningful dialogue, which, as I said earlier, is speaking the truth. It is talking about what is real, important, and factual. Meaningful dialogue is critical in any profession where you must accomplish tasks either with other people or for other people.

Many organizations are filled with jobs where people have much responsibility and essentially no authority. This is common in matrix organizations where a team member represents a certain functional area—finance, marketing, production, research, and the like—but has no real authority to punish or reward. All authority comes from his or her ability to build relationships and coalitions with others to get things done.

Each functional area has a certain spin on how it would like events to unfold, but the team has its own spin that may well be different. How individual team members juggle conflicting agendas can be tricky. But it is much easier to do it if they have good relationships with the people who can influence either the team's success or the functional area. Project managers in one recent seminar concluded they didn't have very good relationships with the very people who were critical to their success. They agreed, however, that if they could build better relationships with those people, they could get a lot more done—and have a lot more fun doing it.

In cross-functional organizations, people usually know very little about the issues, challenges, and objectives of other groups. If you don't know anything about finance, but you need a good relationship with finance, become close to somebody in finance. Have that person educate you; most people love to teach. The concept is simple, but it works nonetheless. If you can get more people to understand what you are trying to accomplish and why, the mere fact that you ask someone in another function about his or her goals and challenges will improve your relationship. Often people are surprised because nobody ever asked before.

At the end of the day, we all are trying to accomplish a specific objective and that objective usually has two parts. One is some organizational initiative, imperative, or goal. The other is some personal thing, usually intertwined with the organizational. If I get this accomplished . . . if I make this sale . . . if I meet this deadline, it makes me look better with my boss . . . my client . . . my customer. In addition, accomplishing this makes me feel better about my job and better about myself. It is easier to realize both parts of an objective if you have positive relationships with people.

And of course, to have a positive relationship, you must have meaningful dialogue.

You can usually have a meaningful dialogue only with someone who trusts you, so establishing your integrity is a condition for such a dialogue. When you are at the top of the Relationship Pyramid, you have, almost by definition, established your integrity, and you can have a meaningful dialogue. But until you get to the point where someone respects you, it's difficult to stimulate such dialogue on a routine basis.

THIRTEEN FACTS ABOUT HUMAN BEINGS

To move up the Pyramid and build strong relationships, you need a natural curiosity to ask questions other people wouldn't ask. You need to think about things other people wouldn't think about. But before I talk about the questions, let me establish a context for them.

Research shows 13 fundamental facts about human beings. Because relationships are interactions between two human beings, you need to keep these 13 facts in mind as you continue reading:

1. In general, people have a desire to be important.
2. They want to be appreciated.
3. They are not nearly as interested in you, your interests, or your concerns as they are in themselves.
4. Most people want two things out of life: success and happiness.
5. They want you to listen to them with your full attention.
6. People will connect with you only if they feel you sincerely value them.
7. Most people make decisions emotionally and defend them logically.
8. The average person's attention span is very short.
9. People with common interests have a natural rapport.
10. People want to be understood.

11. People are drawn to people who are genuinely interested in them.

12. Most people love to teach.

13. People want to associate with others who they believe can help them in some aspect of their lives.

Clearly, not every one of these characteristics applies to every single human being. Many would argue that while the attributes broadly apply to other people, they don't apply to themselves.

Obviously, some people (your mother, your spouse) *are* interested in you, your thoughts, your concerns. But in general, most people are more interested in themselves than in other people. You both distinguish yourself and build relationships when you demonstrate more interest in other people than in yourself.

In addition, different people define success and happiness in different ways, so you cannot assume values are universal. One person may define success as a big house and expensive car; another, as teaching or working for a nonprofit organization.

Nonetheless, these 13 generalities are the place to start. Think of your own good relationships. Does your spouse make you feel important and appreciated? Do you and your best friend have common interests? Do the people to whom you feel closest listen to you with their full attention? Do you feel they are genuinely interested in you? As Dale Carnegie wrote in his classic *How to Win Friends and Influence People*, "You can make more friends in two months by being interested in other people than you can in two years by trying to get other people interested in you."[1]

Again, you only move up the Relationship Pyramid when you are sincere and genuine. If you do not sincerely value other people or if you are not genuinely curious about them and their lives, you cannot reach the point where they will value a relationship with you. If you are not genuinely interested in other people, they will sense your hypocrisy and neither respect you nor value a relationship with you.

Remember that everyone we meet and everyone we do business with wants us to read his or her invisible tattoo. The tattoo is a command that, if heeded, will bring about dramatic results. We can sell more, we can manage better, and we can be more effective parents if we read this invisible tattoo and then genuinely and sincerely do what it begs us to do.

And what is it? Invisibly tattooed on the forehead of every person we come in contact with are four words: *Make Me Feel Important.*

These words can change lives. Psychologists tell us the deepest desire in human nature is the desire to be important. It is man's strongest, most compelling, nonbiological hunger. We want to associate with, do business with, and live with people who cause us to value ourselves. There is an almost uncontrollable urge to do things for the people who make us feel important.

Make me feel important and I'll probably like you. I'll listen to you. I'll most likely buy from you. I'll even follow you.

All you have to do to make me feel important is listen to me. Let me do the talking. Don't talk about yourself; talk about me. Notice me, learn something about me, learn something from me, do something special for me. I want to amount to something. I want to be special and you can help me be that.

Look at your prospects and customers. Look at your coworkers. Look at your friends. Look at your spouse. Look at your children. If you look carefully enough, you'll see their invisible tattoos.

LET THE OTHER PERSON TALK

A critical question to ask yourself is: What percentage of the time does a prospect or client talk and what percentage do I talk? If you scrupulously track these two percentages over a month and find that you're talking 90 to 95 percent of the time, you're talking way too much. A writer friend says that when he began recording his interviews, he was appalled to hear himself spending much of the interview talking about himself, his qualifications, his accomplishments, his interests. It went a long way to explain why his interviews were not very informative.

If the other person is not talking enough and if you do not really know what is important to him or her, you have a major problem. I would go further: It explains why you're not getting anywhere with the relationship. If what you're doing is not working, do something different.

When people talk about themselves, they smile, they engage, and they are easy to interact with. If you look at the people in your business life who are difficult but with whom you need a relationship, wouldn't you rather have them smiling, engaged, and interactive? Get them talking about themselves.

Every salesperson has stories about customers who could spare "just five minutes" until they started talking about themselves and only began to wind down a half hour later. Using this book's process, you can consciously, systematically, and routinely create those experiences.

Sometimes the interaction—the colleague chatting about vacation plans, the client reminiscing about high school—is more important than whatever you think you must accomplish. Because in the end, you need to be focused on the relationship, not just the sales activity. Remember that without meaningful dialogue, there is no selling. Sometimes the best call you can make is the one in which you never mention your product or service or idea.

Because Mike Accardi has been one of the top five salespeople in his company (of more than 40), a representative from a New York distributor came to Memphis and rode with Mike one day to pick up sales pointers. When they left one account, the representative was clearly irritated so Mike asked, "Is something the matter?"

"Yes, something's the matter," his guest said. "You realize in the last three hours we've made three calls? In that time, half the time's been spent talking about your kids. Nine-tenths of the balance of the time has been spent talking about Memphis State basketball."

Mike held up his order book. "But I got a book full of orders here."

"I know, and that's what ticks me off. Where I come from, you walk into a buyer's office and he says, 'You got ten minutes. Go.' You'd never make it in New York."

Mike agreed. "I wouldn't even try to make it. But customers have to spend their money with somebody, and they have to spend most of their waking hours at work, so why not try to make it enjoyable to be at work? I tell customers that 'You have to spend your money with somebody; why not spend it with somebody you like?' There are some cold-hearted situations where the deal will be only on price, and I spend minimal time on them. But a big part of my time is spent visiting."

SELL BY NOT SELLING

Years ago, the pharmaceutical company I was working for developed a value-added service for doctors: how to improve quality at the point of care—how to see more people in less time yet be more patient focused. The program required the doctors to study a continuing education lesson for one hour and then watch a 20-minute video once a week for six weeks.

We offered the program only to doctors who did not see drug representatives. The representatives told each doctor's nurse we were inviting only a few doctors, which was true, and we needed to ask the doctor personally to establish an interest level.

In roughly half the cases, the doctors who would not see representatives agreed to see them when they made that presentation to the nurse. Of those we saw and offered the program, 80 percent signed up for the program. In other words, for every 100 doctors who would not see drug representatives, approximately 40 agreed to attend the course.

Our representatives had to come back once a week to moderate a session on what the doctors were learning. We told the representatives they were not to talk about our product—they were there simply to deliver this service.

In an overwhelming majority of cases, the doctor would look at the representative after the second or third visit and ask, "What is it you sell? Because I'd like to know more about it."

When you provide real value to people in an unselfish way, they want to reciprocate. People—most people—want to return kindnesses. But you have to give first. You have to make deposits before you make withdrawals—yet as I pointed out in the last chapter, you're not keeping score.

We are drawn to others who are genuinely interested in us, and nothing conveys genuine interest more than active listening. Active listening is that process where we not only hear what they say, we process what they say, we ask questions, we embellish, and we clarify. It is all those things that tell the other person we are really focusing on this conversation. Active listening convinces people we are interested in them.

START WITH THESE 20 QUESTIONS

The other point I should make is that, contrary to the chapter title and the list that follows, there are not just 20 questions. There are hundreds—thousands—of questions. I use these 20 to start, but as conversation flows, you need to continue to probe to learn more.

These questions are the way you start. You are not filling out a questionnaire. This is not an interrogation. I am not suggesting you obtain answers to these questions and stop. You are not taking a survey. This is not market research. You are not asking to understand the customer's business so you can design products and technical solutions to their problems, although that may well be part of the process. Nor is the point merely to make a new friend, although that may also happen. The point is to build a winning business relationship and have fun doing it.

If you ask the following 20 questions properly over time, you will move up the Relationship Pyramid with most people. (The next chapter is all about how to ask a question properly.) The questions are:

1. What do you do when you are not working?
2. Where did you go to school (and how did you choose it)?
3. Where did you grow up and what was it like growing up there?
4. What was your high school like?
5. What do you enjoy reading when you have the time?
6. How did you decide to do [whatever it is he or she does] for a living?

7. Tell me something about your family.

8. Where is your favorite place to vacation?

9. What kind of vacation would you like to take that you have not yet taken?

10. What community associations, if any, do you have time to be involved with?

11. What sports, if any, do you enjoy participating in?

12. What sports do you enjoy watching?

13. If you could have tickets for any event, what would it be?

14. How did you decide to settle in this area?

15. Tell me something about yourself that would surprise me.

16. What things would you really want to do more of, but don't have time for?

17. What challenges/issues in your work might I, or my company, be able to help you with?

18. What is the most frustrating thing about being in your business these days?

19. In your opinion, what two or three qualities make a top-notch sales representative [or account executive . . . or management consultant . . . accountant . . . or whatever you are]?

20. If all work paid the same and you could go around again, what would you do?

Note that these questions—like all good questions designed to draw out information—are open-ended. They have no wrong answers. They are designed to get people talking about themselves. Only when people talk about themselves can you uncover areas of common interest and discover what is truly important to them. By asking the right questions in the right way and getting other people talking about themselves, you can move up the Relationship Pyramid to form closer connections with your key business contacts.

I know that different readers will be more comfortable with different questions. Some want to focus heavily on the business questions because they are not comfortable asking personal questions. (But how difficult is it to ask, "What was your high school like?" Start with the easy ones.)

Similarly, some people you meet in business will be uncomfortable talking about anything personal. But to build a relationship, you must learn what is truly important to the person you are having the conversation with. At a given time, that person might be thinking about the weekend, an upcoming vacation, or his or her family. Or, as John Fuqua, the Birmingham area sales manager discovered, they're worrying about organizing a meeting.

Every doctor's practice is busy, John says, and this particular group was in charge of the program for a statewide physicians meeting. The group president was the program chairman, and that year the meeting was to be in Montgomery, Alabama. The day John called on the group, they were so overcommitted that they were about to call off the annual meeting.

As a routine practice, John says he tries to find out what is going on in the customer's world to see how he can help them. That day, that customer needed help with the meeting more than anything John might be selling. John asked questions: "Tell me what you're looking for. Tell me the audience. Tell me the topics you're looking to cover. How can I help? Can I do the printing?"

As it turned out, John's company was able to sponsor the meeting. John did all the legwork. He had the invitations printed and mailed. He found speakers. The company held a picnic cookout at an area ranch for the 150 physicians and their families who attended the meeting. "We were able to provide the barbeque and the music," John recalls. "Everybody got a cowboy hat. We were there throughout the entire event and basically all the cups, napkins, and everything had our logo on them."

John says the situation was a win-win for both his company and the physicians. The doctors talk about that meeting to this day, John says. "It was probably the most fun meeting they ever had, and they were about to call it off until I asked: What are you looking for? How can I help?"

MEMORIZE THE QUESTIONS, BUT THINK FORM

The 20 questions attempt to give you specifics that you can plan to ask those people who are key to your business success. If you have trouble memorizing the questions, think FORM.

A "Dentist in McPherson, Kansas" suggested in a letter to the syndicated newspaper column "Annie's Mailbox" (October 23, 2002) that the acronym FORM can help you remember conversation-starting questions. The dentist's letter:

F is for family. Ask people about parents, children, or siblings.

O is for occupation. Ask what they do, what they would like to do, what they are studying, and what they like best about their job.

R is for recreation. Ask what they like to do in their spare time. This leads to a conversation about hobbies, sports, books, traveling, and music.

M is for motivation. Ask what motivates them in life. This is when the conversation gets more involved with religion and politics.

The dentist wrote that he tried FORM with his sister-in-law, and "she said it was the best conversation she'd ever had."

Good questions and attentive, active listening open doors. "Tell me what you do when you're not working" is much more effective than asking, "Do you have a hobby?"

First, many people do not have hobbies. Or they have them, but they don't call them hobbies. Second, everybody does something when they're not working. (And if they claim to work except when they're sleeping or eating, that tells you something significant right there.)

What they do when they're not working may tell you something about their feelings for the job. They hate it and it's only a means to support their nonwork activity. They love it and will be running the company one day. It may indicate their family life, their social feelings, or their ambitions:

"I play with my kids, get them ready for bed, read them a story."

"I've been helping on a Habitat for Humanity house."

"I'm taking a distance-learning MBA."

If you know for a fact that the person attended Virginia Military Institute because he tells the world he did on his LinkedIn profile, you can ask, "How did you happen to go to VMI?" If you know she went to college but don't know where, you can ask, "Where did you go to college and how did you choose that school?" If you are not sure the person attended college, ask, "Where did you go to school?" People who went to college tend to answer with its name. But do not assume everyone went to college, especially people who may be hypersensitive about not doing so.

You want to be as alert as possible not only to coming events, but also to what has just passed. If a colleague just returned from two weeks in Rome, it's a good time to talk about the vacation. How did you decide to go to Rome? Had you been to Rome before? What do you like about Rome? Would you want to go back?

The goal is to listen carefully so you can follow up with something related. Plan to ask the questions, but don't write them on your cuffs as if preparing for an exam. You should not be thinking, "Okay, what is the next question I have to ask?" You should be actively listening to what the person is saying.

These 20 are designed to get another person—a prospect, a coworker, the company president—to open up and begin to talk. Once someone begins to talk, two essentials should take over on your part: a genuine interest in and a natural curiosity about other people. If you have a genuine interest and a natural curiosity, follow-up questions will come to you naturally.

TELL ME SOMETHING THAT WILL SURPRISE ME

If you are able to set it up properly, the request "Tell me something about yourself that would surprise me" can open amazing doors. A good friend of mine, Dr. Mark Cohen, suggested the question.

Dr. Cohen, a prominent gynecologist in Birmingham, Alabama, can be a very imposing figure and is socially active in the city. A brand new representative for a company that sells birth control pills called on Dr. Cohen. When she asked if this very formal, buttoned-up doctor could tell her something that would surprise her, he said, "I have two passions other than my family. One is Elvis Presley, and the other is NASCAR—and that's something no other representative has ever known."

You would never suspect these passions from looking at Dr. Cohen or by the artifacts in his office. But he has a room in his house jam packed with serious Elvis memorabilia including tapestries and videos. He even went to Las Vegas where he and his wife reaffirmed their wedding vows, with most of his family in attendance, in an Elvis chapel with an Elvis impersonator officiating.

Dr. Cohen's point to me: "This representative knew more about me in two minutes than any other drug representative who had ever called on me." Once you learn that someone is a NASCAR fan, or he likes Elvis, how many other questions can you ask? What makes you like Elvis? How did you begin to like Elvis? Who is your favorite NASCAR driver? Do you get to go to the races? Whom do you go to the races with? There are a million things you can ask once you have a key bit of information.

I once took a key customer who had made a speech for our company to the airport, a 17-minute drive. In the car, I asked, "How was your talk?" He said it had gone fine. I then said, "Tell me what you do when you are not working." For the next 16 minutes, he told me how he loved to play racquetball and beat taller guys because it made him feel powerful. He told me about his love for wine and his love for travel, and I never spoke another word. When I got out at the airport to take his bag from the trunk, he said to me, "You are the smartest guy I have ever met. You will be great in this business." He did not know anything about me. I had asked only two questions.

The power of getting someone to tell you about himself or herself is incredible because most people desperately want to talk about their favorite subject—themselves.

John Fuqua recalls a lunch with a representative and a customer. "The doctor is very introverted, but we landed on his hot button, which was his family. He has three children, and when we asked about the family, he became a different person. It changed from a very tight-lipped, not-going-anywhere lunch. When we hit on that, it opened up the entire lunch. We got to know about his kids, their ages, what they like—going to the mountains to camp and fish."

John says that what he and the representative learned helped them understand a little more about what this doctor truly enjoyed, what he wants to do, what his children are thinking about, and, as they get older, what they might want to do. "That was fun, and the doctor enjoyed it so much he even said, 'Well, this has been a very nice getaway for me, and I really enjoyed getting to know you all and talking to you.'" As John concludes, this is a physician a representative can see only at lunch, and once a year at that. "Better make it count."

RESPECT THEIR TIME AND OPINIONS

You make it count by respecting the other person's time and opinions. Lance Perkins says that his physician wife resents salespeople who do not respect her time, try to force her into a conversation she is not ready to have, or do not have product knowledge. And she thoroughly dislikes those who come across cocky or arrogant.

For example, a representative was promoting his product. He asked, "Are you using this product?" Dr. Perkins said she was not. The representative responded, "I know how it is. Old habits die hard."

She gave him a look. "No. It is not a habit. It is my choice." The sales representative may have been trying to be quick on his feet and sound cool, but he came across as patronizing and condescending. (And this illustrates my earlier point that salespeople sometimes have trouble building relationships with prospects who buy competitive products.)

Julie Wroblewski was selling her firm's software and services to financial institutions. She once found herself in a difficult business situation, but her client said he could give her only a half hour to address it. It would not be enough; she estimated they needed at least an hour. Nevertheless, she decided to cover as much as she could in a half hour.

She kept one eye on the clock, and when the half hour was up she said, "We're at the half-hour mark. I respect your time, so perhaps we can pick this up later. I want to hold to your time frame and let you go."

The client said (in a remarkable admission), "That was a fictitious time limit, so let's continue talking."

The lesson Julie draws—and I agree with: You must take at face value what the other person says, whether you believe it is true or not. In time, people who respect you and value a relationship with you will not lie to you.

As we talked about respecting another's time and circumstances, Julie thought of another situation. She had driven four hours to meet with a woman who was the director of a home health agency. When Julie arrived, she learned that a terminally ill patient had just died. The client was clearly distraught and Julie told her, "This is obviously not a good time. Let's do this another day." Julie turned around and drove the four hours home.

Julie asks rhetorically, "Now, did my superior appreciate that? Probably not. But the client went out of her way to spend time with me the next time, and she did allow me to sell something. I think a lot of my success has to do with respecting someone's life and the situations around it, not just going through my presentation or my mission." Sometimes your goal for the day may have to be put aside for the next visit.

PLAN WHAT YOU WILL ASK

If you have prospects, customers, and colleagues who are key to your business success, don't just plan what you are going to tell them about your company, about its products and services, and about yourself. This is hardly an original thought; sales trainers, consultants, professors, even books tell you that business success depends on customers. Mike Gold, who manages Pat's Cleaners, a Scottsdale dry cleaning business, and who develops relationships with people as well as anyone I've ever met, says, "Without customers, you have nothing. Everything else takes a back seat. I always think I can get back to the other stuff—restocking, bookwork, or whatever. My customers come first." Of course, everybody says customers come first, but I can tell you from personal experience that Mike Gold lives it.

As Lance Perkins says, "So many times in life we know what to do, but we don't do what we know. We get caught by the constant drive coming down from the top executives of our organizations saying, 'You have to get this sale! You have to make the kill!' And you lose focus on what you are really trying to do." This should be building a relationship so that you can convey the value of your product and worth of your ideas.

To help maintain that focus, plan what you are going to ask so you can learn something about your key individuals to build a relationship. Before you talk to them, ask yourself: Which of these questions am I going to ask? Indeed, write down the name of the person and the question you are going to ask the next time you talk (see Figure 4.2). If you can get an answer to all 20 questions over time, you will move up the Relationship Pyramid with most people.

Remember that even if you know the answer, you still want to ask the question and get the person to tell you. Even if you know she loves golf or you know he is nuts about NASCAR racing, you want to get them to tell you about it because a dynamic occurs when they are talking to you about what they like. This dynamic makes them like you better and feel differently from that moment on. It happens because you allow them to tell you something about themselves that makes them feel better about themselves.

When you ask these questions, you are looking for the activities, goals, and dreams these people treasure. If you can get people talking about what they treasure, whether personally or professionally, they will talk for a long time and you begin to build the relationship that counts. But again, don't assume, don't guess, and don't presume. Ask them questions that help you understand what and who is important to them, and focus on both the personal issues and the professional.

What is the person's company trying to accomplish? What is this person trying to do within the company? If you know people well, they will tell you almost anything. I even ask people to explain how they are evaluated. If they are evaluated on a matter where you can make a contribution, you can help them and benefit yourself.

Figure 4.2
What Will You Ask at Your Next Meeting?

Contact name: _____

Question: _____

Contact name: _____

Question: _____

Contact name: _____

Question: _____

Contact name: _____

Question: _____

Contact name: _____

Question: _____

Contact name: _____

Question: _____

Contact name: _____

Question: _____

Contact name: _____

Question: _____

Contact name: _____

Question: _____

This goes back to the whole concept of meaningful dialogue being truthful.

You should use the information from the 20 questions for two specific purposes. One is to plan the conversation that builds a relationship. If I know Dr. Cohen likes NASCAR and Elvis, I have many more questions to ask. If I know the company is planning a major expansion, I can suggest suppliers, job candidates, or lenders.

The second purpose is once you learn what people treasure, you can plan unselfish and unexpected acts that demonstrate that these individuals are important to you.

If you really want to get to know people and to find out what is important to them, you have to ask them the right questions. There are hundreds of questions you can ask people, and once they begin to tell you what is important, you will think of other questions. But for a start, plan to ask one or more of these 20 questions the next chance you get.

Of course, to avoid sounding like a market researcher filling out a questionnaire, you have to set up the question properly.

CHAPTER 5

ASK THE QUESTIONS PROPERLY

Asking a good question is an art. It is often important to preface questions so the answers encourage meaningful dialogue. Asking the Link 20 questions in the last chapter as if you were filling out an opinion survey, however, will not build a positive business relationship. In many cases, you must request permission to ask the question. Good questions asked properly beg to be answered; bad questions elicit superficial answers. Good questions seek information honestly; bad questions seek data to serve a selfish purpose.

I believe we can promote good answers in two important ways:

1. The atmosphere of comfort and safety we create when we are with the other person.
2. The quality of our questions to further facilitate that safe feeling so the person wants to answer truthfully and candidly.

Indeed, the only way to have a genuine relationship is to be honest and open, to be truly curious, and to share information. This may sound very warm and fuzzy but not very practical. Does it do anything for the bottom line? Will it help a consultant or an accountant bring in more business? Will it help an employee in a matrix organization do the job? Will it help salespeople sell more?

In fact, it will.

If people trust your word and trust your intentions because they have learned over time that you are honest, open, and willing to share, they will be willing to work with you, to buy from you, to take your ideas into account. In time, you will move to the top of the Relationship Pyramid. However, as Mike Accardi knows, you have to get on the Pyramid in the first place.

MOTIVES MATTER

My friend Mike Accardi in Memphis tells of visiting a new prospect for his firm's packaging supplies and asking to see the company manager. The secretary said, "He only sees people by appointment." Mike said he was sorry, that he does not make appointments, and would come back another time.

Three weeks later when he was back in the area, Mike returned to the building. The same secretary said the same thing, "Sir, he only sees people by appointment."

The manager could see Mike standing at his secretary's desk through a window in his office. He came sprinting out of his sanctuary wearing an angry look. "You were here three weeks ago, weren't you?"

Mike said, "Yes, sir."

"She told you I always see people by appointment."

Mike said, "I'm sorry, sir. I thought I made it clear that I don't make appointments."

The manager looked surprised. "What are you talking about?"

"I don't have an agenda for you. Why should I schedule some of your time when I don't know what I am going to sell you—or if I'm going to sell you anything? I just try to stop by to serve as a reminder to look at the area of your business I deal with because over time I have found that my stuff doesn't matter a whole lot unless you have a need for it. So, my coming by just serves as a reminder in your busy day to look at these few areas to see if there might be some way I can help."

As that was sinking in, Mike continued, "I don't mean to be a smart aleck. I can make appointments. But what am I going to do? Make an appointment to come back to say, 'Hey, do you need anything?' "

After a moment, the manager said, "Well, come on back," and they went into his office.

Mike says that after that appointmentless beginning, he learned the business *did* have needs his company could satisfy. He was able to get meaningful dialogue because his motives were healthy. He wasn't there just to sell his company's products; he was there to learn whether the firm needed the products. Once the prospect saw Mike as different, he treated him differently from other salespeople. What is more, Mike and the manager became such good friends that their families hung out together.

SETTING UP A GOOD QUESTION

Let me talk about the art of setting up a good question because a part of what you need to do is to make sure that the people you question will want to answer.

Not that they always will. If you are sitting next to somebody on an airplane (as I was not long ago) and you say to your seatmate, "Where do you live?," he may say, "Birmingham."

You could then ask, "What made you move to Birmingham?"

"I was born there."

You try another subject. "What do you do for a living?"

"I'm a carpenter."

"How'd you get in that business?"

"My father was a carpenter."

This is not an exchange that is going much further. The brief answers tell you this person does not feel safe with you and does not want to have the conversation or is focused on something else. You may meet someone on a bad hair day who simply is not interested in anything but the matter at hand—if that. As I said at the beginning of this book, this relationship-building process does not work with every single person every single time. A few people will not be responsive no matter how you set up a question.

(In all fairness to the Birmingham carpenter, we were strangers on a plane. He did not expect to see me again, and I did not see him as a potential client and was not trying to start building a relationship.

Also, his mother may have impressed on him it is dangerous to talk to strangers.)

Usually, of course, you have to give information if you expect to get any. If you treat the situation as an interrogation, you are very quickly going to shut down the flow of information. The other person's degree of openness very often reflects your own. If you won't tell other people what you do when you're not working, or where you went to college, or where you grew up, why should they tell you?

Suppose you ask, "Where do you live?"

The other person says, "I live in Skokie."

You then have the opportunity to respond, "I live in Evanston. My wife and I moved there a couple of years ago because she was teaching at Northwestern" (assuming all this is true). With your openness, he will feel safer with you. Most people will show you their cards if you show yours. But it has to be a roughly equivalent exchange. I'm not showing five if you're showing three.

I often say, "Tell me about your current job." Most people will tell you about their current job, but some will tell you about every job they've had since college. Other people will tell you about their current job and stop. If someone gives you that kind of answer, it would seem to invite the question, "That is interesting. I've always wondered if I had a chance to start all over again, what I would do. If you had a chance to start all over, what would you do?" That might open up a dialogue.

ANALYZE THE BRIDGE TO THE QUESTION

Consider the way the sales representative set up the question, "Tell me something about yourself that would surprise me," with my friend Dr. Mark Cohen. Because that particular question can shut down a relationship instantly, the way she prepared him for the question is a superb example of how you get somebody to answer a question many people find embarrassing or offensive. Indeed, I tried that question on the investment banker wife of a good friend without any preparation. She bridled, "If somebody asked me that, I'd throw him out of my office."

So while the question can open doors, about half the people, by my admittedly rough estimate, will not answer. I suspect they won't because they do not think there is anything interesting about themselves that would surprise you, and they are not out-of-the-box thinkers. But the half who will answer are worth asking.

Much depends on how you set up the question. Listen to the way the representative set it up with Dr. Cohen. It was her first meeting and she said, "I'm new." That was absolutely true.

"I'm going to be calling on you for a long time." Again, most likely true.

"I'd like to differentiate myself from other reps." The statement makes sense on its face, so it's probably true.

"It occurred to me it might benefit me to know a little something about you personally." At some level, most of us believe it would benefit the other person if he or she knew a little something about us, therefore we would agree with this.

"Would you mind if I asked. . .?" Dr. Cohen could withhold his permission.

"Tell me something about yourself that would surprise me." The representative's entire body language and tone of voice conveyed sincerity and genuine interest. Dr. Cohen, like most people in the same situation, felt she truly wanted to know, and, as a result, he wanted to tell her of his Elvis and NASCAR passions.

I suspect that had I prepared my investment banker acquaintance for the question in this way, she would have said something like, "Well, there's not really anything about me that would surprise you." Not everyone has a secret—or semiprivate—passion. Not everyone wants to tell you something that would surprise you.

On the other hand, she might have said, as a well-dressed, professional woman once told me, "I'm a biker; I'm a Harley bitch." I am sometimes shocked at things people tell me. One guy told me his brother died in a car accident saving him. A woman told me (and a roomful of 200 people) that she performs nude in the theater. Another woman told me she was "Miss Teen D.C." A third woman told the group that she was adopted when she was three years old.

"Tell me something about yourself that would surprise me" is a particularly interesting question because, by answering it, the person reveals something not immediately apparent and something important to him or her. It can be a door into a private life and a path to lifelong friendship.

WHAT DO YOU NEED TO ACHIEVE TODAY?

My friend Tony Buckalew sells Oracle software solutions to colleges and universities. He says that when he visits with a client, "I have a plan in my mind on what I am looking to achieve. It may be just to get down the field two yards, so you have to look at your strategy—what do you need to achieve today?" Because it takes a year to 18 months on average to sell a system, Tony has plenty of time to build relationships with his customers.

He feels that a salesperson should have an end goal in mind for every sales call. The goal may be to learn what sports the client likes to watch or how the family decided to settle in the area. It may not be a business-related goal, but if you don't have a plan in mind, says Tony, "and you just go in there loosy-goosy and open, you are never going to maximize your potential with the client."

If you preface the Link 20 questions correctly, most people will answer them most of the time (but not always; again, this does not work all the time). As I said at the beginning of this chapter, good questions seek information to build the relationship; bad questions seek data to serve a selfish purpose. Before you ask the 20 questions, think how you might preface them to set them up or buffer them so they do not sound preemptory or intrusive.

All good questions seek truthful, honest, candid answers. But they often must be introduced in such a way that the other person responds with truthful, honest, candid answers. So the way we ask, the language we choose, and the way we introduce the question can dramatically affect the quality of the response. We should use the same rigor to plan these questions that we use to plan for an important sales call, our performance appraisal, or our meeting with the big boss.

Julie Wroblewski says she formulates her questions before a meeting. She feels you should prepare questions appropriate for what you want to discuss with the flexibility to junk them if it is apparent the other person wants to go in another direction. More often than not, however, if you have prepared and thought through your questions ahead of time, you can set the agenda. "Asking open-ended questions and letting someone talk is not rocket science," says Julie, "but I do pay close attention to those things."

Ewell Hopkins says that every Sapient client has unique needs, and the company can offer unique solutions tailored to each client. "But even if I were selling automobiles, where one car is much like another, each client is unique," says Ewell. Automobile salespeople sell more than a piece of machinery. They sell the sense of freedom, an expression of self, and a statement of status. Car buyers satisfy those needs through the automobile they buy. To be successful, the automobile salesperson must determine each prospect's emotional need.

At a somewhat more sophisticated and complex level of selling, Ewell says, "I use questions to probe for needs, goals, and to obtain more information. The more open-ended the questions, the better. The more continuity in the probing questions—so they don't seem disjointed—the better. I think questions need to demonstrate a pattern of thought or a rationale so the person being asked doesn't grow bored or confused. People have to understand where you are heading, and I like questions that have some aspect of explanation. 'This is why I am asking this' indicates the goal and the kind of information you're looking for—but not necessarily a specific answer. You don't want people spending a lot of time wondering why you're asking what you're asking. Explain why you're asking the question." And listen to the answer.

Active listening demonstrates your empathy to the business requirement or the needs you are about to explore. "Beyond the obvious of gathering information and obtaining a better appreciation of the challenges ahead, all of which are critical," says Ewell, "I think it demonstrates a sense of professionalism. If you start off talking, the client is going to believe you are not prepared to listen and understand his or her unique needs. You have come in with a predetermined conclusion." Active listening shows you respect the other person's time, situation, and ideas.

ASK PERSONAL QUESTIONS FIRST

If it is important you talk about business—and not every business call must be about business—you can set up the personal question and bridge to business questions. One way to do that is to say something like, "Before I give you my commercial . . ." or "Before I talk about my product, I thought it might make some sense for me to ask you a different kind of question. Do you mind if I ask what you enjoy reading when you have the time?"

Tell people at the beginning of the meeting that after we have this social, personal interaction, we still need to talk about business. I know this is not always easy or possible. Setting up these questions is not effortless. It takes practice, practice, practice. Great salespeople plan their sales questions in advance, and when they get a good question, it is like a talisman and they use it forever. Planning these buffers or prefaces is no different. Once you get a great setup to a question, you can use it again and again. Crafting a great setup that feels right for you may not be natural to do, but it will dramatically impact the quality of the response that you get to your questions.

Some of the 20 questions are innocuous enough that you can probably ask them of almost anybody under most circumstances. Few people bristle when you ask, "Where do you live?" "What do you do for a living?" or "How did you get into it?" You can ask most people "What do you do when you're not working?" without much introduction or preparation. On the other hand, "Where is your favorite place to vacation?" may be too personal to ask someone without a little bridge to the question or setup.

By a bridge, I mean saying something like, "I'm trying to decide where to go on vacation. One of the ways I thought might make sense for me to do that is to ask some people I respect what kind of vacations they like and see if we can come up with something unique or unusual. Do you mind if I ask—what kind of vacations do you like to take?"

If you're not trying to decide where to go on vacation, this is not an appropriate bridge for you. Don't lie to the person with whom you want to build a relationship. Do not say something untrue even for an innocent purpose. If you're not open to a new place to go on vacation, create your own introduction from your own true situation.

Brenda Stapleton, a hepatology representative with Roche Laboratories, tells me she has found a good bridge to the vacation question for her busy customers is something like, "You are so busy taking care of other people all the time. When you have time for yourself, what is something that you like to do that just takes care of you?"

Brenda finds they often talk about family activities and vacation plans. She will often ask, "Hey, when are you going to get a chance to take some time off work and get away from all of this?" That question "gets them to talk about their vacations and their families."

Does Brenda find customers resenting her questions? Not really. Occasionally someone is having an off day. She says, "I talked to one customer whose partner had just gotten back from a conference and I said, 'Well, you had to hold down the fort, so when is it going to be your turn to take a little bit of time off? Do you have a vacation planned?' He said, a little more abruptly than usual, 'No, not this summer.' A few minutes later he said, 'I apologize. I'm not really talkative; I feel like I'm getting the flu, and I don't feel well today at all.' That was probably the reason for his response."

The permission question—"Do you mind if I ask?"—can be answered "Yes" or "No." In my experience, however, virtually no one ever says "No." The people I ask inevitably answer the open-ended vacation question. They talk about the vacations they like to take (or their current reading . . . or the community associations they're involved with . . . or whatever they are interested in).

Nevertheless, I always request permission—"Do you mind if I ask?"—because it makes the other person feel he or she is consenting, permitting me to go into an area where I would not naturally go.

You have to consciously think about the situation and plan what you should say to obtain permission, but most people don't do it.

Most salespeople plan carefully what they are going to say on a sales call, and they spend hours figuring out how they can overcome this objection or answer that question. Consultants will rehearse the presentations they plan to make for hours. But virtually no one plans what he or she should say to build the relationships that are key to their business success.

They have not memorized the 20 questions they should be asking or the bridge to those questions so that the other person wants to answer. Many of the more penetrating questions need thought and preparation. You don't walk into a meeting and ask the prospect you've never met, "What things would you want to do more of, but don't have time for?"

Take that specific question as an example. You don't drop it on someone. You listen for the right occasion. If you ask someone what he does when he's not working and he says, "I'm always working," you have an opportunity to say something like, "I know that feeling and I've always wondered what I would do if I had time to do it. Have you ever thought about what things you would like to do, but don't have time for?" Virtually everybody will answer the question if you set it up that way.

I suspect that people who are uncomfortable asking questions of a personal nature are uncomfortable sharing notions of a personal nature. They have cognitive dissonance. They don't want to ask where someone goes on vacation because they don't want to be asked where *they* go on vacation. They don't want to ask what someone does when not working, because they don't want to be asked.

It could be they were raised with the idea that a person's private life is private, and a person's business life is entirely separate. They may feel ashamed or embarrassed. They feel a kind of competition in college experiences, vacation plans, or leisure activities. They may feel their alma maters, vacations, or hobbies cannot be as glamorous, interesting, or sophisticated as someone else's. To ask where someone went to college is to risk an invidious comparison with their own school.

This is unfortunate because the likelihood these people will be able to develop many relationships at the top of the Relationship Pyramid is not good. Others may respect them for their technical knowledge and their ability to answer technical business problems, but they will probably never have an emotional connection with customers and colleagues.

Remember that people tend to decide emotionally and defend logically. If your ultimate objective is to persuade someone to your point of view, you need an emotional connection, not just a logical connection. Without the emotional, you are going to fail much of the time. The American philosopher William James said 85 percent of decisions are emotional, not logical. You need an emotional connection with people if you are going to be ultimately successful in persuading them (which may be why successful politicians rely more on emotional appeals than cool logic to accomplish their goals).

But because we are building better business relationships, how do you set up a business question?

HOLD UP A BOOK

Years ago, I found that an almost infallible way to open a business dialogue was to carry a book. In those days, I carried around *In Search of Excellence* by Tom Peters and Robert Waterman. Another business book that has impressed you will do just as well. (You could even—modest cough—use this one.)

In a customer's office, I would hold up the book and say, "I've been reading this book," which was true. "You know what this book tells me? It says we will never be a great company unless we ask our customers what they think, and it occurred to me we rarely do that. So what I would like to do today is to ask you some questions. Is that okay?"

Over eight years, I must have asked a thousand doctors that question. Of the thousand, every one—100 percent—said, "Go right ahead."

I would ask three specific questions about the kinds of products we were selling, how they could use those products, and how they make a decision about which product to use. If these three questions are not appropriate for your situation or your industry, ask one of the 20: "What challenges in your work can I, or my company, help you with?" or "What is the most frustrating thing about being in your business these days?" or "What two or three qualities, in your opinion, make a top-notch sales representative or account executive?"

You can use a more recent book such as *Made to Stick* by Chip Heath and Dan Heath and say something like, "I've been reading this book, and it says if you are going to be a great company you have to get to know your customers. You have to understand how your customers think. And with that in mind, I'd like to ask you some questions if that's all right with you." If you don't know what to say, a book is always a great bridge to use. And you can use it again and again.

Always keep in mind that you are not going to learn everything you need to know on one call, in one meeting, or in one visit. As I said earlier, building a winning business relationship takes time. In some meetings, you may learn almost nothing new; in others, you may learn a person's entire business history.

And never forget that many people love to teach things. They like to share their knowledge if you demonstrate you are truly interested. When you ask people to educate you, you almost automatically make them feel important.

You are not asking for proprietary information (or shouldn't be), so they should help you understand what two or three issues the organization faces today. When you sincerely ask people to educate you, their guard comes down and they feel they can open up and tell you. The conversation then becomes a dialogue and the relationship grows.

It is always a good idea to use a book. It's even more effective if you read it first. But it is not difficult to find a business advice book that suggests you ought to know your customers.

DON'T SUGGEST AN ANSWER

If you want to gain information—as opposed to scoring points or forcing a choice—you have to ask questions that do not point toward their answers. A question such as, "Wouldn't you like to increase the quality of your promotional brochures?" has only one reasonable answer, which is why inexperienced salespeople tend to ask a version of it in every situation. That is not the kind of question I'm talking about. Nor is the traditional forced choice that assumes a sale, with the slick salesperson asking before the prospect has made any commitment: "Given your production schedule, would you prefer delivery on Wednesday or Friday?"

There are entire sales scripts designed to force prospects into a corner where the only answer is "Yes, I'll buy your product/service." Salespeople who use these scripts are feeding the stereotype of the callous, manipulative salesperson. They may make sales, but they are not building good relationships. They are making their own jobs harder than they need be because, without good relationships, they have to continually find fresh prospects or force customers back into the corner where they'll order. It's an old-fashioned and less and less effective way to sell.

People who don't know you well sometimes tend to give the answers they think you want to hear or they think makes them look good. If you can ask a question in a way that doesn't presume an answer, you are liable to get better information.

In fact, your ability to gain valid information is a function of your ability to be sincere, genuine, and to demonstrate a natural curiosity. You are not seeking any specific answer; you are seeking to learn. It is almost like due diligence. You are trying to learn as much as you possibly can because the other person and his or her business/organization/industry interests you. That the information you learn about the business may ultimately pay some dividend is almost a side benefit. The goal is to build the relationship through your genuine interest.

FIND COMMON GROUND

Remember that building a winning business relationship requires two kinds of information: what or who the person treasures personally and what he or she needs professionally.

Also remember that although the 20 questions appear in a numbered order, there is no rule that you must ask them in that order.

Figure 5.1
Topics to Establish Some Common Ground

- Cars
- Clothes
- Sports: spectator or participant (coach or play)
- Hobbies: collecting coins, stamps, antiques, toys, books; fishing, hunting, diving, photography, golf, gardening, reading, movies, theater, travel
- Pets: dogs, cats, birds, horses, snakes
- Family: spouse, children, spouse's interests, children's interests
- Friends
- Heroes/mentors/colleagues
- Art: painter, sculptor, museum attendee
- Music: classic, opera, swing, jazz, rock, country, alternative, rap. Play an instrument?
- Dance: ballet, modern, jazz, country
- Alma mater: prepschool, college, graduate school, military, fraternity, sorority
- Clubs: Rotary, Kiwanis, Elks, Civitan, Scouts
- Home town
- Home state
- Home country
- Charities involved in or associated with
- Neighborhood or area in which they currently live
- Goals, dreams, wishes, or plans

Indeed, depending on the individual, you may want to ask all of the business-related questions before asking any personal questions. In my experience, however, the personal questions often lead you to find some important common ground.

This is key because you build relationships on common ground. Common ground is something—anything—you have in common with the other person and, as Figure 5.1 shows, covers a wide spectrum.

For example, you ask, "What do you do when you're not working?"

"I'm into watercolor painting."

"Really? My brother is a painter. What kinds of things have you been doing?"

Or you ask: "Where did you go to college?"

"University of Pennsylvania."

"My best friend went to Penn. When were you there?" You ask the second question to see if there's any possibility he was there at the same time your friend was. If their times overlapped, you ask, "Is there any chance you knew. . .?" Given the university's size, the odds are small that the two knew each other, but you never know—and if your best friend and this person turn out to be fraternity brothers, you move up the Relationship Pyramid in a jump.

Simply asking where people live, what part of town they live in, and where they grew up are opportunities to find common ground. You look for these commonalities because, as research has repeatedly established, we like people who are similar to us. "This fact seems to hold true whether the similarity is in the area of opinions, personality traits, background, or lifestyle," says Robert Cialdini in his book, *Influence: Science and Practice*.

Cialdini warns his readers against salespeople who claim to have backgrounds and interests similar to their prospects. "Car salespeople, for example, are trained to look for evidence of such things while examining a customer's trade-in. If there is camping gear in the truck, the salespeople might mention, later on, how they love to get away from the city whenever they can; if there are golf balls on the back seat, they might remark that they hope the rain will hold off until they can play the 18 holes they scheduled for later in the day; if they notice that the car was purchased out of state, they might ask where a customer is from and report—with surprise—that they (or their spouse) were born there, too."[1]

Salespeople like these are not building relationships. They are using a basic human attribute to manipulate prospects for their benefit. But while the manipulative can (and do) use the characteristic, so can (and should) the sincere and genuine use it to build relationships.

The common ground need not be strong and may be only a starting point.

But a relationship usually starts with common ground. First you learn this, then you learn that ... and the next thing you know, he is telling about his child who has an alcohol problem. He tells you because he is comfortable sharing it with you. Because he trusts you and respects you.

The common ground is, for lack of a better metaphor, the onion's outer skin. It moves you to the next level of information—of intimacy—and the more you can peel back layers of the onion, the more you can intensify the relationship. The illustration indicates that discussing common ground over time gradually increases the value of the relationship. When you get to the top of the Relationship Pyramid, you will have done a lot of peeling. If people value a relationship with you, they know a great deal about you, feel safe with you, and

Figure 5.2
Relationship Development Usually Takes Time

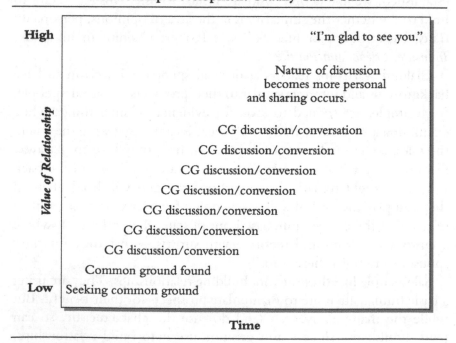

respect you, just as you know a great deal about them because they have told you (see Figure 5.2).

Finding common ground is not chitchat. It is not useless. There is a reason for it. Once you find common ground, continue to build on it. The more common ground you find, the deeper the relationship is likely to be. This is why when you talk for three hours with a stranger on an airplane with whom you find common ground—the reason you can talk for three hours—you exchange cards when you deplane and you are introduced to the spouse who is meeting the plane. Such contacts usually go no further than the airport terminal, but you feel the beginnings of a relationship because you have shared common experiences, ideas, and feelings.

Ultimately, you want to go beyond the common ground. The common ground is to feel secure in what you say. Once other people feel secure with you, they are willing to open up more, to trust more, and to share more kinds of information. The personal questions of the Link 20 help you find common ground, and they form, I think, a continuum from the least to the most personal.

MAKE THEM THINK

One of my salespeople and I once called on a urologist in Anniston, Alabama. The doctor was committed to a competitive product to treat infections, and before we went in to meet the doctor, the representative told me, "You will never sell this guy."

I said, "I'm not trying to sell him. I'm trying to learn if there's a fit between what he is looking to do and what we have."

We met the doctor, and I told him the same thing. I was not trying to sell him. Indeed, I promised I would not sell him. I was visiting only to learn if there were a fit between his needs and our products. Was it all right to ask a few questions?

The doctor agreed it was all right, and I asked my questions. Once he answered the questions, I got ready to leave and said, "The next time the representative comes in, he'll tell you why you should be thinking about prescribing our drug."

The doctor looked surprised. "Why don't you tell me right now?"

"No. I promised you I wouldn't do that. I'm not going to go against my word."

The doctor said, "You are not leaving here until you tell me why I should consider your drug."

That was such a flat command, I said, "Do you mind if I argue with you then?"

The doctor sat back in his big chair to hear me out. "No, go right ahead."

"You said you chose a drug because it kills the bacteria e-coli." He nodded in agreement. "You told me that 90 percent of what you see is e-coli, but the other 10 percent, you told me, is all kinds of stuff." He agreed again.

"You also told me that when you're sitting at the nurses station trying to decide which drug to use, you have no idea what the bug is, even though you know 90 percent of it is e-coli. So, I don't think e-coli is important for this reason: Almost all antibiotics kill e-coli. Your issue is not what drug kills e-coli. Your issue is: What drug has the greatest likelihood of success every time you prescribe it? Now, if that's what you are looking for, the drug you're using doesn't fit that description. Our drug does," and I explained why.

Because he looked thoughtful and did not contradict me, I went on, "Now, let me back up and say that what I just told you, while true, is not statistically significant. If you use the drug you're currently using, you're probably going to cure 98.99 percent of patients, and if you use ours, you're probably going to cure 99 percent—statistically insignificant. But, if you want the drug with the greatest likelihood for success every time you prescribe it—it's not what you are using right now."

I never said, "Will you use our drug?" "Will you try it?" "What do you think?" But after hearing me out, the doctor picked up the phone, called a local hospital, and changed two people who were on the other drug to ours. Without hanging up the receiver, he called another operating room and told the nurses to change his preprinted orders to our drug, so that every appropriate patient received our drug and the doctor didn't have to think about it.

As we were leaving, the doctor said to me, "You have a great representative here, but you know something? He never made me think."

STIMULATE REAL THINKING

Those five words—he never made me think—were like a light bulb going on over my head. It finally dawned on me, after years of selling, that when you are trying to persuade another person, you must provoke thought. You cannot sell a product, a service, or an idea if you don't stimulate real thinking. Without real thinking, the likelihood you will see any change in behavior is probably close to zero. This means you have to think about what you can do to make the other person think.

This is another reason why the relationship is so important. It is much easier to have a dialogue with somebody with whom you have a good relationship than when you have no relationship. When you have a good relationship, you can trigger real thought (in your head, as well as in the other person's). When you have no relationship, the only thought in the other person's head may be how quickly he or she can get rid of you.

Like everyone I've talked to for this book, Julie Wroblewski says she consciously tries to listen more than she talks when building a relationship, particularly with a new prospect. She notes that salespeople are notorious for spewing words. "Many salespeople seem to ramble on just for the sake of hearing themselves speak and hope they will say something that triggers the prospect to buy something."

Julie says she not only asks questions, but also asks permission to take notes of the answers. By using her time to ask questions—the opposite of what many prospects expect from a salesperson—and taking notes, Julie gains the other person's attention and invaluable information about the person and the business.

Julie also mentions eye contact. "To me, you cannot do anything better than make eye contact in a first meeting. To me, looking into someone's eyes instills trust. I've met salespeople who don't look me in the eye when I'm the prospect. I don't buy from them. I need to see a salesperson look at me. It gives me a sense of comfort, and I think you need to feel comfortable before you buy anything from a salesperson."

WAYS TO GAIN RESPECT

Because mutual respect is so important in building winning relationships and creating a meaningful dialogue and an atmosphere of comfort, let me take a moment to talk about it.

How do you gain respect? I suspect that when we meet someone for the first time, the needle on the Respect-O-Meter is usually in the neutral zone. The person feels neither respect nor contempt. From your first action—a firm handshake, looking the other in the eye, smiling—and your first words—"I really appreciate your taking time out of your busy day to speak to me"—the person begins to form an opinion, one that either holds you in respect or not.

Often we do and say things that send the needle into the "disrespect" zone. We're late. We're unprepared. We appear to be biased. I respect someone who is objective, and I don't respect anybody who seems to be biased. I can like someone who is biased—I might enjoy a round of golf with someone who believes all poor people are lazy and untrustworthy, for example—but I will not respect his views on Welfare or the criminal justice system.

A salesperson I knew well came up to me after one seminar and said, "I now know why my customers don't respect me." I asked why she thought that was so. She said, "I realized while you were talking. It's because I don't respect me. They will never respect me any more than I respect myself. I know why they like me, because that's been my goal, but I've never asked them to respect me because I don't have as much respect for myself as I should."

I said, "As a religious person, Vicki, you don't need to get your greatness from anywhere other than from the person upstairs. You are just as worthy as any other human being, and you of all people should understand that." The seminar had been a revelation to her.

Figure 5.3
How Will You Preface the Questions You Ask at Your Next Meeting?

Question: ______________________________

Preface: ______________________________

Question: ______________________________

Preface: ______________________________

Question: ______________________________

Preface: ______________________________

Question: ______________________________

Preface: ______________________________

Question: ______________________________

Preface: ______________________________

Question: ______________________________

Preface: ______________________________

Question: ______________________________

Preface: ______________________________

Question: ______________________________

Preface: ______________________________

Question: ______________________________

Preface: ______________________________

Some people don't like themselves because they are overweight, or have a bad complexion, or are shy. They wish they could change things they don't like about themselves, but they don't change and so they beat themselves up for not changing. A certain amount of self-acceptance must take place before you will be effective in developing relationships. Most of us are harder on ourselves than anybody we will ever meet (possibly excluding our families).

To function effectively, you must accept that you are doing your best. If you're truly not doing your best, you probably shouldn't respect yourself. In that case, you should do what is necessary to change. Try to correct what you do wrong, but don't overreact because you make a mistake. Don't lie. Keep your word. Do what you say you are going to do and accept that all you can ever do is your best.

Ewell Hopkins says, "At the end of the day, the key word is sincerity. You had better bring sincerity to the experience or you are going to be found out real quick. If you are not sincere about what you are doing, you shouldn't be doing it." If the other person experiences your sincerity, you are more likely to engender meaningful dialogue.

But even if you are sincere, you have to ask your questions in a way the other person wants to answer truthfully and candidly.

Think about the people and the questions you plan to ask that you wrote down at the end of the last chapter. How will you preface those questions? Write down the exact words you plan to use and practice saying them aloud (see Figure 5.3).

Remember that you often must ask permission to ask the question. Although almost everyone will give you permission, not everyone will respond to every question. Not every visit should be entirely about the personal or the business, although there will be times when it is appropriate to talk only about personal interests just as there will be times when you should talk only business.

Another issue you should pay close attention to is the unexpected personal connections you may have with someone if you look hard enough.

CHAPTER 6

PROBE FOR SMALL WORLD CONNECTIONS

Here are three quick it's-a-small-world examples that could be multiplied endlessly.

I was giving a speech to a pharmaceutical company and mentioned I was in from Memphis. Later that morning, a young man, Stephen Bell, came up to me and said, "You mentioned you were from Memphis. Did you ever know a guy named Bud Garrett?" Bud Garrett, as I wrote in the Foreword of my first book, was the single greatest motivator of people I'd met before I was 25. Garrett was Stephen's grandfather. He had an incredible impact in my life, and I've now developed a terrific relationship with Stephen.

Another example: I was having breakfast with a client who is a good friend, Mike Hartman. We got to talking and he said he played football at Lebanon Valley State. I said, "Really? Did you happen to know Jim Monos?" He said Monos was his coach and had taught him everything he knew about leadership. I said, "Well, I played college football with him." Monos and I then reconnected and every week we carried on a running discussion about what was going on with his successful Lebanon Valley State team.

One more: I was in a meeting with a client I'd never met before. As Gary Casto, the vice president of sales, talked during this meeting, it was clear to me he's from the south. At a break I went up to him and said, "Hey, man, you're not from around here."

He said, "No, I'm from Memphis."

I said, "Really? I'm from Memphis. Did you go to school in the south?"

"Yes, I went to Memphis State. And played baseball."

"Did you know Bobby Kilpatrick?"

"He was my college baseball coach."

I said, "He was my high school baseball coach." That was the beginning of our relationship—we had the same baseball coach. Gary has become a terrific client and an even better friend; he is one of the most savvy, effective sales leaders I've ever met.

As you uncover information about people, stay alert for connections. You are looking for connections among all of the things you know about yourself, your world, and the people you deal with and all the things and people they know. Whenever you make a connection—whenever you find a mutual friend, colleague, or acquaintance—it helps you move up the Relationship Pyramid.

CONNECT FOR YOURSELF

One important reason you ask questions is to see if you can make connections. If you can make the connection, you can accelerate your trip up the Pyramid. If you find a mutual friend, you have some common ground, and common ground, as I pointed out, gradually improves the value of the relationship over time. Even better, I can go from not knowing your name to liking you almost instantly if I know someone at the top of my Relationship Pyramid likes you. It's the old "The friend of my friend is my friend . . ." adage in action.

If I know my friend likes you and I value and trust my friend's opinion, you are up the Pyramid in a fraction of the time. We experience a version of this every day when we ask someone we trust, "Do you know a good mechanic? A reliable plumber? A skillful tailor?" The plumber you call based on a friend's recommendation is several levels above the "People that know me by name" level on your personal Relationship Pyramid.

This is the principle behind such websites as Angie's List (www.angieslist.com), Yelp (www.yelp.com), and the dozens of product and service review sites on the Web. While you may have no relationship with the person recommending the butcher, baker, or plumber, the ones they recommend are still further up the Pyramid with you than the plumber you found in a Yellow Pages ad.

The small world phenomenon is even more significant when you are trying to gain someone's trust. As John Maxwell writes in *Becoming a Person of Influence*: "People are reluctant to trust you ... when they are worried about whether they are safe with you."[1] If other people feel safe with you and trust you, however, and they know the person whose trust you are trying to gain, you want to make those connections. Moreover, the extent to which somebody is willing to leverage your relationship says volumes about how much he or she trusts you.

I should make it clear that connecting is not networking. A good definition of networking comes from David Lewis (president and founder of Operationsinc.com, a Stamford, Connecticut, consulting practice), writing in the *Fairfield County Business Journal*. Business networking is "the connection between businesses and their representatives with the common goal of sharing information about the available pool of prospective clients. By developing an effective network, a business can exponentially increase its pool of prospective clients, securing leads from those with whom you partner."[2] While there is nothing wrong with this—leads are good—it does not give you a Relationship Edge.

Many books tell readers how to network; for example: *Nonstop Networking: How to Improve Your Life, Luck, and Career,* by Andrea R. Nierenberg; *Power Networking,* by Donna Fisher et al.; *Masters of Networking,* by Ivan R. Misner and Don Morgan; *Make Your Contacts Count: Networking Know How for Cash, Clients, and Career Success,* by Anne Baber and Lynne Waymon; *Dig Your Well Before You're Thirsty: The Only Networking Book You'll Ever Need,* by Harvey Mackay; and *Breakthrough Networking: Building Relationships That Last,* by Lillian D. Bjorseth.

Networking organizations have sprung up all over the country to help businesses large and small obtain contacts. Most cities have at least one such group and some have several. The groups usually allow only one representative from any one industry, and many require that newcomers be nominated by a member and approved by a majority vote. This is serious business. Ann Field reported in the *New York Times* that members of the Business Forum, which operates in 15 cities, must generate three to five leads per quarter.[3]

Building a strong business relationship has elements of networking, and clearly people who network may also build strong business relationships. You can use the strategies in this book when you network. The key difference, it seems to me, is that the Relationship Edge gives you a strong connection with a relatively few key people. Networking is an effort to make some connection with as many people as possible.

USE THE SMALL WORLD PHENOMENON

Brenda Stapleton at Roche Laboratories was able to use a small world connection and an inexpensive, unexpected, and unselfish act brilliantly to improve her relationship with one of her prospects.

One August, when Brenda and other salespeople took computer training classes in New York City, the group went to see a musical on Broadway. On the bus to the theater, a co-worker remarked to Brenda that it's a small world—Kelly Sheehan, a member of the show's chorus, had been a high school buddy of his daughter. He hoped to go backstage at the end of the performance to say hello to her.

As it turned out, Brenda and her associate were both able to go backstage and say hello to Sheehan—making the evening much more memorable for Brenda than it might otherwise have been.

Back home in Indiana, Brenda was talking to one of her prospects a couple of months later. "I asked if he was going to one of the upcoming conferences," she says, "and he said, no, he wasn't able to do that. I asked if he was going to take any vacation time, and he said, no, his daughter was in musical theater and was going to be involved in rehearsals and then a show she was doing."

Brenda asked about the show and mentioned that she herself had been a theater major as an undergraduate and had been involved in a lot of musical comedy and dance. "The more we talked about theater, the more he opened up and discussed his daughter's aspirations." He walked Brenda out to his car where he had a demo CD his daughter had made. "She has a beautiful singing voice," said Brenda, and the doctor said his daughter wanted to send the CD to *American Idol* or *Star Search*. He said she had a keen desire to graduate from high school and go off to college or, better yet, go to New York and audition for a job performing on Broadway.

Three weeks later, Brenda was back in New York City taking her parents to the same show she'd seen in August as a Christmas present. As they went into the theater, she told them, "It would be really nice if somehow I could figure out a way to see Kelly Sheehan again. Maybe she'll remember me, and I could get her to autograph a Playbill for me."

It had occurred to Brenda that Sheehan had done just what the doctor's daughter wanted to do—go to New York after high school, audition, and be cast in a Broadway show. An autographed program could inspire the doctor's daughter. It could suggest that she was not dreaming an impossible dream.

Brenda not only saw Sheehan after the performance and had her sign a Playbill, but also the actress gave Brenda a big poster with pictures of the entire cast with all their autographs. She also gave Brenda a book, detailing the history of the show's development.

The next time Brenda was able to visit the doctor was an exceptionally busy day at the practice. At one point, the doctor hurried past, saying, "It might be a few minutes; I am really busy."

Brenda recalls, "He wasn't avoiding me, just letting me know that he really didn't have time for me. So, the next time he walked past, I said, 'I understand you're busy, and I'm really not here to talk about product to you. I just wanted to deliver something for you to give to your daughter. And you don't even need to take the time to look at it now. Look at it at your leisure and give it to your daughter; I think she'll be excited by it."

With an introduction like that, the doctor could not leave the package untouched. When he pulled the autographed poster, the autographed Playbill, and the book from the bag, he was overwhelmed. "I can't believe this! You did this for my daughter?"

Brenda said, "Well, in the conversation we had, you talked about her desire to be in musical theater. I thought she'd like to know it could happen."

Brenda's inexpensive, unexpected, and thoughtful gift (which I'll talk about in more detail in a chapter ahead) put her at the top of the doctor's mind. Her considerate gesture had (and continues to have) practical, positive consequences.

This chain of cause and effect may sound tenuous—from the daughter of Brenda's colleague to Kelly Sheehan, from Kelly Sheehan to Brenda to the customer's daughter—and it's not something you could plan. Brenda could not have known she would be meeting a cast member when she went to New York for training. She could not have known a customer had a theater-struck daughter. Could not have known that Kelly Sheehan would be so generous. Could not have known the extent of the customer's appreciation.

We all have small-world stories. Bob Holman, the CPA in Birmingham, says that when he first went into practice in 1976, one client was an insurance business that consisted of two brothers and a secretary. "They went through some difficult times, getting started and trying to make enough money the way they were trying to do it, which was a little unusual."

Added to the ordinary stresses of starting a business, the brothers often battled with each other. The secretary got caught in the middle, and Bob was called in to act as referee. "I had to tell them this is the way life really is, guys, and you have to get on the ball. You're doing this wrong, and you're doing that right—just be honest with them, which is what they were looking to me for."

Ultimately, the secretary quit the brothers' insurance business; she liked both brothers but did not like being in the middle. Thirteen years passed before Bob heard from her again. When he did, she was married to a local business owner. The business is fairly large and they were very unhappy with their CPA. "She wanted me to come and talk to them about taking on their account," says Bob. "I had not heard from her in 13 years. No contact whatsoever. It was a relationship I'd built, and I'd built it on sometimes being the bad guy, but by being honest and being what they needed. I think she realized that and that was what they were looking for, and now they're one of the best clients I have."

I recall meeting John Fitzgerald, an independent financial planner associated with the Acacia Group in Phoenix, at a Cardinals football game. As John tells, "I am in the stands and the guy in front of me is wearing a VMI sweatshirt. I went to Virginia Tech, and Virginia Tech and VMI used to play each other all the time. I grabbed his shoulder, turned him around, and said, 'Hi, my name is John Fitzgerald, did you go to VMI?'" It's a small world. I did go to VMI, and John and I began talking.

We had a lot in common, so the conversation took off from there. I sat in front of John at the football games for the rest of the season and enjoyed seeing him every week and talking to him. He finally asked if we could get together sometime and really talk about what he does.

Now the second small-world part: The financial planner my wife Maryann and I were working with had worked at John's firm and John knew him. "He is a good guy and everything, and if you have a good relationship with him, you should stay with him." But we did not have a good relationship with him; he didn't help us understand what he was doing and would not return calls consistently. John said, "If that's the case, I'll try to get you comfortable with what we're doing. If you have questions, I'm here to answer them, and I will follow up with you." Maryann gave John her account, and we ultimately gave him much more of our business.

Sometimes these small world stories result in nothing more than an interesting anecdote that illustrates once again how coincidence (if it is that) colors daily life. I led a program in North Dakota at a hotel on an Indian reservation about 12 miles from the Canadian border. I had never been to North Dakota in my life, and I know only one person in the state. I had not seen that person in seven years, but because he lives 300 miles from where I would be speaking, I did not tell him I would be visiting. I flew to North Dakota, led my program, and at the lunch break I looked out, and who was in the lobby? Pure chance. He did not know I was coming; he had another reason to be in the hotel. The only person I know in North Dakota. There was no direct, immediate business consequence, but what are the odds?

You can increase the odds of making a small world connection in business by constantly looking for a relationship that will benefit you. You do that by really probing and continuing to jump off the information you learn on to something else that will bring you closer. Where did you go to school? Where have you lived? Where have you worked?

Most industries are relatively small islands in the sea of commerce. If you have worked for any time in an industry, you know people who know people. If you have built strong relationships, they can help you build new relationships.

CONNECT FOR THE OTHER PERSON

But you want to do more than connect for yourself. As Zig Ziglar says in *Secrets of Closing the Sale*, "You can get everything in life you want, if you would just help enough other people get what they want."[4] You want to help other people make connections.

For example, Tony Bonelli and I have known each other for years. We worked for companies that had a strategic partnership, then lost touch for six or seven years. One night I was having dinner with a friend who happened to bring Tony along. Tony and I reconnected, and at a breakfast meeting a month or so later, we started talking about what we were doing. I told him that I was trying to talk to Pfizer but couldn't get anybody to call me back. I asked if he knew anybody, and he introduced me to John Woychick, the senior vice president of sales.

I now have breakfast with Tony every two or three months, and recently he told me he was just starting to market and sell a new software product. As he explained the product to me, I was thinking about the people who are my customers who might benefit from the software. I made a list of several people I would contact on his behalf.

I did contact those people and said, "I would like you to see Tony Bonelli. I think he has something you would be interested in." Five of the seven agreed to meet with him, and Tony moved further up the Relationship Pyramid because I leveraged those relationships for him. Also, because it's a small world, he knows a couple of the people I know. If you have ever said, "Call so-and-so and use my name," you are helping the other person connect.

You want to be alert to making connections in the best interests of the customer or colleague. Connecting is not just doing something to benefit yourself. It is also finding some connection to benefit the customer or colleague. You look for things where you may be able to make a connection. Most of the time, of course, you probably will not make a connection, and occasionally you run into a concrete wall.

My friend Tony Buckalew hit such a wall when he was trying to interest one college chief information officer in Oracle's system. This CIO was a former U.S. Army colonel, now retired, who loved to swap West Point and military stories. Tony at the time was 38 and had never been in the service. He was finding it impossible to connect with the colonel; they seemed to have no acquaintances in common and not a lot to talk about outside of very narrow business concerns.

Although the narrow business concerns are absolutely critical (you are not, after all, doing all this simply to make new friends), they are seldom enough to persuade the other person. Particularly when, as in Tony's case, we are talking about multimillion-dollar sales negotiated over a year or more. Remember that people make most decisions emotionally and defend them logically.

Oracle did have a retired U.S. Army brigadier general on its staff, and Tony was able to bring him to the college, introduce the general to the colonel, and sit back as the two built their relationship. Ultimately, Tony made the sale and the general became the system's executive sponsor.

This is another way of considering the small world phenomenon. If you cannot build the relationship yourself (and it happens), perhaps you can bring someone else into the situation. Not all of us can call on brigadier generals to help us out, but, fortunately, we do not often require that kind of heavy artillery. Always be thinking about connections regardless of where you are or what you are doing.

CONNECT WITH DIFFICULT PEOPLE

How do you use the small world concept to connect with your difficult customers or colleagues? First, you inventory all those places where you have relationships high on the Relationship Pyramid and you find out whom they know. How do you leverage those relationships so that it matters? You should always try to discover if the people with whom you have a strong, positive relationship know those difficult people.

LinkedIn can be an invaluable source in researching these connections. Is someone you know connected to someone you want to know? Is there some way your connection could help you with that person? Would they be willing to use their own relationship to arrange an introduction, set you up with a dinner, or make an appointment for you?

I had a difficult prospect in Haleyville, Alabama, who gave me as much attention as he gave a piece of reception room furniture. I finally asked one of my friends if he knew the man. He said, "Of course I do. He's a great friend of mine." He picked up the phone, called the prospect, and said, "I want you to see Jerry Acuff." (I have since learned that this is Pyramid hopping, which I'll talk about in a chapter ahead.)

With that entrée, I went to lunch with the prospect, and by the end of lunch he had agreed to use my product. The one phone call from my friend to his friend on my behalf made all the difference.

You have to proactively look for these connections, however. People are not going to tell you about their other relationships, not because they are uncooperative but because they don't know whom you need to know. With your good relationships—those people who trust and value their relationship with you—you can always ask for help. That, remember, is one of the marks of a relationship at the top of the Relationship Pyramid. They will help you when you need it just as you will help them.

People will only go to bat for you when they really believe and trust you, because your performance, good or bad, reflects on them. If someone will not make the call for you and is evasive about the reason, it may be a symptom your relationship is not as strong as you thought.

I find, however, that people generally do like to share their good contacts because it makes them feel virtuous; they are possibly helping other people. In such a situation, they usually believe correctly that they are helping both you and their friend.

PROBE FOR CONNECTIONS

If you are alert to the small world phenomenon, you can use it to accelerate your movement up the Relationship Pyramid. It cannot, and should not, replace time exploring common ground, asking the 20 questions, and doing inexpensive, unexpected, and thoughtful acts. It will almost always take more time to build a strong relationship than we might like in our fast-paced business world. But when the small world phenomenon kicks in—or you kick it in—building a relationship can speed up somewhat.

When I first started doing business with Patrick Higgins, the vice president of sales and marketing, Roche HCV, for Roche Laboratories, he told me he wanted me to work with the company's Phoenix representative, who was one of their top salespeople. No fool I, I said I'd be glad to. Pat told me the representative's name was Tim Hutsko.

There are approximately 90,000 pharmaceutical representatives in the United States. One of them happens to be my wife's cousin. The cousin happens to work out of Phoenix ... happens to work for Roche (I thought he worked for Glaxo) ... happens to be named Tim Hutsko. It's a small world. I immediately had more credibility with Pat Higgins because of my relationship with Tim.

But you have to be looking for those connections. LinkedIn can help, but not everyone is on it, and not everyone is connected to your contacts. Sometimes, as in this case, the connection is serendipitous, but sometimes it results from your continuing to dig to see if some link exists. Whom do you know and whom do they know? Probe to

Figure 6.1
"What Questions Will You Ask to Establish Connections?"

Question: _____

_____

Question: _____

_____

Question: _____

_____

Question: _____

_____

Question: _____

_____

Question: _____

_____

Question: _____

_____

Question: _____

_____

Question: _____

_____

Question: _____

_____

find if there are connections. Indeed, fill out the form in Figure 6.1 with the questions you could ask to learn if you can connect the dots from one relationship to another.

The more often you can make the connections and the small world phenomenon kicks in, the faster you accelerate up that ladder. Look for connections and commonalities, and don't assume there are none. Memphis is a big city. Why would someone assume that because you grew up there you knew Bud Garrett or Bobby Kilpatrick? You wouldn't, but as you probe, you may find a connection exists when it is difficult for you to imagine such a link could exist. Bonding happens faster and can be more lasting when a real connection takes place.

But all this is not enough. You must do more than talk; you must actually do things to show that you listened to the other person and that you care about what he or she says.

CHAPTER 7

BUILD RELATIONSHIPS
ON ACTIONS

Relationships aren't built on your mind-set or the information you gather—necessary as those both must be. You build your relationships on your actions. You build them not on what you say but on what you do and how you do it.

Good relationships exist because people trust you and feel close to you. Your objective in building strong relationships, therefore, is to draw people closer to you and to trust you. To build trust, you must demonstrate your professionalism, integrity, caring, and knowledge over time. To show you care and in order to get close to people, you do inexpensive, unexpected, and thoughtful acts for other people based on the information they have shared with you.

By continually demonstrating your professionalism, integrity, caring, and knowledge, you can move to the top of the Relationship Pyramid, the point where people value a relationship with you. How much time? Again, the only honest answer is, "It depends." But certainly more than a couple of weeks or a couple of months.

Your professionalism is how you do what you do. It is the skill, competence, and character one would expect of people in your profession who are really good at what they do.

Your integrity is the quality of possessing and steadfastly adhering to high moral principles, professional standards, or both. It is reflected in the persistent, consistent, predictable actions that say who you are over time. You show it by your willingness to take a stand and to be a person who is perceived as having strong convictions but also an open mind. You have principles, but you are not pigheaded. You are always willing to listen to another point of view and change your mind when new evidence convincingly refutes something you believe.

You demonstrate your knowledge by what you know and know well. You want to be a person who has demonstrated some superior knowledge and understanding of either a subject matter or of the other person's field. The better you understand another person's field, the more penetrating questions you know to ask.

Sales representative effectiveness in face-to-face situations is a function of mastering three areas: knowledge, messaging, and relationships (KMR). If you believe that, you will put forth the effort to become proficient in all three. If you believe that KMR is important, your mind-set forces a decision—what am I going to do about this?

It is important to recognize immediately that *just* knowledge or *just* messaging or *just* relationships is not enough. Sales success requires the combination of all three as well as a mental commitment to all three. Knowledge, messaging, and relationships are not just three critical concepts; they also involve your mind-set. Mastering knowledge, preparing every call, and using words that will resonate with prospects and customers play a significant role in the success of KMR, because without the right mind-set, you will not behave differently enough to have a profound effect on the people you are trying to persuade. And one of your goals should be to differentiate yourself from all other salespeople, engineers, accountants, or whatever your contacts may be.

Your professionalism, integrity, and knowledge tend to be specific to what you do professionally. These factors apply differently to a machine tool salesperson, an engineer, or an accountant. For that reason, I will devote the rest of the chapter to caring, because that is not specific to any one profession. Actions that demonstrate you care transcend business, profession, industry, and job description. When you demonstrate that you care, you draw people closer to you, and if you have also demonstrated the professionalism, integrity, and knowledge relevant to your position, you have done all you can do to build that relationship.

SHOW YOU GENUINELY CARE ABOUT OTHER PEOPLE

You establish you care by your compassion, concern, and thoughtfulness for others. When you have demonstrated over time that you genuinely care about other people—their feelings, desires, and dreams—and not only about yourself, you have shown you are a caring person.

One way to demonstrate that you care is to use what you know other people treasure in unexpected, thoughtful, and—preferably—inexpensive acts to demonstrate you have listened and that these folks are important to you. These actions show you are genuinely interested in the other person and want to build a closer relationship. They also demonstrate you are not like most other people.

Here is an example of what I am talking about. Several years ago, I hired Valerie Sokolosky, who heads Dallas-based Valerie & Company, to teach business etiquette to a group of national account managers so we would know which fork to use at a formal banquet or how to introduce someone properly at a reception. During the day-long program in Dallas that October, I learned that Valerie's son was an actor in Hollywood. She told me his name and the name of his TV show, but I'm afraid I didn't recognize either one.

Back home, I asked my 16-year-old daughter if she'd ever heard of Brandon Douglas. "Brandon Douglas!" She couldn't believe her old man had any connection with fame and brilliance. "Of course I do! I love Brandon Douglas!" I mentioned my daughter's reaction when I next talked with Valerie a few weeks later, then put it out of my mind.

On Thanksgiving Day, my home phone rang at 10 A.M. It was Valerie. I wondered why she was calling me on Thanksgiving, but after we chatted for a minute, she asked, "Is your daughter there? Can you put her on the phone?" Suddenly I knew why she called. Who was home for Thanksgiving at Valerie's house? Her kids—specifically Brandon Douglas.

I gave the phone to my daughter and Valerie gave hers to Brandon. My daughter could barely believe she was talking to a real live star she routinely watched on television. They chatted for perhaps five minutes, and she floated through the rest of the day. Brandon sent her an autographed picture that she kept for years.

Valerie's call was an inexpensive, unexpected, and certainly thoughtful act. It touched something I treasure—my family. Valerie's action moved our relationship to another level on the Relationship Pyramid. Valerie was no longer just another training resource, someone I might think of when I needed help. Valerie had demonstrated a sincere interest in something other than my ability to hire her. She and I still have a close business relationship, and we routinely help each other with contacts.

It is not enough to know what someone treasures to build the relationship. Asking the Link 20 questions gives you only information. To develop the relationship, you must act on it.

BUSINESS GIFTS ARE NOT UNSELFISH ACTS

Let's make a couple of things clear. I am not talking about traditional business gifts—the golf balls, travel alarm clocks, pen sets, and coffee mugs with the company's logo. Nor am I talking about golf junkets, resort weekends, or dinner and a show.

For one thing, such presents may be illegal. The New York State Ethics Commission charged that five information technology companies broke the law when they gave gifts to executives of the Nassau Health Care Corporation (NHCC), a quasi-public health care provider with one hospital and nine community health centers. It receives about $60 million a year in Nassau County aid.

In New York, the law states that executives at publicly funded institutions cannot take gifts worth more than $75 from vendors. Gifts include money, loans, travel, meals, refreshments, or entertainment. Those who accept such gifts face fines of up to $10,000 per violation as well as criminal charges. According to the Ethics Commission, the presents to NHCC's executives, totaling $10,272, included limousine and plane fares, hotel stays, restaurant meals, and playoff tickets to a New York Islanders hockey game.

Even when a gift is not illegal, it may violate an organization's own rules. Walmart's corporate policy is to destroy all gifts to its employees—even a cup of coffee—or give them to charity. If an employee violates company guidelines by accepting, say, opera tickets from you and loses his or her job as a consequence, it's not going to help build your relationship.

The Pharmaceutical Research and Manufacturers of America adopted voluntary marketing guidelines for member company sales-people. These guidelines forbid representatives from offering meals to physicians without some sort of accompanying informational pre-sentation, and they prohibit gifts of substantial value or anything not directly connected to patient care. As *Medical Economics* reported, "Even a $30 gift certificate to a bookstore is a no-no under the new rules, unless the certificate is redeemable solely for a medical textbook or other health-related book."[1]

There are times when you as a generous soul (or as standard business practice in your world) may want to provide a gift, but the other person cannot, for reasons of law or company policy, accept one. When in doubt, call the company's human resources department and ask about guidelines.

But what about the other situation? The prospect/customer/client wants or expects a gift? For example, Greg Davies, director of sales for Action Printing in Fond du Lac, Wisconsin, had taken a prospect to lunch and after leaving the restaurant they passed a country-western store. "All of a sudden, the prospect stopped dead in his tracks, and his eyes lit up," Davies told *Sales & Marketing Management* magazine.

He was looking at the store's window display, which featured ex-pensive cowboy boots. Davies' prospect turned to him, grinned, and said, very slowly, "I have always wanted a pair of boots like this."

"There was no mistaking it," said Davies. "He expected me to buy him the boots." Davies said he simply smiled and began walking again. Action Printing's policy is not to offer expensive personal gifts to clients in exchange for business. Nevertheless, Davies said he felt awkward around the buyer from that day on.[2]

Davies may feel awkward, but he did the right thing. In my experience, people who can be bought are rarely worth buying. They are not worth the investment because they will almost always go to the next higher bidder. If you don't plan to be the highest bidder when the auction ends, don't start the bidding. You do not give gifts—even unexpected, thoughtful gifts—to buy people, their business, or their friendship.

Businesspeople who covet gifts are not the people you want relationships with anyway, because the relationship does not mean anything more than a calculated commercial exchange, and usually a poor one at that.

BE ALERT TO OPPORTUNITIES

Your actions differentiate you from other people. Many people have the same information you have but do nothing with it. The actions you take set you apart from others in a person's business network, and they are the foundation on which you develop meaningful relationships. Once you understand the principle behind inexpensive, unexpected, and thoughtful acts, you can be sensitive to possibilities and opportunities you never realized existed.

Because the people with whom you want to develop strong business relationships are individuals, I cannot give you a list of sure-fire actions you can use with them. I can (and will) give you some principles and examples, but because each person is unique, I am afraid I have no one-size-fits-all suggestion.

Building a strong business relationship requires you to be alert both to what people tell you and to opportunities to demonstrate that you listened. The key is to listen. Indeed, the best way to truly understand the other person is to be a great listener.

As Linda Richardson says in her book, *Stop Telling, Start Selling*,[3] listen to question, not to answer. Often when we seem to be listening to people, we are trying to decide how to respond. What do I say next? Richardson's suggestion: Listen to formulate the next question you need to ask in order to truly understand what the person is saying.

I agree. I believe that very often we are one or two questions short of true understanding. I tell people that when somebody expresses their point of view, the natural tendency is to either agree with it or rebut it. What I've learned to do is say, "Tell me how you came to that conclusion." Because here is what I know: If you are really going to understand the person, you have to know where the belief originated. If the belief came from an article in a newspaper, that's one thing. If it came from an industry expert, that's something else. Once I know the source, I have to decide whether the belief has a solid foundation. Maybe I shouldn't challenge it. If the foundation is not so solid, maybe I can challenge it in a way that is not combative. But I try to understand not just the idea or the point of view, but its origin, where it came from. This process is all about ensuring you are listening carefully and asking the right questions.

The answers to the Link 20 questions generally fall under nine headings: important dates, important names, special concerns, important people, important goals, major events, favorite foods, schools attended, and important places. Here are some ideas—thought starters—of what you might do to show prospects, customers, or colleagues they are important to you.

Important Dates

Obviously, important dates vary by individual, but for most people their important personal dates—the ones they want remembered—are their birthdays and wedding anniversaries (although not every person wants to be reminded of his or her age or marriage). Other possibilities include the date the company was founded, the date the person joined the company, the date he or she earned degrees or graduated from college, and any other meaningful and recurring dates in the person's life.

When you know the date is important, put it on your calendar and do something to recognize it with a phone call, a card, a cake, a pie, or a special meal, which does not have to be expensive.

Other ideas include sending a copy of a newspaper published on the date. Do some Internet research and send profiles of famous people born on the same date.

If you know the person would like his or her birthday recognized, make sure the staff knows the date is coming.

If you are going to—or can make it your business to—visit the office on the date, bring a birthday cake. If not a cake, perhaps a pie, or a balloon. A surprising (to me) number of people never received birthday cakes when they were kids. Homemade is better than bakery, but supermarket is better than none. It does not have to be elaborate; indeed, a cupcake with a candle says "I was thinking of you."

A cake story: I knew a salesperson—I'll call her Kate—who could not get in to see a certain buyer. Kate learned from the buyer's executive assistant that the guy loved chocolate cake. So Kate ordered a chocolate cake to be delivered together with her card to the buyer every Friday for three weeks. At one o'clock on Friday afternoon, the cake arrived, but no Kate.

On the fourth Friday, Kate stayed by her phone. At 1:05, the buyer called. "Where's my cake?" Kate said, "I'll bring it right over."

Of course, you do not have to tie your action to a specific date. How many greeting cards do you get over the years? Dozens? Hundreds? Thousands? I still remember one I received more than 20 years ago from Gene Vezina, a former boss. I had been reasonably successful, and he sent me a card that said on the outside, "This is a list of the 10 people I most appreciate." Inside, "Your name is here 11 times." Thoughtful acts are often fondly remembered, and they say a great deal about who you are.

Important Family Names

These include the names of children, spouses, and other family members close to the person. For most of us, few things are more important to us than our children. Every time you work with someone, ask a lot of questions and use your natural curiosity. Ask about their children; learn their ages. Learn what grades they're in, the activities in which they're involved, the sports they play. Learn their interests,

interests they may share with your children, your spouse, even with you. And—key point—record it somewhere.

Electronic gadgets like laptops and smart phones make it easy to record all this information, the children's names, their birthdays, anniversaries, interests, and more. Likewise, they make it ludicrously easy to recall the information. When you talk with one of your key people, you can ask about Trevor and Tommy and about her husband and about her niece, who is the spelling bee champ.

And you can do much more than simply use the child's name in conversation. A friend's wife, Marian, was chatting with a colleague in another city who told her he had just become the father of a baby girl. Coincidentally, he and his wife had named the girl Rose, the name of Marian's granddaughter. Marian, who loves needlework, bought a plain baby bib and embroidered "Rose" and a rose on it, and sent it to her colleague. The bib cost less than $3 and 30 minutes of Marian's time, but the effect on the colleague was priceless.

One recent weekend, my wife and I took our two-and-a-half-year-old to a hospital emergency room because we thought he had an ear infection. There are two hospitals about equidistant from my house. That Sunday I learned the one I've always gone to in the past does not have emergency pediatric care, so we went to the other one. Two days later, the hospital called to follow up on our visit. Because that call was inexpensive, unexpected, and thoughtful, I've switched hospitals. The original visit was not inexpensive, but the call certainly was and it told me the staff cared about my son.

If you learn that a customer or colleague's children participate in an activity—football, basketball, soccer, theater, dance, whatever—and if your schedule permits, go watch. Even better, get involved in the activity—Boy Scouts, Girl Scouts, Junior Achievement, sports. When my daughter was young, I coached girls' softball both for her sake and because one of my biggest customers also coached girls softball. It was a chance for me to know him away from the office and we became best friends.

Is there a way you can help your customer or colleague's child (or spouse) reach his or her goals? John Fuqua says that the daughter of one of his physician customers wanted someone to speak at her high school's career fair about sales and, in particular, a career in pharmaceutical sales.

John has a particularly good relationship with the physician. "He said I was the first person he thought of, and if I could speak it would help him out a lot because his daughter was one of the students in charge of finding speakers. I told him I'd be glad to."

John says the career fair worked out well. The speakers had an opportunity to talk about what they do, "which is something I really love." He found it personally rewarding because these students are starting to think about what they want to do when they leave school. The doctor's daughter, says John, is very interested in pharmaceutical marketing. "I don't know if that's what she is going to end up doing, but right now she's in business school and we'll see."

Because he knows the young woman's interest, John has offered to let her ride for a day with one of the company's sales associates to see if she likes the job once she sees it firsthand. "A lot of people have the feeling that all we do is take doctors to lunch and we don't really work hard, when in fact it is a difficult job. It's a lot more than eight to five on most days. Most people love it, but we have had some students, once they have a chance to ride with us, go, 'Well, that's really not what I thought.'"

Anne Cobuzzi, a senior brand planning manager at AstraZeneca, says she was touched one day when a woman with whom she works brought in a huge bag of clothes for her daughter. The woman had a daughter about a year older than Anne's and said, "Because my daughter was cleaning out her room, I thought about your daughter and I thought she might like this." Anne points out that she never asked for the clothing, and she earns enough to dress her three children without help. "It was just the fact that they thought of me, which I thought was so nice."

Special Interests

I am calling these special interests for lack of a better term; they include lifestyles and activities. Lifestyles covers things like vegetarianism, committed involvement in social issues (active volunteer in church or charitable organizations), and conscious participation in environmental matters (drive a fuel-efficient car, buy only organic fruits and vegetables). Even a life committed to work could be a lifestyle.

Activities include sports and hobbies: golf, tennis, skiing, bass fishing, hiking, hunting, basketball, Ultimate Frisbee, sailing, woodworking, quilting, gardening, painting, photography, stamp and coin collecting . . . the list is immense (and publishers produce one or more magazine titles for everyone, just as there are specialized websites for most if not all).

Interests include the stock market, international affairs, local politics, religion, books, movies . . . this list is longer than the list of activities because most people have more interests than the activities in which they actually participate.

Once you know someone's special concerns, however, you can be alert to newspaper and magazine articles (printed or electronic) related to the interest. As a general principle, pertinent information is almost always inexpensive, unexpected, and thoughtful. Clip and send the review of a new mystery, an article about the benefits of tofu, a story about religious architecture.

The Web, which makes it too easy to forward jokes, also makes it simple to forward articles and websites that may be of special concern to one of your key customers or colleagues. Google searches billions of sites, so the odds are good you will forward something the other person has not yet seen.

The Web also gives you means to do innumerable inexpensive, unexpected, and thoughtful acts. Does someone with whom you want to have a better relationship have a blog? Comment on the blog posts (most bloggers I know are delighted to see that someone is reading them). Add links to your own blog or to appropriate articles. Show that you are interested and involved.

Similarly on Twitter, comment on someone's article, speech, blog post, or anything that should be more widely known. Retweet appropriate Twitter messages. Tweet comments directly to people such as a question or refer them to something on Twitter. Recommend that people follow someone on Follow Friday. Invite them to join appropriate groups in which you participate on LinkedIn.

If someone has a Facebook page, you can post on his or her wall, birthday greetings, for example. If the firm has a company page, you can hit the "Like" button, post comments, and show that you are interested and involved in what the company is saying and doing.

What else can you do? Greg Genova sells metal cutting tools for Kennametal in San Diego. He once met a prospect at a Los Angeles trade show, a company that had done no business with Kennametal. The firm's shop was almost in Greg's backyard—five or so miles from his house.

The customer manufactures top-of-the-line regulators for the scuba diving industry. The workers have pride in their work and have won awards with their regulators. "I've always had an interest in diving," says Greg, "but I'd never done it. I thought this would be a good opportunity to build my relationship with the customer and do something for myself—so I took up diving. I got one of my sons involved. I bought this manufacturer's equipment, and my son and I both got certified."

The shop's management was so impressed by Greg's commitment that the firm now buys virtually all cutting tools from Kennametal. (It would be all, but Kennametal cannot provide a few niche market items.) Greg says, "I am always his first choice to see if we have an item. If we do, he buys from us." And the relationship continues to build. "I have got some of the guys in the shop now who are going to be certified, and we're going to dive together."

If you share an interest with a customer or colleague, so much the better. At one time, my wife Maryann was a pharmaceutical sales representative in Edison, New Jersey. She once called on one of the most important doctors in the territory, a physician who, as a matter of policy, did not see drug representatives. Maryann walked in just as UPS was delivering a motorcycle windshield. She recognized the doctor as he accepted the package, so she asked him, "What's in the big package?"

He said, "Well, I needed a new windshield for my bike. I ride motorcycles. You know anything about motorcycles?"

She said truthfully, "I love riding on motorcycles. I just haven't ridden on one in a long time."

"Come on," he said, "I'll take you for a ride on mine."

She might have turned him down—it was a workday, she wasn't dressed in jeans and a leather jacket, she didn't know the man or how he drove—but she agreed. The doctor took off his white coat, she stashed her briefcase, and they took a spin around Edison on his bike. From then on, the doctor and Maryann were good buddies. She could see him whenever she wanted, all of which because they shared a common interest and did something that made him feel as if she cared. They talked about motorcycles, and when the opportunity was right, she talked about her product.

Greg Genova once learned a new prospect was a fervent Harley-Davidson owner. Greg also learned the prospect was looking for something to add to his bike, but nothing on the market satisfied him. Greg, by the nature of his job, happened to know a metal-working shop in a different town that was starting to manufacture a part Greg thought the prospect would like. The part is a chrome-covered, bullet-shaped cap that covers the motorcycle's hex bolts, "and they fit the bike perfectly."

Greg bought a number of the caps, which were a couple of bucks apiece, and gave them to the prospect. "He was very impressed," says Greg, "and excited to put them on his bike." Here Greg used his special knowledge—the manufacturer had only begun to turn out the part—and what he knew of his prospect to build the relationship with an inexpensive, unexpected, and thoughtful act.

You don't have to have special knowledge of a factory's new product to do something thoughtful, however. Julie Wroblewski says that if you learn someone is interested in Harley-Davidson motorcycles, "go by a Harley café and pick up a coffee mug and send it to her." Julie says that as you go through life, there are times you can spot things that will be meaningful to a customer or colleague. "They don't have to cost a lot, but they definitely give the person a sense that, boy, she not only hears me, she cares about me."

Brenda Stapleton at Roche says she has been buying inexpensive novelty picture frames as she spots them. "For one nurse practitioner who trains dogs, I found one with little dog bones. A couple of my customers go on vacation in the Bahamas, so I got a couple of

$5.99 frames that had tropical fish on them. When I gave them, I said, 'That is a moment to savor with your family, so if you get a picture, put it in here.' The frames are not expensive, but they are specific to their lives and what is meaningful to them."

Important People

Think about the people who might be important to the other person—the way Brenda thought Kelly Sheehan could be important to the customer's daughter. Important people could be industry figures, well-known executives, or ordinary people who are, or should be, significant to the other person.

If somebody is well-known in the industry, or is published, bring copies of the person's work. If the important person is local and accessible, make an opportunity for the three of you to be together; go have coffee, a drink, or go to dinner. Help customers and colleagues get access to the people they think are important.

Richard Sanders, who was a sales representative for our company in Mississippi, learned that I liked books by John Grisham, who also lived in Mississippi at that time. Every time a Grisham book came out, not only would Richard get the book, but also he would get it autographed. I now have four autographed novels that say, "To Jerry, from one Southerner to another, John Grisham." Richard was one of 650 representatives and quickly became someone I felt I should know, because I appreciated the fact he learned something about me and did something about it. As I got to know him, I really liked him. We promoted him; he came to the home office and did a great job for us.

All these anecdotes may make the process sound too easy. You do something inexpensive, unexpected, and thoughtful and nice things happen as a result. These stories may give that impression because we tend to remember the incidents when something did happen. The more dramatic the something, the better we remember. We don't recall the times when the gesture, the action, the occasion had no apparent effect, which may be most of the time.

But, as they say about state lotteries, you can't win if you don't play. If you don't habitually look for opportunities and act on them, you cannot build a strong relationship with the people most important to your business success. Finding opportunities requires a kind of heightened awareness, a sensitivity to the other person and to possibilities in the world. If relationship-building is crucial to your success, ask the 20 questions, listen intently, and continue to think inventively about what inexpensive, unexpected, and thoughtful things you might do to build the relationship since many business relationships are built this way.

Important Goals

What does the other person want to accomplish in his or her business and personal life?

Find commonalities in your personal goals and the other person's. Suppose you know a woman whose personal goal is to run a marathon. You may not be ready to run a marathon, but you may be able to be present when she runs hers.

Suppose you know someone who wants to create an English garden. You can pick up tips and suggestions even if your green thumb touches nothing more than a window box. Just to know the person's personal goals makes you able to reference them in conversation, to be present when they're being achieved, and to find some commonality between yours and theirs.

You can find publications relating to their goals—building their own boat, hiking the entire length of the Appalachian or Pacific Crest Trail, vacationing in the Lake District, or retiring to North Carolina. You can search the Web to find articles related to the goals.

When I decided I wanted a new, updated life insurance policy because I was building a new house and did not feel I had enough coverage, I asked John Fitzgerald, who I'd met at the Cardinals football game, to get me the policy. He called one day to tell me the policy had been approved, but he was not going to write it. I asked why. "Because I think I can beat the rate," he said. "This policy is $11,000 and I think I can get the same coverage for $9,000."

I had no clue what the policy should cost, and I would not have known a $9,000 option existed had John not told me. He cut his commission to do the right thing by me, and by doing it he pole-vaulted up the Relationship Pyramid in my eyes. His act was certainly unexpected and thoughtful. And because it was clear John cared more about our long-term relationship than his immediate income, I have asked him to manage our other financial assets.

Major Events

These are the big events in people's lives. They may include national or religious holidays such as Thanksgiving, New Year's, Christmas, Yom Kippur, but they also include events such as marriage, promotion, or a death in the family.

This last category is especially important because some people turn away when something bad happens. They act as though illness, accident, or a business reversal were catching. But usually they're not, and a thoughtful act at a stressful time can have an incalculable impact.

"I had gotten to know a customer over the course of a year," says Julie Wroblewski. "One day he told me he was going home to Michigan because his mom was dying of cancer. He ultimately took a leave of absence because she had passed away. I sent a handwritten sympathy card that tried to tell him I cared." Her simple card had a huge, positive effect on the relationship.

Debbie Wilson had scheduled a program and had a commitment from an exceptionally influential physician to be the keynoter. A week and a half before the program, her keynoter called to cancel the program. "At first he didn't give me a lot of explanation," says Debbie, "and while I was not happy about it, I couldn't imagine, with the relationship we'd built, why he didn't have a good reason. He finally asked me to come in and meet with him."

She did, and the doctor apologized profusely for canceling on such short notice. Debbie told him, "I know you have your reasons and I'm going to have to try to replace you—not that I can replace you—but I have to respect your reasons."

The doctor then revealed his wife had cancer, had to have surgery, and they were going through a terrible crisis at home. He apologized again, and Debbie thanked him for telling her as soon as he could, and adding, "Obviously, your family has to come first."

Debbie feels that because she was so understanding, even before she knew of the wife's cancer, "the doctor paid me back a hundred times. I got to know his kids; my kids met his kids. We did programs together. We developed a real friendship and when I run into him, he still treats me as if I had seen him yesterday."

Find ways to commemorate special events, whether with a note—handwritten or electronic, a fax, a card, or a phone call. Drop a note to say, "Thinking of you." Julie says she recently sent a congratulations card to a prospect who had become engaged. Julie tries to set herself apart from other people by sending cards and notes at times other than the holidays. "You almost expect to get a card at those times," she says. "But it is those times when someone was promoted or after a meeting, these handwritten notes go a super long way to build the relationship."

We should always be aware that customers and colleagues may be very different from us, with different holidays, different traditions, different histories. Many of our customers are Hispanic, Asian American, and African American. If they are Hispanic, it is important to know the difference between Mexican, Cuban, Central, and South American backgrounds. If they are Asian American, are their roots Chinese, Japanese, Korean, Vietnamese, Thai, or something else? Depending on our situation, we may want to build a relationship with someone who is Islamic, Jewish, Russian, Indian—someone otherwise very different from ourselves.

I believe it is often easier to develop a relationship with someone who is dramatically different from me than it is with someone who is more like me. I find it easier to learn things about someone who is Jewish or Greek Orthodox or Islamic. If you have Jewish customers or colleagues, you should understand the difference between Yom Kippur and Rosh Hashanah. You would do well to know what greetings you give on those holidays. You should learn what sitting Shiva is and why somebody would do it.

I usually say to someone, "Pardon my ignorance." I admit I do not know much about Islam . . . or Buddhism . . . or Mormonism. But it is okay to be inquisitive. People love to teach; they love to share with you. Major events can be religious dates, and to the extent you know something about the religion and act on the knowledge, they will be surprised and responsive.

Mike Accardi says that he tries to avoid giving business gifts. His company does not have a budget for such perks, so gifts come out of Mike's pocket, which, in the early days, was exceedingly shallow. Nevertheless, he did want to do something for certain customers for a major holiday. "When the Disney Store opened their distribution center here in Memphis, they bought everything from me. I knew everybody in the building. I couldn't afford to buy everybody in the building a gift, and I wasn't going to give the executive staff something and have people along the line wonder why didn't they get anything."

A Christmas tradition in the Accardi family is to make a special Sicilian sausage, salcicci, that one cannot buy in Memphis. "My dad and I would make two hundred pounds at a time," says Mike. On a Monday or Tuesday during the second or third week of December, Mike rose early to cook up 10 pounds—"a lot of sausage." He cut it into bite-size cubes, sliced Italian bread, and his wife made apricot nectar cakes to satisfy those people with a holiday sweet tooth. Mike took it to the building, offered everybody toothpicks and a bite of salcicci. "It had an amazing effect—giving them something of myself."

Favorite Foods

Speaking of food, what can you do when you know someone enjoys Mexican food, or Japanese, or Indian? What if someone loves chocolate-covered coffee beans . . . smoked herring . . . Danish wedding cookies?

Not long ago, I was working with Shari Kulkis, a Roche Laboratories sales representative in Atlanta. At one of the offices we visited, the staff was having a birthday party for an employee. The party included a box of Danish wedding cookies. I remarked that you cannot get Danish wedding cookies in the Northeast or the Southwest, only in the South. Shari asked how I knew that. I told her I've tried to find them, but I can't. "The only place I buy them is when I go to Memphis to visit my family," I said, and thought no more about it.

While I was in Atlanta, I loaned Shari some poster presentations I thought she might find useful. Because I had only the one copy, I said, "Just mail them back to me whenever you finish." The following Saturday, UPS arrived at my front door with a carton containing the posters . . . and three boxes of Danish wedding cookies.

I had hardly talked to Shari about the relationship-building process, but she was obviously alert to what I was saying and did something unexpected, inexpensive, and thoughtful about it. She is also one of the top representatives for her company, which does not surprise me at all.

Julie Wroblewski says that one of her unmarried customers once told her the one thing he really missed was homemade Christmas cookies. "So that Christmas I made him a giant batch of Christmas cookies." Now that Julie has changed industries, the man is no longer a customer, "but we still keep in touch."

Krispy Kreme donuts were first available on the West Coast only in Los Angeles. Whenever Greg Genova had a meeting in Los Angeles that required him to spend the night, he would get up especially early, "pick up fresh Krispy Kreme donuts, and drive the 150 miles back to San Diego to give them to my first two or three calls. That was phenomenal. Here's something nobody can really get, and here's the Kennametal guy coming in with them. They knew I had to go the extra mile to get the donuts."

Other possibilities: Refer people to restaurants—good new ones in the area, or restaurants you know in an area they'll be visiting. You might buy a cookbook on the cuisine they like. Share recipes.

The crucial point is to know the other person. Shari Palant, a Roche Laboratories sales representative, says that one of her customers does not give representatives much time and does not attend dinner programs. Only after she scheduled a lunch with him did she learn he has celiac disease and is, therefore, unable to eat anything containing gluten or wheat. His diet is very limited, and he has researched the disease extensively and presented papers on it. Learning all this, Shari began looking for foods and information on celiac disease for him.

A few months later, she attended a gastroenterology convention. One exhibitor displayed a large variety of foods for celiac patients made from gluten and wheat substitutes. "I got to know the people at the booth really well by the end of the convention," says Shari. "I told them if they had any samples they did not want to ship back to the factory, I'd be happy to take them off their hands. I ended up with half a suitcase of food samples. I brought a 20-pound box of foods like cereal, bread, pastas, and granola bars—all things my doctor was ordinarily unable to eat."

When Shari brought the food to the doctor, he was so affected by someone doing something so thoughtful that, while not normally a man who showed a great deal of emotion (or at least not to a salesperson), he gave her a hug and a kiss. Has it helped her relationship with the customer? Immeasurably.

Schools Attended

If you have a customer or colleague for whom college was a peak experience, what can you do with that information?

At one time I lived in Charlottesville, the home of the University of Virginia. One of my customers, Charlie Miller, was a fanatic University of Virginia alumnus and lived in Elkton, Virginia, about 60 miles away. One year, the University won the National Invitation Tournament basketball championship, and the local paper did a special section on the team and the competition. I clearly remembered going to the trash to throw away the section and thinking, "I'll bet one of my doctors would like to have this . . . but who?" Asking the question gave the answer: Charlie Miller.

I wrote a quick note—"Dr. Miller, thought you'd like to see this"—stuck it to the section, and sent the package to him. Two weeks later on my next trip to Elkton, Charlie greeted me as if I were a favorite relative and ordered as if I were his only vendor. We'd had a good relationship before—that's how I knew he was a University of Virginia enthusiast—but that Sunday supplement kicked the relationship up another level or so.

If you are part of a national sales organization and if you have a customer who still talks about his days at Notre Dame and Notre Dame football, or the University of Texas, or Ohio State, it is pretty easy to call the representative who covers South Bend or Austin or Columbus and say, "Send me Sunday's paper," which has a report of Saturday's game. It will cost you about two bucks, and if you're living in Boise, Idaho, you're probably not getting the Sunday South Bend paper.

Of course you can always give school paraphernalia, mascot stuff for the sports teams, or school logo-type materials. If you know people in the community who graduated from the school, you can connect with them over lunch or at a special event. Use them as a resource for children of customers or colleagues who are considering the school. "Colin is thinking of the University of Virginia? He should talk to Charlie Miller. If you'd like, I'll try to set something up."

Important Places

Some people love to vacation at the same place every year; others want something different every year. Some people are nostalgic about the towns in which they grew up; others are thinking ahead to retirement. Knowing that a place is important to a customer or colleague and why it's important, what can you do about it?

A few years ago, John Fuqua and one of his representatives called on a busy physician who happened to be going to Disney World within the next couple of days. "He had not been there in a number of years," says John, "and he was really excited about going, but he was sure things had changed since his last visit."

John said that from what he knew, it had changed, and he hoped the doctor and his family would have a good time. "We did our sales call and the minute we walked out of the building, I looked at the representative and said, 'What do you think we should do with what we learned this afternoon? He's going to get on an airplane and take his family to Disney World. What comes to mind?' "

The representative thought for a bit and suggested Books a Million. Pick up a Disney World guidebook the family could read on the plane to Orlando. John says, "We picked up a relatively quick-reading guide and put it in a little basket of goodies for the kids." John and the representative returned to the office and told the receptionist they needed to see the doctor for a moment.

"The whole thing was very inexpensive," says John, "but you'd have thought we'd given him a gold brick. I've never seen him as appreciative of anything I've done. To this day, he mentions he really appreciated the gesture and he and his family had a great time."

If you know a customer or colleague is planning a vacation in Florence . . . or Prague . . . or Kyoto, clip and send news articles about the country or the city. Spend time on the Internet and forward a bit of information about sights, restaurants, or activities. If you know a country, a district, or a city and can recommend a spot, a town, or activity that you know someone would like, do it.

Do the Right Thing

Doing something inexpensive, unexpected, and thoughtful doesn't always produce immediate results—indeed, it may not produce any results at all—but it is still the right thing to do. There are very few, if any, acts of kindness that are wrong. Not every seed you plant is going to sprout, just as not every popcorn kernel is going to pop. But if you want a garden, the more seeds you plant, the better the odds you'll have vegetables someday.

Knowing what you now know (or will know) about the key people with whom you want to build a relationship, what actions could you take? Create a form like the one shown in Figure 7.1, and use it to think about opportunities for inexpensive, unexpected, and thoughtful acts.

Your actions over time do demonstrate your professionalism, integrity, caring, and knowledge; they set you apart. But they have to be done over time. You can't expect to do one thing one time and then get a quid pro quo—and always remember, you're not keeping score anyway. Doing inexpensive, unexpected, and thoughtful acts over time demonstrates this is how you operate. This is who you are.

Figure 7.1
What Action Could You Take with What You've Learned?

Important dates: _____

Action: _____

Important names: _____

Action: _____

Special concerns: _____

Action: _____

Important people: _____

Action: _____

Important goals: _____

Action: _____

Major events: _____

Action: _____

Favorite foods: _____

Action: _____

School attended: _____

Action: _____

Important places: _____

Action: _____

Our housecleaner Rosa brings inexpensive gifts about every other time she comes to our house. She will stop to get bread because she knows I love a particular Mexican bread. She knows I like model elephants and will bring me an elephant she found at a garage sale. I do not care that it wasn't bought at Neiman Marcus. I care that this unique woman does something—has done it for years—to set herself apart. Rosa does these things because that's who she is.

We really do like a person who does things in an inexpensive, unexpected, and thoughtful way for us, whether she is our housecleaner or he is our financial advisor. I feel different about you when you show me you care about me. Unexpected, inexpensive, and thoughtful acts say, "I thought about you. You matter to me. And I am different from every other person in your business life."

Relationships are built on actions—inexpensive, unexpected, and thoughtful actions that are small acts of kindness that make a huge statement of who you are and how you treat other people. They say you care, and often they result in people getting closer to you. That doesn't mean an act can never be expensive, but inexpensive is probably better.

Now that you know the three steps to building strong business relationships—think well of yourself, ask the right questions in the right way, and do the right thing with the information—you should begin to map your key relationships.

CHAPTER 8

MAP YOUR KEY RELATIONSHIPS

Virtually everyone who has been in business more than a day or two understands that positive business relationships can help them do their jobs. Not everyone understands, however, that the more good relationships you have and the more diverse those relationships are, the more effective you can be at whatever you do.

Most of us take an accidental or serendipitous approach to relationship building. We tend to just let relationships happen. A more effective life and professional approach is to build relationships strategically—not because you want to gain or be successful in life (although that doesn't hurt), but because you want to have a more fulfilling and rewarding life. Again, the quantity and the quality of your relationships in many ways determine the quality of your life.

Take William Dawes and Paul Revere, for example. Each rode from Boston on the night of April 18, 1775, to alert the countryside that the British were coming. Dawes rode south, Revere rode north. As Brian Uzzi and Shannon Dunlap point out in the *Harvard Business Review*, the towns they traveled through were demographically similar. "Both men came from the same social class and had similar educational backgrounds. But only Revere raised a militia and only Revere's name became famous." What did he have that Dawes did not?

He had a network of diverse relationships! Paul Revere was an information broker, Uzzi and Dunlap say, "a person who occupies a key role in a social network by connecting disparate groups of people. Because Revere targeted other well-connected people during his ride, his news spread widely and quickly." The key is a diverse network—many kinds of people who know many people.

In contrast, "William Dawes was not an information broker, so he didn't know which doors to knock on when he entered a new town. As a result, the information he carried was circulated within a small group of people instead of expanding outward."

In Chapter 6, I talked about the difference between networking and connecting, but there does not seem to be another word that works as well as "network" to describe a large and widely distributed group of people who communicate with one another and work together (web? group? set of connections? set of contacts?), which is what I am talking about in this chapter. Whatever the word, Uzzi and Dunlap say that "networks determine which ideas become breakthroughs, which new drugs are prescribed, which farmers cultivate pest-resistant crops, and which R&D engineers make the most high-impact discoveries." Networks are powerful because they give you private information, access to diverse skills, and power.[1]

Social media sites make it easier than ever to build these kinds of networks within an organization. Yammer, Jive, and Salesforce Chatter[2] are three sites that allow people to communicate and collaborate efficiently. All three act to limit participation to people within the organization. On Yammer, for instance, you can ask a question and, if somebody within the company sees it and has an answer, he or she will respond. You don't have to spam the inbox of everyone in your company. You can share news, links, and photos—any kind of information—without having to direct who the recipients will be.

David Sacks, Yammer's CEO, argues that by posting on Yammer, information will flow to where it needs to go. People can search for it. "They can find it by tags; they can decide to follow you because you post relevant content to them." Yammer, like Jive and Chatter, is a way to share information in the company and let it flow more freely than it could by e-mail. In the process, you begin to be seen as a valuable source within the company.

Strong personal networks don't just happen: They have to be carefully constructed—which means you probably ought to think consciously about mapping and cultivating your relationships to build a truly effective network.

MAP RELATIONSHIPS WITH FOUR GROUPS

Relationship mapping is creating a list of people with whom you must build or initiate relationships. Although most relationship building is done reactively, I believe you ought to consciously, deliberately, and strategically map your relationships with four groups of people to proactively build positive relationships.

1. *People within the organization who are important to your success.* You need these people to get your job done. They may be customer service reps, warehouse clerks, finance people—anyone who can make your work easier ... or impossible. They should be a diverse group, not simply your peers in sales or accounting or engineering, but from many parts of the organization. The more diverse, the better.

2. *People external to the organization who are important to getting your job done.* They may be customers, vendors, regulators. They could be anybody, as long as they are not within the walls of your company.

3. *People who are important to the success of your career.* These individuals may be your boss, the human resource director, a mentor, or other people within the company. You need to meet and develop a relationship with these people if they can help you either to understand something about a future opportunity or help you have an opportunity. These resources may also be outside the company: coaches, friends, or a spouse. They are people who will share their insights and experiences, tell you when they believe you are making a mistake, or suggest options you might never consider.

4. *The people with whom you need to repair a relationship.* You know them: They are the folks you or the organization have alienated

with whom you'd like to improve your relationship or must improve it to do your job. You may be lucky and have no one in this group, or these people may exist whether you identify them or not. You are much more likely to be successful if you are clear about who they are. You are much more likely to be successful if you consciously, systematically, and routinely build and maintain positive relationships with them.

PEOPLE INSIDE THE ORGANIZATION

Ron Cleboski realized the importance of building a network of relationships when, after success in one field, he changed careers. Ron is a former police officer who got into high tech, started his own business, grew it from zero to $6 million in two years, sold it, and, to stay close to his daughter, restarted his career in 1994 as an entry-level salesperson selling long distance telephone services. He is now director of business services sales and marketing for the Wisconsin division of Time Warner Cable. "As a salesperson, building a career from scratch," he tells me, "I found it absolutely necessary to create relationships with the internal people who could make my job easier."

Ron says that one of those people has always been someone in customer service, whether a supervisor, a manager, or just a person on the phone. "I wanted someone who would watch my back and I could pass customers on to and know for sure that they would be taken care of. It would make me more efficient, and be the person to call at all times."

He says that, like many salespeople (but not, unfortunately, all), he intuitively recognized that having a good relationship in customer service was important for his own success, because his time was best spent being a salesperson. When a customer service issue developed—and it always does—Ron was able to say, "I appreciate your concern. I know just the person to put you in contact with. She is the supervisor of my customer service department. I'm going to call her right now, ask her to give you a call, and I promise you will be taken care of within the next 30 minutes."

He would call his associate and she would say, "Okay, Clebo, gotcha. I'll take care of you," and she'd do it. Once a quarter Ron would bring her roses, take her out to lunch, or do some other inexpensive, unexpected, and thoughtful act to maintain the relationship and help him with his new career.

Henry Potts, the national sales manager for Melillo Consulting in Somerset, New Jersey, points out that the category of people within the organization is not always obvious. They include both the people you work with and the people you work for. Melillo is a business and technology systems integrator and reseller of Hewlett-Packard products. Henry spent 26 years at Hewlett-Packard before joining Melillo. "It's easy to identify the people you work for that you should target. It is not so easy to identify the people you work with and the people who are important to your success, but that's a key component to being successful inside the organization—figuring out how to get work done through people who are either on your level or not in your organizational stream." It is important to have really positive relationships, says Henry, with the people who neither report to you nor to whom you report. "I think that is the hidden nugget, the thing that often you are not thinking about if you are just a manager in an organization."

In many situations we have to try to build these relationships from afar. You may live in Portland, Oregon, but your headquarters is in Detroit. How do you ensure that the people you are mapping are the right people? Then how do you go about building relationships with them from the edge of the country?

Most people use e-mail, telephone, and voice mail, but those are not always the most effective ways to communicate. The most effective messages are communicated simultaneously by the words you speak and your expression and body language as you say them. This is why a live speaker is more effective than a television image, and a television image is more effective than a radio speech. Whenever you use e-mail or voice mail you reduce the likelihood that you are going to communicate effectively because the recipient cannot see you, your expression, or your eyes.

Although technology is helping companies make it easier to communicate visually with video conferencing, you still don't get the full impact of being in someone's presence. But it is still better than a voice on the phone.

Perhaps the best way to build long-distance relationships is to make use of the times when you are together at sales meetings, conventions, trade shows, and the like. Before any gathering, make a list of the people you want to know better and create a quick plan for moving those relationships forward while you are together. Make a point to spend time at breakfast, lunch, or dinner with those key associates, ask the questions in Chapter 4, and listen to the answers.

Having said that, I should also point out that you can use in-house social media like Yammer, Jive, Chatter, and others to prepare the ground for any personal meeting. If you post relevant content—suggestions, ideas, experiences that can help another person in the organization—you tend to become someone worth knowing. If you answer questions, you are a resource. When you are seen as a valuable resource, people want to have a relationship with you. If you note and congratulate the successes of others, you are sensitive and thoughtful. All of these may make it much easier to connect with your Detroit colleague when you finally meet at the annual sales meeting in Arizona.

PEOPLE OUTSIDE THE ORGANIZATION

You don't need a book to tell you that on any list of people outside the organization who are important to you, customers tend to be right at the top. David Sokol is the Berkshire Hathaway executive responsible for turning around NetJets, the fractional-ownership jet company. Sokol created cross-functional teams that are responsible for knowing an owner's needs. They are responsible for knowing that Mr. X likes caviar and Coke Zero, and more. "Just knowing the owner, knowing anniversaries and birthdays, helps to build strong relationships," says Adam Johnson, NetJets' senior vice president.[3]

But in a complex sale, it is not always obvious who all is involved or their role in the final decision. For example, Melvin Boaz is a national sales manager in the orthopedics division of Smith & Nephew, a global medical devices company.

"We sell to hospitals, and physicians are the key drivers within the hospitals. So the physician may say, 'Yes, that's what I want to do,' but he has to get the hospital administration to agree to it. I need to leverage my relationship with the physician in order to secure a relationship with a hospital administrator."

How easy that is depends mostly on the hospital's size; as in the corporate world, the larger the organization, the less accessible the highest levels tend to be. Mel tells me that "For the most part, the physician can give me credibility to speak to the key person in the organization I need to speak to. If I need to speak with the CFO or the CEO to get the deal done, the physician's entrée or the physician's relationship I currently have gives me the credibility to ask for the appointment."

Once he has the appointment, Mel says it is his responsibility to develop a deeper relationship, not just accomplish a business transaction. "If it's strictly business, then after the deal closes there's probably no going further. But if you find some common ground with the people you know, things that interest you or other things within your industry, then you can have an ongoing relationship. You can then go back to that person after the deal and still have access ... and sometimes you even develop friendships."

Henry Potts says that at one point in his career he was a client manager at Hewlett-Packard, responsible for all of the General Electric businesses in the Midwest. HP salespeople were responsible for selling the various product lines into his accounts. He had to map an exceptionally diverse corporation—appliances, lighting, aircraft engines, and medical devices were in his territory—understand the specific GE customer's business problem, relate that back to a solution, and help the HP salesperson take advantage of the opportunity.

Jack Welch, GE's legendary CEO, indirectly helped Henry by making it clear to the GE executives on whom Henry was calling what Welch expected from them in the year ahead. When GE executives left their annual planning meeting with Welch, they knew the year's business imperatives. "The IT guy knew what he needed to do to match his IT initiatives to the business initiatives. So I would go and try to understand what those initiatives were. I would look across the broad spectrum of Hewlett-Packard products and figure out what we offered to solve that IT problem. Then I would go to the HP people who were selling those solutions and help them understand what was going on."

The salesperson didn't waste a lot of GE's time on irrelevancies, and Henry became such a trusted advisor at the appliance division that the CIO was inviting him to staff meetings.

Henry says that the value of mapping your relationships laterally is not always immediately apparent. In his new company, however, "It didn't take me long to figure out there are some very critical players inside the organization who are not above or below me, but who can have a serious impact on my success in terms of their responsiveness to me. I need to demonstrate a desire to support them in their success, so they will want me to be successful. It's no different than selling. It's just selling inside the organization."

Tom Wilson, who is an Open View account manager for Hewlett-Packard, spent 18 months to close a major contract. It required relationship mapping across both the customer's organization and HP, from technical to vice presidential levels in both corporations. When the process started, Tom did not know who all was going to be involved, so he began by first talking to the customer's employees and started building relationships with them. Those relationships enabled him to begin mapping the organization: who reports to whom, who has the budget, who has signing authority, and who are influencers even though they don't have signing authority.

One of the biggest challenges in a large, complex sale, says Tom, "is that a lot of people are going to have visibility in it, and there are a lot of people who have to weigh in on the decision, and you have to get buy-in across multiple groups. There was probably a group of 30 to 40 people who were evaluating solutions to needs." His task was to identify the key leaders among the group, the people HP needed to influence to help persuade others.

Key to winning the deal, Tom feels, was the relationships the customer executives built throughout HP's organization. "If at any time this project started to go south or turn a corner they didn't want, they could call very high up in the HP organization to get any issues corrected." Obviously, for this kind of a sale to happen, Tom could not manage everything; he let customers talk to associates within HP he had no control over. "I had to understand that I am not as important to the customer as an individual within the HP organization," says Tom. "I am not going to be able to sell to all their needs. I had to put the business case together and explain the customer situation to my people—the HP opportunity—in executive summaries, through e-mails and phone calls, and start enlisting the support from HP executives."

By mapping the relationships within the customer organization and understanding the map of the HP organization, Tom was able to encourage a web of relationships that assisted both.

In some cases, your association with someone outside the organization may be as simple as the printer you hire to print business cards. You have two options: You can place your order and return three days later to pick up your business cards, or you can work to build a relationship that may bring future benefits.

If you take the first option, typically when you need new business cards in a year you will have forgotten where you had them printed. It was a transaction and not worth any more attention.

But if your business will be doing any other printing, I believe it is more productive to approach the printers with a different attitude. You tell them at the first meeting what you plan to be doing and try to build some sort of relationship. Similarly with your banker. Even if the bank doesn't require monthly statements, build a relationship with an officer at the bank and send him or her a P&L and balance sheet. These businesses are not "a printer," they become "my printer;" not "a bank," they become "my bank."

PEOPLE IMPORTANT TO YOUR CAREER

The third group of people you should map consists of those who are important to your career. These are not necessarily people who can help you get promoted, because a lot of people don't want to be promoted. Many people are happy doing what they are doing, living where they are living, and they understand exactly what they want to do.

For those people, the issue is not getting promoted, but how to continue finding fulfillment, excitement, and interesting things to do in a job that make it rewarding.

People important to your career can be inside or outside the company. They can be family members, preachers, rabbis, coaches, mentors, friends, former teachers, anybody. The important relationship outside of your organization may be a family member. Allen Zimmerman, a senior vice president of Solutions Group at AmerisourceBergen, considers that his wife and children are critical to his career success. "The nature of what I do, the hours, and the travel are extremely demanding. I have almost four million miles with American Airlines alone, so I am gone quite a bit, and my wife functions as a single parent when I am on the road two, three, or four days at a time. Her and my family being willing to make that great personal sacrifice is critical to my success and to our harmony as a family—and without that harmony, it would be difficult to continue on in my career."

What would Allen say to a valued employee who came to him and said, "I'm having a real problem at home. I love my job and I understand the need for the travel, but I am getting some pushback from my wife. Do you have any ideas?"

Allen says, "I think family comes first. I think each family needs to find within itself their level of tolerance for travel. Because of the nature of what we do, our organization has a very large consulting division. We also have a very large staffing division. We have a lot of implementation personnel in our technology companies who travel quite a bit. So my advice to someone in that situation is to find what is tolerable for your family. My advice would be to put the family first. I would respect any valuable employee who might have to give up a traveling position, and I would certainly try to keep that person within the organization."

PEOPLE WHO ARE UPSET WITH YOU

People inside the organization, outside the organization, and important to your career may in many cases be relatively easy to approach and to build a positive relationship with. It may not be so easy to approach people who are upset with you.

Few of us deliberately offend an associate or a customer. By the nature of their task, managers may inadvertently offend subordinates; some people resent being held to a standard—any standard—of performance. That is a discussion for another book, however; here I'm talking about the people, often customers, who are important to your business success but who you or the organization have managed to upset.

Invariably, many of us will have somebody who is upset with us and we have to try to figure out a way to deal with that. It is not uncommon for a salesperson to learn that a customer has been offended. A key to sales success is being able to recognize offense and find a way to repair the relationship so you can continue to do business with the individual. The offense may not be on a personal level. The person may be offended because your product didn't perform to specification or the competitive situation forced you to behave in a certain way or because your competitors put you in a bad light. Perhaps someone else in your company at some point in the past promised something and didn't deliver.

I see three steps to repairing business relationships.

Step One: Apologize and mean it. Acknowledge the perceived offense even if you don't think it was an offense, because the perception is reality. And it's the perception of the other person you're concerned with, not your own.

Step Two: Take responsibility. Even if you don't feel the issue was your responsibility in the first place. If the other person thinks it was your responsibility and that relationship is important to you, it is your responsibility. Then explain your side of the story, about why you believe the rift occurred, and then listen.

Step Three: Take actions to prove you are doing your best to rebuild the trust.

146

Researchers have found that people who are wronged in business are more likely to say that they were reconciled if the offender took responsibility and offered a sincere apology. When doctors honestly apologize for medical mistakes, people are much less likely to sue.

How about repairing a relationship that you had and now have a problem with?

"I always tell my sales team that Elton John said it best when he remarked, 'Sorry seems to be the hardest word,'" says George C. D. Griffith, who is a co-founder and with two partners owns four different operating companies: M2 Communications, Super Nova, XSCITE, and ConneXion360, all of which support the pharmaceutical/biotech device industry in different capacities.

Many salespeople—and perhaps most people in general—do not ask themselves where they went wrong in a relationship gone bad. George notes, "They will seek to blame a thousand things other than themselves. The first question I ask myself is, 'What did I do wrong here? What could we have done better?' It can be like any relationship. You get busy and don't love and cultivate the relationship, so they go out and start dating someone else. You really need to sit down and have some open, honest dialogue."

Most people in such a situation go wrong, George observes, when they say in effect, "Well, they're going out with somebody else now and we had our chance; we were working with them, but I'll try to find someone else," versus fighting to repair the relationship, expressing what they mean as a client, and seeking to understand their dissatisfaction. As Stephen Covey said, 'Seek first to understand, then to be understood.'" Most people don't really figure out where they went wrong or ask the questions to find out, although most people are willing to tell you how you failed.

Let's say you find out. Now you know what you did wrong, but they're still angry. "As in a situation I inherited," says George. "I took over an account that had really gone bad. We had not delivered to the proper level." True, there was a little back and forth and the client had contributed something, "but at the end of the day you always have to take the blame."

When George went to see the client, his goal was to neutralize the situation. All George wanted at that point was that the client not spread negativity around his company about George's business. George did not want or expect to get any more business from him (although the client was very defensive at first, as if George was coming to sell him on other things). At the first meeting, George simply listened, as if he were a therapist.

"One of the great techniques I've found is what I call the 'feel, felt, found.' Tell somebody you understand how they feel: 'Heck, if I was in that situation, I'd have felt the exact same way. But what I've found through my research is . . . ' A simple feel, felt, found can let the person understand you know where they're coming from, and you feel the same way. Then, through some research, help put things into perspective a little bit."

This client unbent somewhat and he and George actually started developing a bit of a friendship. After that first meeting to stabilize the situation, George called the client to invite him to lunch. They did not talk about business the entire time. "I knew he kept thinking it was coming, but I never said anything. I dropped him off and said good-bye. A couple of weeks later we had another lunch, and he started opening up to me." Eventually, he brought George back for tactical planning and gave the company some new business about six months later.

Address the Problems Early

The worst thing you can do is to ignore the situation when mistakes have been made and a relationship has gone sour. You have no more contact. George says that he tries to teach his team members as well as tell all his company's clients whenever they start a project that it's like planning any event. Something along the way is not going to go perfectly. "That's not to say we're not a great company, but I think it's a lack of maturity if you think any relationship or marriage is going to be perfect."

George points out that if you date anybody for three months, something is bound to go wrong. He tries to set the expectation up front with all clients that this may be the case. Then should something happen, he can call them and say, "Remember a couple of months ago when we first started? Well, here's our current situation." He emphasizes the importance of communicating as soon as the problem occurs—something a lot of people don't want to do.

That's the situation when you are aware of the snag before the customer is. What if the customer calls first? George describes a not-uncommon sequence of events:

8:30 A.M.: The client calls with a problem, complaint, grievance, leaving a testy voice mail.

9:30: The responsible salesperson, fortified with his morning coffee, assembles a team to consider the issue.

10:30: The group has an approach but needs more input. The necessary source is in meetings until 1:00.

1:00 P.M.: The group reassembles with the key person.

2:00: The group now has a game plan, but it needs clearance from legal, public relations, operations, and senior management.

4:30: The salesperson responds to the customer.

By 4:30, of course, the customer has gone from steaming to boiling. What began as a grievance has blossomed into a full-blown crisis. Far, far better, says George, is to call back as soon as possible to say something like, "I got your phone call. I don't completely understand what's going on. I have heard your voice mail. I know the situation. You might want to tell me a little bit more. But I'm going to figure out what's wrong and I wanted to call immediately and acknowledge that I hear you. I'll call you back at ten o'clock. And when I do, I might not have any answers, but I am just going to call you back at ten to let you know that I'm still working on it." For customers, the belief that you are working on their issue may be as important as any solution you offer.

Not long ago, I had a situation with a client who clashed with one of my key account executives. I heard about the meeting and realized that whatever relationship we'd built with this person we were about to destroy because we weren't really listening to the customer.

Although I had a conference call scheduled with the client five days later, I called him as soon as I learned about the situation. I told his administrative assistant, with whom I'd built a relationship, that I really needed to talk to Doug. "I know I have an appointment with him, but I wanted to speak with him today."

When he answered, I said, "I just got off the phone with one of my folks and got the sense that the session you just had with our folks did not go well. I am really, really bothered by it, because what it says to me, unless I heard it differently, is that we are not listening to you as a customer. I am deeply bothered by that. So if you have the time, can you tell me a little bit about your perspective?"

He then gave me an earful of how we didn't listen to the customer. We are this company that talks about thinking like a customer, but we're not practicing what we preach. When he'd said his piece, I said, "I want to assure you that that is not the organizational philosophy. That might be the perception you got from this person. I can tell you she was well intended, but I own the company, so it is my responsibility. I accept responsibility and if I can't repair this relationship with you, then so be it, but I am going to do everything I can to make it right."

I said that the first thing I would do is assign somebody else to the account—a specific action to demonstrate I am trying to build trust. I said that the next thing I would do is meet with him in person. And I said that the third thing I would do is send a letter of apology to the people he felt we had most inconvenienced and copy him on the e-mail.

I apologized. I explained my side of the story. And I took actions to prove that I was doing my best to rebuild trust: a new person, a meeting, and I made sure we delivered on the plan. The result? At the last meeting he gave us two referrals to other companies.

Melvin Boaz at Smith & Nephew recalls working on a large deal in which the hospital administrator was part of the purchase process but Mel had not understood how important he was to the deal, and during the process Mel did not pay enough attention to him. "I didn't give him the credit he was due for his position and his title. I clearly offended him and found I had no access to him. It reached a point where I was not going to get this million dollar order."

Realizing he had made a serious mistake, Mel went to his biggest supporter in the hospital, said that he had not intended to offend the administrator, and asked what he could do to repair the damage. The contact explained that Mel needed to understand the organization's workings and to develop relationships with a couple of other key people who were on the administrator's staff and gain credibility. "So I worked through those people, got their respect, got their buy-in, and used them to get me back in front of the administrator. I had a chance to make amends and saved the deal."

Ron Cleboski at Time Warner Cable came into a situation where the company and a major customer were at each other's throats. The company provided cable services, billing hundreds of thousands of dollars a month, but through misunderstanding and a lack of response, the customer was threatening to sue Time Warner Cable and Time Warner Cable was threatening to sue in return.

"We had different viewpoints on the letter of the contract. Let me emphasize: the letter of the contract versus the intent of the contract. Because that was instrumental," says Ron. The situation had reached the point where the customer administrator was calling the division president—Ron's new boss—once or twice a week, complaining that he wasn't getting information. The administrator felt empowered because he was talking to the division president rather than someone lower, when, in fact, the president was not the most appropriate executive to deal with the situation.

"The first thing I did was read the contract to understand the difference between the intent and the letter," explains Ron. He then asked his boss to refuse the administrator's calls, to "tell him I am the man with the plan and am empowered to make any and all decisions, because we have got to bring him back down to a level of controllability." Ron's boss was hesitant because they had been working together for only two or three weeks, but she agreed to it.

The next step was to meet with the administrator. "I was adamant and forthright, and I said, 'I understand your problem. I am here to fix it. As far as the company is concerned, I will make the final call. With that said, you and I can have a relationship of prosperity and work toward what I consider to be the intent of the contract.

Or we can have a relationship of adversity and work to the letter of the contract. If we want to go down that route, I don't think you and I need to talk any further because we'll let the lawyers make all the money. I'm not going to ask you to respond to me now, but I want you to think about our relationship and send me an e-mail as to which kind of relationship you want to have.' And I didn't give him a chance to speak."

About a day later, the administrator called the division president. The division president forwarded the call to Ron. "So he tested the waters, learned the waters were as I said them to be, and at that point he said, 'I'd like to work with you to the intent of the contract.' Our next meeting was a very good one. It was a meeting of 'Here's what we see' and 'Here's what you see.' And 'Here's what I plan on doing with your assistance, but it is not going to happen tomorrow. It is going to happen over the next year.'"

Ron says that two years into the relationship—from the point of having to tell lawyers on both sides to give the two a chance to work out the difficulty—Ron had a meeting with the administrator, his supervisor, and his two subordinates, and they gave Time Warner Cable a perfect rating for the relationship.

BUILD RELATIONSHIPS STRATEGICALLY

We will be dramatically more effective if we build our relationships strategically. In my personal situation I have a list of 115 names of people I am trying to build and maintain relationships with, people in my own company and people outside the company who I ought to know. Some of these are customers; some are people such as the editor of this book, my accountant, and my travel agent. I believe that, like Paul Revere, I need relationships with a wide range of people to be successful.

I look at the list once a week, and I ask myself: Who, if anybody, should I add to the list? And how do I touch this person this week, if at all? Because building and maintaining relationships starts with touches. It starts with some kind of interaction.

For example, I recently had dinner with a sales and marketing executive who I'll call Dave. This was our first meeting. He came to dinner with a client who is at the top of my Pyramid, as I am at the top of his. We were all together for three hours and really connected. I was already working on Dave's brand so he knew me by reputation, but we had never worked together.

On the plane home, I added Dave to my list and then considered, when do I need to touch him again? I needed to follow-up on the dinner. I had Dave's e-mail address because I knew the company's formula. (Here's a tip: If you want to e-mail somebody you've met and you didn't get their address, you can figure out their company's e-mail formula; it's usually one of these: jerry.acuff@. . . .jerry_acuff@. . .jacuff@. . .whatever.) I also had his cell phone number.

I didn't want to appear to be too close to the interaction, but when I landed in Phoenix—8 o'clock my time, 11 o'clock his time—I sent him a text message: "Dave, it was great to have dinner with you last night. Look forward to seeing you the next time I am in town." Within 10 seconds he sent a message: "It was really great to spend time with you; let's catch up soon." I sent him another text: "Look, I am at the firm next Thursday. If by chance you are available, I can do breakfast, lunch, or coffee." Within 30 seconds, I had his text: "I am open from 10:30 to 11:00. Meet me in the cafeteria."

But you have to ask yourself: Who should I actively list and when and how do I need to touch them? Do I need to call them? Do I need a conference call? Do I need to see them on Skype? Text them? E-mail them? See them in person? I consciously decide not to touch 95 percent of the people on my list every week. I don't have any real reason to. But I also decide I need a meeting with so-and-so, a call to so-and-so, a text message to so-and-so. It could be someone's birthday. I might need a meeting. It could be that I just haven't seen them in a while.

I regularly determine how to best touch the key people on my list. If you continue to ask yourself who are the important individuals with whom you should continue to build relationships—and do something about it—you increase the likelihood you will maintain the momentum of moving up in their Relationship Pyramids.

Relationship mapping means you take a more strategic approach than most of us usually do. You actually write down names, and then write down what you might do to meet with and interact with these people. Who do you know that they might know? (This is Pyramid hopping, which I discuss in the next chapter.) What can you offer them? Information? Contacts? A business opportunity? Think about how you are going to interact with them, and how often.

Nobody can tell you how to relate to a contact or with what frequency. That's up to you. But I can tell you that you can't build or maintain a relationship without touches. I occasionally call somebody when I know they are unlikely to answer. I don't need to talk to them at that moment; I just want them to know I am thinking of them. I would not mind talking to them; if they answer the phone I'll be glad to talk. But more important is letting them know they are important to me. They are important because I like to develop relationships with people and not because I am trying to get anything out of it. I am simply trying to figure out who I need relationships with and how to build those relationships.

My very good friend and exceptional sales manager George Summerson always reminds me that you can't hit a target you don't have. You must have targets. Begin to identify the people that are important to your success, a list that constantly changes. If you get a new job, if you meet someone new, if you get a new client, ask yourself: Does this person go on my list?

As you learn things about these people, you would be well served to develop some system to record, store, and retrieve that information so it can be useful to you. If I find out that someone loves to hunt and fish, I ought to capture that. If he likes to restore wooden furniture, I ought to capture that. If she collects John Grisham signed first editions, I ought to capture that. I store the facts in a way that works for me: in a paper notebook, in an iPhone, on a laptop, or some other means so that I can find it when I need it. How else will I keep it all organized and easy to access?

While building a relationship you are trying to learn about and understand other people. When you learn about and understand other people, you will naturally understand ways you might be able to help them. If your focus is on how you can help them get what they want, you must seek to understand them, their issues, their challenges, their wants, their desires, and how they became who they are. You will be dramatically more successful and will have a far more fulfilling and rewarding life than if you have only a few and limited relationships.

The mapping concept points out the four groups who are crucial to most people in business and in having a high quality of life. Think about who they are, think about developing a systematic approach to building a relationship with them, and think about staying in contact with them so they know they are important to you.

Most relationship building just happens. You meet this person; you meet that person. Relationship mapping gives you a strategy, which is further enhanced when you have knowledge of other people's Pyramids. This knowledge enables you to begin to develop the concept of Pyramid hopping. As you hop onto other people's pyramids, they become people you add to your map. The more relationships you have, the more opportunities you have to access and leverage people on those acquaintances' Pyramids. So let's talk about Pyramid hopping.

CHAPTER 9

HOP FROM ONE PYRAMID TO ANOTHER

Pyramid hopping is actively pursuing contacts by leveraging the relationships you have with people on your Relationship Pyramid. It is networking on steroids—making a *good* connection, not just *a* connection. The strength of the connection is based on where you are on someone's Pyramid. By Pyramid hopping, you can be more productive and effective because you are able to access people who can help you. It is proactively doing something most of us do unconsciously all the time: asking for recommendations from someone we trust.

When a friend asks, "Do you know a good plumber?" and you recommend a reliable one, you've helped the plumber hop from your Relationship Pyramid to your friend's. When someone recommends you as a possible resource and you follow up, you hop from one Pyramid to another. (The phrase "Pyramid hopping" was actually coined by Debbie Warner of AstraZeneca in one of my seminars.) Most of us do it to some degree, but we could probably develop the skills to do it much better.

PYRAMID HOPPING IS NOT NETWORKING

Once again, Pyramid hopping is not networking in the ordinary sense. Networking is handing out as many business cards as possible at a business mixer. Networking was what Ron Cleboski, now at Time Warner Cable, did early in his sales career when he was selling long-distance telephone services. He would make it a point to go to golf outings and networking events where, if he could find one person to talk to him, he regarded it as time well spent. One day he paid his own way to go to a Houston golf outing of the British American Business Association. "I didn't know anybody; it was just something that I was told about. I got hooked up with a foursome, one of whom was a guy by the name of Peter, an importer/exporter running a small seven-man shop. He turned out to be a really nice guy. We had a great day, and within two or three months I was able to sell him our services."

At the same time, Ron was trying to approach another Houston company, a huge user of international calling to and from the United Kingdom. Not unexpectedly, Ron wanted as much international calling as possible, and he knew this company was spending six or seven thousand dollars a month on calls to and from the U.K. Because they were using another long-distance supplier, however, he couldn't get the time of day from them.

Six months or so after Ron met Peter, they had a golf date. Peter invited one of his friends, also British and, through no coincidence, a decision-maker at the company Ron was trying to approach. "I recognized the guy's name and he recognized mine, and he said, 'I've been avoiding you, but Peter said you took good care of him. Why don't you come in and talk?'" Two months after their first meeting, Ron signed his business and was able to achieve about a three-month quota with one signature. This is an example of successful networking. If Ron had asked Peter to introduce him to the contact directly, it would have been an example of Pyramid hopping.

Networking is what people do when they put their personal profiles on websites such as LinkedIn, Facebook, MySpace, and more than a hundred more.[1] A job-search website called SimplyHired is edging toward the kind of Pyramid hopping I'm talking about here. SimplyHired has a deal with Facebook, so that its users see who among your Facebook friends are employed by a company in which you are interested. You can search LinkedIn for company affiliations.

This is a kind of technological approach to Pyramid hopping that's probably better than nothing, but what I'm suggesting is much more personal.

For example, people e-mail me their resumes with a note asking if I can help them find jobs. They expect me to e-mail the resume to somebody else. But this is not Pyramid hopping. The actual "hop" or move between Pyramids occurs when you take the process further, to accessing that relationship. So, if someone knows me well enough to send me her resume, she could call me to say, "I'm in the process of looking for a job. Here's what happened. . . . Who do you know that I might contact in the pharmaceutical business who'd be looking for somebody in Texas?" I would tell her who I know and she could legitimately ask, "How would you suggest I go about contacting him? Or would it be better if you contacted him on my behalf, if you're comfortable doing that?"

I am glad to call rather than send an e-mail. If someone asks me to forward a resume, I will gladly forward the resume, but the chances of making a connection that way are not very good. If you ask me to help you hop from the top of my Pyramid to an acquaintance's Pyramid, I will help. I will always recommend people at the top of my Relationship Pyramid if I'm asked. If a sales manager knows that I have contacts, she may ask if I could recommend a salesperson, and I will recommend someone (or two or three people) who is at or near the top of my Pyramid.

Depending on the situation, someone does not have to be at the top of the Pyramid to get my recommendation. I will recommend a reliable mechanic or an accurate accountant who may not value a relationship with me. Even if you are not at the top of someone's Pyramid, he or she is usually willing to introduce you to other people as long as they believe they run no risk of looking stupid or malicious. That's a hurdle you must clear. Who recommends an inept mechanic or a back-stabbing salesperson? You may not be at the top of my Pyramid, but as long as I'm sure you won't embarrass me, I'll recommend you.

True, the higher you stand on someone's Pyramid, the stronger the endorsement you are likely to get when he or she introduces you and allows you to Pyramid hop. It's the difference between, "I don't know him very well, but I've been in some meetings with him and it seems like you two might have something in common" and "You need to meet Jerry because he can help you."

FRIENDLY IS NOT THE SAME AS FRIENDSHIP

Here is another key point: Pyramid hopping is not the same thing as making new friends. Friendships in business are not necessary. They may develop, but they are not necessary. Being friendly in business, however, *is* necessary. One may have a valued business relationship without friendship, but a friendship does not necessarily mean you have a valued business relationship.

Friendships are characterized by significant and more intimate interactions between people. Friendship tends to include mutual understanding, sympathy, esteem, affection, and honesty, even in situations in which it may be difficult for you to tell the truth. Friends welcome each other's company and are loyal to each other, often to the point of altruism. Their tastes tend to be similar and they share enjoyable activities. They help each other, exchange advice, and share hardship.

Synonyms for "friendly" include welcoming, forthcoming, responsive, sociable, open, pleasant, and affable. A friendly person is not antagonistic, belittling, or sarcastic. It's easy to get along with someone who is friendly. The primary objective in relationship building isn't to create friendships; it's to create valuable business relationships. Being friendly is important, because it is virtually impossible to build a strong, positive relationship when you are unpleasant, nasty, or irresponsible.

I should make the distinction between professional friendships and social friendships. I have some professional friendships, people with whom I have great professional relationships and I love being around them. I know their families, but when we get together, it's usually around something business-related. We are not friends, but we are friendly. I have never done anything socially with one of my best clients. We've had dinner together, but other people were present.

I enjoy his company and he seems to enjoy mine, and we are friendly; we have a professional friendship. At the same time, like most of us, I have friends with whom I have no professional relationship.

Many people think you have to develop a social friendship to move up the Relationship Pyramid. You don't. Even a professional friendship isn't necessary as long as you are friendly. You can be at the top of the Pyramid without friendship. Many people who value a relationship with you are friendly toward you and consider you a friend, but they don't have a friendship with you. Social interaction outside of work is not necessary to get to the top of the Pyramid. If you do have social friendships with colleagues outside of work, you still have to remember that the objective is not socializing outside of work; it is the professional business relationship where the person values a relationship with you.

Consider friends toward whom you have no professional feelings. For example, you may have an attorney friend, someone you like and enjoy hanging out with, but whom you would not recommend professionally because you have reason to believe he's not a very good lawyer. The only way to reach the top of the Pyramid on a professional basis is through performance. You have to deliver. If you don't deliver, you can have a friendship, but you are not going to have a valued business relationship.

Here's another point: Pyramid hopping allows you to be in two or more places at once. Even as you hop from one person's Relationship Pyramid to another's, you remain on the first person's. If you maintain your relationships (or don't commit some blatantly offensive act), you never leave the top of someone's Pyramid.

PYRAMID HOPPING IN PRACTICE

Here is how Pyramid hopping works. Not long ago I had lunch with an executive I was meeting for the first time. He is the director of professional relations at a major corporation, and the first thing he said to me was, "Man, Dane thinks you hung the moon." I know that I am at the top of Dane's Pyramid as he is at the top of mine, and I had asked Dane to set up this lunch. Where am I starting on this stranger's Pyramid? I'm certainly not at the bottom. He knows my name and, thanks to Dane, he is predisposed to like me and to be friendly toward me. If his relationship with Dane is strong enough, he may even be predisposed to respect me. He sees there may be value for him in a relationship with me, just as I see there may be value for me.

Both parties seeing value is a key point. The ultimate objective is to get people to value a relationship with you, and the earlier in the relationship people begin to think there might be value in having a relationship at all, the faster you are likely to move up the Pyramid. If someone sees no value in the relationship (or, worse, that the relationship will actually cause mischief), you will never move from level 1, "People who know me by name." The value in the relationship may be obvious; for example, you have information or skills the other person wants. But it doesn't always have to be so clear-cut. It could be as squishy as the fact that you are fun to be around, that you have interesting ideas, or that you share a common interest.

The director of professional relations was going to send me his daughter's resume and I promised to try to help her get a job with my contacts. He in turn would introduce me to the director of training at his corporation. During lunch, I explained the concept of Pyramid hopping. Once he understood, he said, "So I hop on your Pyramid and you help my daughter get a job, and you hop on mine and I help you get in to see the director of training." Exactly. In addition, if the relationship develops, there may be more than that basic exchange. He added that he might be able to think of other people who could be helpful to me, and I told him the same.

PYRAMID HOPPING REQUIRES QUESTIONS

You start the process of Pyramid hopping with an inventory of your relationships, part of the mapping exercise I described in Chapter 8. But that is only a start. You cannot Pyramid hop unless you consciously uncover who those people know, their networks of acquaintances, friends, and colleagues. If I am at the top of your Pyramid,

I can leverage a relationship you have with somebody else. The problem is, if I don't have any idea who is in the upper echelons of your Pyramid, I'll never be able to leverage those relationships. As you identify those people who have put you at the top of their Pyramid, it is helpful to know who else is on their Pyramid so you can leverage the relationships. People who value a relationship with you will help you Pyramid hop, but they can't do it unless you ask the right question.

Here is an example. Recently in a training session, Mel, one of the participants, said he didn't know how he could Pyramid hop. He owns a business training insurance brokers, most of whom work for only three or four insurance companies. With such a limited field—possibly no more than 15 or 20 prospects in total—he felt there were only a few places those contacts could send him.

Yet every one of those brokers is selling insurance. I asked if they have clients who might be sales leaders in companies that would be potential clients for Mel's training business. Rather than ask these brokers "Who do you know at Blue Cross/Blue Shield?" ask: "Who in your client base is a district manager, a regional manager, a senior sales or marketing executive, or a manager working for a reasonable size company?"

If you assume your contacts have only three or four relationships themselves, you artificially limit the number of possibilities. You have to seek information about who else they know, colleagues or customers for whom they would be willing to use their relationship on your behalf. To do that, you have to learn to ask specific questions: Who do you know in a senior sales and marketing position? Who do you know who is a buyer for a company that sells widgets? The questions have to be specific, because people aren't mind readers. They cannot know whom you need to meet unless you begin to probe.

Note also that the higher you are on someone's Relationship Pyramid, the more likely he or she is to volunteer to help you Pyramid hop. But that person cannot help you unless you describe what you need, what you are looking for, or what you have an interest in—that is, what kind of Pyramid do you want to hop on to? As the *Harvard Business Review* article I talked about in Chapter 8 points out, it is important to have diversity in your network. "Linus Pauling, one of only two people to win a Nobel Prize in two different areas and considered one of the towering geniuses of the twentieth century, attributed his creative success not to his immense brainpower or luck but to his diverse contacts: 'The best way to have a good idea is to have a lot of ideas.'" The more diverse your network, the more you can develop complete, creative, and unbiased views of issues. "And when you trade information or skills with people whose experiences differ from your own, you provide one another with unique, exceptionally valuable resources."[2]

Henry Potts at Melillo Consulting says that successful business people typically limit themselves to a narrow band of what they know, what they're particularly good at. "You continue to exploit those things to gain more success in your career, and don't consciously look outside that specialty." Henry has one easy suggestion to experience something outside your norm: "Go to a magazine rack and pick up a magazine you've never seen before on a totally different topic from what you usually read and look through it."

Diversity, Henry points out, requires two things: "One is to consciously go do it, like getting a different magazine. And then be open to it." Henry goes on to say that in the past few years, he's begun opening up to taking people's calls even though it may not be immediately apparent what value the call has for him. "If somebody suggests, 'How about talking to this person about that subject?' whether it's in my realm or not, I'm open to talking. So I think one of the first steps is to be open to doing these things even unconsciously, whenever it involves a relationship or whenever it appears you might be doing something for someone else's benefit. Be open to someone taking the time to pick up the phone and call you or send you an e-mail or ask you to do something. It's an opportunity to help them. And if you take those opportunities, opportunities will come back your way."

Mel, in my seminar, was thinking in a linear way. He was thinking insurance, insurance, insurance. But he also has a training business in which he would feel comfortable training people who sold paper for Kimberly-Clark, Fiberglas for Owens Corning, or power tools for Black & Decker. So why not ask about people who are sales managers in consumer goods companies? As Henry says, the key is being open to opportunities to expand your business by asking for help from others—and reciprocating those opportunities as well.

PYRAMID HOPPING USUALLY REQUIRES SPECIFICS

Pyramid hopping takes place when I want to meet somebody because I need something specific done, and to be effective I must be specific about who and how I ask for it. The quality of the endorsement plays an important part. I might be looking for a good baker because we are going to host a party. I might be looking for a great Greek restaurant for a client who likes Greek food. I might need somebody to tutor my child, so I will ask people I respect if they know someone who could do that.

If someone at the top of my Pyramid says, "My son is being tutored by Freddy Jones and he's great," I will obtain Jones's phone number. If someone I barely know says, "I heard that someone named Freddy Jones does tutoring," I will be less eager to contact him. Still, many people believe you can Pyramid hop only with people at the top of the Pyramid. That's not true. You can Pyramid hop even if you are on no more than the "People who like me" level. Somebody will introduce you to somebody else, but the quality of the endorsement will be different.

Again, the only way you can learn who somebody knows is by asking. I've been talking about asking specific questions that force colleagues to think about a specific type of person with a specific skill or specific set of experiences. The classic referral question, "Who do you know that [sells power tools ... designs software ... writes books]?" can lead you to the right person. With initial Pyramid hopping, people ask the "Who do you know ..." or "Who have you met ..." questions systematically. You're trying to learn: Who do you know that I need to meet? It is the combination of network and referrals. You might also ask: Who do you know that might be able to help me at another pharmaceutical company? Who do you know that is in a position like yours at another company? Who do you know in your company that might benefit from the stuff we're doing?

LinkedIn may be able to help you with some of these questions. Melvin Boaz said he did not fully appreciate this resource until he was looking for another job.

He tells me he was between jobs. "I had taken a severance package from another company, and my wife and I decided to make a change in lifestyle because our kids are grown. We had been living in the Cleveland area and wanted a change in climate, so we moved to Charlotte, North Carolina."

Mel explains, "When I arrived in Charlotte, I started reaching out, trying to find people who might know of some openings. I came across a recruiter who was a friend of a friend. Traditionally, if recruiters are not looking to fill positions directly related to you, they're not a whole lot of help. This one was an exception. He suggested that I look at a the LinkedIn website, so I did."

At LinkedIn, Mel found job openings for Smith & Nephew, a company he knew very little about, but the jobs listed seemed to match his skills and interest. "I then searched for somebody who might have a relationship to Smith & Nephew, and I found an individual. I sent him an e-mail through the LinkedIn site; he responded, saying he didn't know anything about the division I was looking at, but thought my background was interesting and inquired if I would be willing to talk with him about a project his division was working on."

They were working on a new product launch and wanted to pick Mel's brain. He and the contact talked on the phone two or three times and he gave them a few ideas, and that was that.

About three months later Mel's Smith & Nephew contact called him back to say the product was doing well and they were about ready to go to market, adding, "I keep thinking of you, and I thought you would be a good fit to head up this project. Would you be interested?"

In this case, there was a chain of relationships, hopping from one Pyramid to another: "I met somebody who gave me some information and pointed me in the right direction, which led me to a high-level executive within the organization, and that got me the position that I have today," says Mel. He had to have the skills and experience even to be considered, and he had to talk with the company, but if he had not deliberately built his relationships he would not have his job today.

Who Are the People You Should Meet?

Pyramid hopping is really our personal word of mouth, and there's nothing more powerful than word-of-mouth advertising. But most of us neither ask nor are asked the questions. We probably know many people who could help colleagues, associates, or customers if they simply asked us, but most of the time we do not volunteer the information unless it is obvious a friend needs help.

Let's think about our questions again. To be more effective from our Pyramid hopping results we need to get very specific with our questions. Perhaps an even more powerful question is "Who are the two people you know that I don't know that you think I ought to meet?" Or "Who have you met in the past three to six months who you think is intriguing and who I might like to know [or ought to know]?" Or "Who are the two or three most interesting people you've met in the past few weeks?" Virtually no one asks these questions, but they can open remarkable doors.

A friend tells me that when he was a trade magazine editor, one salesperson, Ed, dramatically outsold every other salesperson. In this trade, the advertising agencies that placed the ads believed all the magazines were about the same; no one was clearly superior. Over time and almost by default, Ed had become a one-man employment agency. He helped advertising agency people find new jobs when they needed one. Two-thirds of his clients got their jobs because of an introduction and recommendation he had provided. As a result, space buyers who believed it made no real business difference which magazine they chose to run their ad, thought, "Why not run it in good old Ed's magazine?"

The story speaks to the value of helping someone Pyramid hop. Here, the law of psychological reciprocity kicked in, which says

"I need to give back to you what you have given to me." When I need something, you are more likely to want to help me because I have helped you. The point to keep in mind is that you never know where the help will come from. Remember when I talked about inexpensive, unexpected, thoughtful actions? Ed was using this skill by constantly helping, and he was able to build a significant network of colleagues because of his generosity. His time and ability to Pyramid hop enabled him to help people find jobs.

Ed did not help his friends obtain new jobs because he expected them to buy his ads; he did it because that was his character. He would have helped even if no one had reciprocated. You do the right thing because it's the right thing to do.

Allen Zimmerman at AmerisourceBergen points out that Pyramid hopping within professional organizations can be invaluable for introductions, recommendations, and testimonials to the quality of the firm's personnel and of the work it does as an organization. "I have found there is a tremendous network available through professional organizations. Also, some of our largest customers tend to be well connected around the country. I have found leaders in the societies and professional organizations to be tremendously valuable in introducing us to other health care thought-leaders and providing us with access that normally of our own accord would be very difficult to obtain."

Allen adds, "I've found that 90 to 95 percent or better of the time I spend with those individuals we never talk about business. I genuinely like them as human beings. I recently spent three hours with one of these senior people, and we spent so much personal time together that we had to set up a call later on in the weekend to talk about business."

My trade magazine editor friend says that he used to report on the industry's annual convention and attend an annual weeklong industry management training session at Notre Dame University. "I didn't do it deliberately, because at the time I didn't know enough," he tells me, "but I stumbled into building relationships with the executives who were the most interesting, articulate, and successful in the industry. Because they tended to be the people who are willing to participate in trade associations and industry groups, they are also able to look at a bigger picture than just their own little business. The relationships I built at Notre Dame were invaluable for information and news—and I used those relationships to make contact with other key industry executives."

People in seminars say they never thought of consciously, deliberately, and systematically asking colleagues or contacts who they know. They, like all of us, have no idea who people know. In many cases, they take their relationships for granted and don't try to probe for the relationships they have. To identify the relationships other people have, you've got to ask them. You have to ask very specifically: Who do you know that . . . ?

This does not mean you won't have a setback every now and again. But if you help a lot of people get what they want, the help will come back to you. Pyramid hopping is about strategically meeting people through others. There is a purpose: You are actively looking for someone an associate has a good relationship with, whom you think it would benefit me to know.

But to develop good relationships, you have to build respect. So let's talk about how you can do that.

CHAPTER 10

GAIN RESPECT THIRTEEN WAYS

Business relationships go two ways: Even as you ask questions of customers and colleagues, they silently ask questions of you. They may not consciously be aware that they even have questions, but you should always be sensitive to the questions in the air. Everyone with whom you hope to build a strong relationship wants to know:

- Is this person good at what he or she does?
- How will this person's work reflect on me?
- Does this person want what is best for me and my organization?
- Does this person understand my challenges?
- Is this a person I will like working with professionally?
- Can this person be trusted?

To simply announce to a prospect, customer, client, or colleague, "I'm good at what I do, my work will make you look great, and of course you can trust me," is not sufficient.

Value and mutual respect are key elements in building a strong business relationship. So how do you gain someone's respect?

169

IDENTIFY QUALITIES YOU RESPECT

Think about the person you most respect. This individual need not be one of the people with whom you want to have a better business relationship; it might be a parent, a teacher, a former boss.

Write down four or five qualities about that person. What are the significant traits of someone you respect? (To obtain the most value from this exercise, you should stop reading and write down the person's qualities on the form in Figure 10.1 or on another sheet of paper.)

I ask participants in my seminars to do this exercise. Here are some of the responses they've given.

- We respect people who are appreciative, enthusiastic, modest, honest, intelligent.
- We respect people who are trustworthy, refined, polite, respectful.
- We respect people who are driven, committed, direct, fun.
- We respect people who are genuine and caring, knowledgeable and interesting to talk to, good listeners.
- We respect people who are competent, articulate, well read, humorous.
- We respect people who are reliable, positive, genuine, and caring.
- We respect people who are nonjudgmental, loyal, who can resist temptation, are courageous.
- We respect people who are other-focused, unflappable, well rounded.
- We respect people who are diplomatic, family-oriented, faithful, reliable.
- We respect people who have integrity, who are intelligent, who teach, and who are dependable.

Certain qualities tend to come up again and again: dependable, honest, trustworthy, and respectful. Does the person you most respect have these qualities?

IDENTIFY QUALITIES YOU RESPECT

Figure 10.1
List Four or Five Qualities of the Person You Most Respect

We respect these qualities in others, and others respect them in us—if we have them. To the extent that we can be good listeners, competent, dependable, and trustworthy, we are more likely to earn the respect we look for in others. More to the point, if you don't embody the qualities of people you respect, should you reasonably expect other people to respect you?

True, I've just listed more than 40 qualities, and it's unlikely that one individual has every attribute to the same high degree. It would be a better world if everyone did have them, but that is not going to happen as long as we remain human. Nevertheless, if you recognize that you are entirely deficient in any one of these traits, or if you have a negative quality—if, for example, you are at times impolite or disloyal or easily upset—you might start considering ways to make a change.

Even if you are dependable, honest, trustworthy, respectful, and all the rest, you may still have difficulty because you are a salesperson or a lawyer or a consultant or a whatever. When I ask salespeople, "What do your customers think of salespeople in general?" it's usually nega- tive: "They're pushy. Inconsiderate. Thinking only of themselves."

Then I ask, "If that's what your customers think of salespeople in general, what do they think of you?" The question forces individuals to consider their relationships from a new angle. Most of the time salespeople say their customers' attitudes are not what they would like them to be.

I am using salespeople as the example here, but the issue affects everyone in business. If you are an appliance service department manager, what do your technicians think of managers in general? What do they think of you? If you are a magazine editor, what do your colleagues in accounting, circulation, and advertising sales think of editors in general? What do they think of you? What do corporate research directors think of consultants—of you? What do marketing executives think of advertising agency people—of you?

Let's extend the exercise a little further. Beyond what your key customers and colleagues—the people with whom you want to have a strong relationship—think of you, what would they tell others about you? If you were a fly on the wall as one customer talked to another about you, what would you hear? "She's all right . . . for a salesperson"? Or "She's the most trustworthy, responsive, thoughtful person I know"?

If a key customer had to prove you were different from all other salespeople (or different from all other lawyers, service managers, magazine editors, consultants, advertising agency employees), how would he or she prove your difference? Most of the time we are not different. We do what we do and we don't change. We tend to wear a stereotype because it fits so well.

THIRTEEN WAYS TO GAIN RESPECT

Your consistent and reliable actions over time and the way you interact with another person, the questions you ask, your knowledge of your product and of your competition, and the actions you take to build a relationship are the tools you use to climb the Relationship Pyramid. Here is a baker's dozen of the things you can do to gain respect.

1. Be genuinely interested in the other person.
2. Do what you say you will do when you say you will do it, or say nothing.
3. Be knowledgeable, be inquisitive, or be quiet.
4. Control your emotions; anger manages everything poorly.
5. Be honest and straightforward.
6. Be objective and avoid appearing biased.
7. Be persistent, but never be aggressive.
8. Be a learned person with some expertise and share your knowledge when appropriate.
9. Be courteous to everyone.
10. Always listen to the other person intently.
11. Seek to understand other people and their points of view.
12. Do things that demonstrate your unselfish nature.
13. Find out what people want, and help them get it.

Figure 10.2
Do's and Don'ts of Interacting with Other People

Do	Don't
• Be confident	• Criticize, condemn, or compare
• Smile	
• Make people feel important	• Judge
	• Be overly anxious
• Treat people as special	• Have a wandering eye
• Make eye contact	• Try to be impressive
• Be impressed	
• Listen intently	• Interrupt

I know this list does not exhaust the things you can do to gain respect, but it is a good start. I also know that nothing on this list or on the list in Figure 10.2 is brand-new information to anyone reading this book. Rather, consider this a refresher course in how to gain respect. The following are some examples of these precepts.

EXAMPLES OF BUILDING RESPECT

All business people prefer to work with others they can trust and find reliable. In today's highly competitive marketplace, someone who knows how to move up the Relationship Pyramid with customers and colleagues enjoys a definite edge.

You prove you have integrity by your actions over time. One does not demonstrate integrity overnight. (You can, however, destroy your integrity overnight with a flagrant misdeed—embezzle, cheat, lie—just as you can undermine it with small offenses: a minor betrayal, a white lie, an insignificant cheat.) You show your integrity by doing the right thing even when it is uncomfortable. Perhaps especially when it is uncomfortable.

You earn professional respect by demonstrating that you have exceptional knowledge or expertise in your product or in its application, in your customer's business, in your customer's industry, or some other specialized expertise that impresses the customer. (I never said this was easy.)

So what about the 13 ways to gain respect?

BE GENUINELY INTERESTED IN THE OTHER PERSON

"The one common denominator to all success and happiness is other people," says Les Giblin in *How to Have Confidence and Power in Dealing with People*.[1] But being other-focused is very difficult because it's not in our nature.

It's not just you. Almost everyone has trouble being genuinely interested in others. But once you recognize the difficulty (and if you agree that other people hold the means to your success), what can you do to change? Ask yourself: What is there about this person I find off-putting? Why, exactly, am I not interested in this person? If you want any true business success, tap into your genuine interest in learning why you find some people entirely uninteresting. At that point, you may develop a genuine interest. When I had to find one thing to like about Dick McDonald, I found many things.

If you are genuinely interested in other people to begin with, show it. How? By asking the Link 20 questions in Chapter 4 and attending to the answers.

Mike Accardi says that to generate respect for yourself, you must respect others. "It has to come from within. It has to be genuine." Mike feels he may have an advantage because he naturally likes people. "I just like them. I am fascinated by people, and people pick up on that. People like to know they have your attention. Probably the most important thing in their life is their name. I remember people's names. When I walk into a warehouse, I call the staff by name."

If you don't want to be seen as a typical salesperson (or lawyer, or accountant, or accounts payable manager), don't act like one. If you want to differentiate yourself from other salespeople, why act like every other salesperson? To be different, you have to decide to be different and you have to act differently.

One good way to be different is to focus more on the customer—be genuinely interested in the other person—and less on what you've got to sell, always remembering that you want the relationship so that you can do your job better, more effectively, more enjoyably.

DO WHAT YOU SAY YOU WILL DO

I know that many of these 13 suggestions sound squishy and obvious. They are things we learned in kindergarten: Be nice. Share. Don't tell lies.

In fact, most of the time, most of us do the important things we say we will do. We certainly do those things important to us. We say we'll prepare for a meeting that has career-building potential, and we're prepared. We say we'll make sure a key document is delivered, and we hand-carry it.

Things become sticky when the issue is not obviously important to us. "I'll get back to you tomorrow on this" may be a throwaway line at the end of a routine phone call with a colleague. Is it going to kill your career if you don't call back? Probably not. If you thought it would—if the call were from your boss's boss—you'd call back. But either you don't say you'll do something – or if you say you will, do it.

BE KNOWLEDGEABLE, BE INQUISITIVE, OR BE QUIET

If you can contribute something substantive to the discussion of the issue at hand, do so.

If you believe you might be able to contribute if you understood the situation better, ask leading, open-ended questions.

If you can't contribute and it does not appear you will be able to, shut up and listen. Now, was that difficult?

CONTROL YOUR EMOTIONS; ANGER MANAGES EVERYTHING POORLY

Anger makes us say and do things we would not do when clear-headed. As the proverb puts it: Anger is a wind that blows out the light of the mind. But what can we do when provoked? Perhaps the best tactic is to back off.

Mike Accardi says he once had a customer who was routinely abusive. The customer was a successful Memphis merchant and cocky about his success. "I would go into his office, and he would start ranting and raving." He knew Mike's bosses socially and apparently felt he could abuse their salesman. One day, he pushed Mike too far. "I came in and he started cussing. I stopped him. I said, 'Whoa. I obviously upset you. You don't have to worry about having your day messed up like this anymore. I will never come in here again.'"

"Oh yes, you will," said the customer. "You're going to keep coming in here and calling on me."

"No, I'm not. I am not going to deal with somebody like this. I am never going to curse you, and I am not going to listen to you curse me." Mike walked out of the customer's office, drove straight to his office, and went to his boss. He reported the confrontation, adding, "You know him, and he's getting ready to phone you and demand I call on him, if he hasn't called already. I don't want to tell you no, so please don't ask me to call on him, because I won't."

Mike's boss started laughing, and said, "Don't worry. I know him, and I'll take care of it."

It's always better to fire an abusive customer than to trash his office or hit him with your briefcase.

BE HONEST AND STRAIGHTFORWARD

Honesty, as someone said, is not the best policy. It's the only policy.

If your product or service will not do what the customer needs or wants, say so. Greg Genova at Kennametal believes that to gain a customer's respect, "You always have to be truthful. You have to be, because you will get caught so quickly—and they'll remember the incident forever."

Customers love the truth, especially if it comes from a salesperson, because many of them have been conditioned to expect an evasive or equivocal response. They believe that although there may be only a small difference between competitive products, salespeople will try to inflate the difference. Admit the truth (if it is the truth) that there's only a small difference between your product and the competitor's, and customers will be nonplussed. They do not expect a straightforward answer, and the truth is a powerful strategy.

BE OBJECTIVE AND AVOID APPEARING BIASED

Salespeople violate this proposition all the time. They don't appear to be objective. Yet, it is very difficult to get people's respect when they think you are always biased—which is true not only for salespeople but for people in general.

Therefore, think hard about how you present your products, your services, and your ideas. When you say, "This is the greatest invention in the world. You have to do this. Everybody is doing it," it has a very different effect from what happens when you present things in a more objective fashion. Even when you present your story logically, the way you present it will come across as biased when you present only your point of view.

If you try to make the differences between your product and the competitor's large, and the customer sees the differences as small, you lose credibility. If the customer sees the differences as small but acknowledges they may be important, and if that's the way you present the differences, you gain respect. This doesn't mean you do not focus on your product's benefits and features; it means that your motives are pure.

There is another issue here, as Lance Perkins at GE Medical Systems points out: Don't take the bait.

What bait? It's the line a customer will toss out that goes something like, "Have you heard about so-and-so? What have you heard about them? I heard they're not doing well." This inquiry may or may not be devious. The customer may be legitimately curious about what is happening in the industry. And our impulse may be to curry favor with the customer, or to suggest through our inside information how knowledgeable we are.

Nonetheless, as Lance says, don't take that bait. It is business poison. Say something like, "You know, the conversations I have with people are just between me and them, and there's really nothing I can share with you on that." It may not have occurred to customers when they ask the question, but eventually they will realize that if you gossip about one company, you'll gossip about every company, theirs included.

BE PERSISTENT, BUT NEVER BE AGGRESSIVE

People don't mind your being persistent, but they don't like your being aggressive—or what they consider aggressive. How do you know if they consider your actions aggressive?

Ask.

Ask before you're back down at the bottom of the Relationship Pyramid because you've pushed too hard. Ask how often they want you to call. Ask if they feel you have been too pushy—or not pushy enough. It does not matter what you think; the other person's perception is the reality here.

The other side of this particular notion is to be responsive. Greg Genova, like George Griffith in Chapter 8, says that when a customer calls, "I respond immediately, whether or not I have the answer or can solve the problem. I respond immediately, because I've been on both sides of the desk. I've placed phone calls and waited for people to call me back. It's very frustrating when you have to wait a day or two."

To the customers, their concern is urgent (and it is important to them even if it's not important in the grand scheme of things). They want a response. "Even if you don't have what they're looking for, you respond, and that is how you build trust and respect," says Greg.

"They know they can pick up the phone, they can page me, and usually within an hour or so I have responded. At least it lets them know I am working on it."

BE A LEARNED PERSON WITH SOME EXPERTISE

People are naturally drawn to those with specific expertise. If you are truly an expert in fly fishing, French cooking, or the American Revolution, many people will respect the fact that you have become knowledgeable in that area. Few of us actually acquire a sufficient level of specialized knowledge to be called "expert" or to be perceived as one.

If you do not have any deep specialized expertise, it might be a good idea to get some in an area in which you are genuinely interested. Through books, audiotapes, and the Internet you can develop considerable expertise in a relatively short span of time. The simple fact is we love to know and associate with people who command vast knowledge in almost any subject, as long as they do not use their learning as a bludgeon to intimidate us. If you have specialized knowledge, you will be able to find places where it helps you get the respect of people who are important to you.

BE COURTEOUS TO EVERYONE

This should be obvious, but it's not. Too often, we give all our attention to the prospect or the customer and ignore the receptionists, secretaries, and assistants. Treat everybody as important because everyone is important.

Mike Accardi says the way he treats people has a lot to do with who he is as a person and the way he was brought up. "I'm from a Sicilian family, a very structured, paternal hierarchy, and I was taught respect. I think if you are going to get respect, you have to give it."

Respect the dignity, the humanity of the human in front of you, says Mike. "A long time ago—and I guess this is just a blessing of my nature—I came to realize that everybody has dignity—everybody.

No matter what they look like, no matter what their position, everybody has dignity. When I go into a building, I address the dignity of the individual. I don't address the title."

Not only is this the right thing to do for its own sake, but the attitude can have practical benefits. Mike says that, in two instances, he has watched janitors became general managers—and good customers—over the years.

ALWAYS LISTEN INTENTLY TO THE OTHER PERSON

As I've said before, listening is hard work. Many of us just do not listen well because we are always projecting our opinions and ideas, our prejudices, our background, our inclinations, our impulses on the speaker. When those things dominate, we hardly listen at all to what is being said. I suspect the only way to overcome this noisy buzz is through practice, to consciously turn down the volume of our clanging thoughts and focus on what the other person is saying. Listen as if to a foreign language, concentrating on every syllable to catch the meaning.

Only after you have heard and absorbed what the other person has said should you respond with your opinions, ideas, and the rest.

SEEK TO UNDERSTAND OTHER PEOPLE

This is related to the previous point. Once you have listened intently to what other people are trying to express, you can begin to comprehend what they want, need, and believe.

You should learn early on what your key customers and colleagues want from someone in your profession or position. What do they value most in the people for whom they have the greatest respect? What do they value most in accountants? In lawyers? Consultants? Salespeople?

Then ask yourself: Given what they want, have I been providing it? In my experience, the answer is almost always no. Often, prospects, customers, and colleagues are not getting what they really want from you because you are giving them what you think they want or need, not what they think they want or need. An accountant may believe customers most want accuracy in filling out tax forms. But the customer assumes, correctly or incorrectly, that accurate tax forms are a given—that's what accountants get paid for—and really wants prompt answers to phone calls.

The challenge is to understand what is actually important to customers and colleagues. It is getting inside their heads and discovering what they appreciate. The higher you stand on their Relationship Pyramid, the more they value their relationship with you, the more likely they will honestly tell you what's important to them.

Few people like to be sold, but most people love to buy. So why do so many organizations try to sell? It makes no sense. If you talk to people about the greatest salespeople they have ever known, they don't see them as salespeople. They see them as colleagues, as consultants, and as partners who understand them in a way that others do not.

DO THINGS THAT DEMONSTRATE YOUR UNSELFISH NATURE

What inexpensive, unexpected, and thoughtful things have you done for the people whose respect you want? Defining moments in relationships often occur as a result of showing your unselfish nature. When you show you are unselfish, good things happen.

Now that you've read Chapter 7, what will you be doing for the people who are key to your business success?

FIND OUT WHAT PEOPLE WANT, AND HELP THEM GET IT

Most people don't know what they want because they have no concept of what is available. Your job is not to sell customers and colleagues products, services, ideas, or plans they don't want. Your job is to learn what they want, to teach them what is available, and to see if there is some way to help them get it.

Bob Holman at Donaldson, Holman & West says he's found that his accounting clients often don't really know what they want. They will say, "I want you to find somebody to buy my business." When Bob begins to probe to identify the real issue, the client is liable to say something like, "I want to get out because I'm having difficulty with payroll. It's always a big issue. Every two weeks I have to deal with this and I hate it. I don't want to deal with it anymore, and the only way I know to stop dealing with it is to sell the business, because it's ruining all the other things I like to do."

Which leads to the obvious (or perhaps not so obvious) question: Why don't you stop doing payroll and do the things you like to do? Give the job to a payroll service. Bob will tell the client, "If you can then focus your time on doing what you really like to do, you'll do much better, you'll make more money, and you can pay the service and still have more money left."

If you have strong, positive relationships with clients, you can discuss hard realities. "If you don't have the relationship," says Bob, "they are going to say, 'That's none of your business.' When you have the relationship, you can say, 'Yes, it is my business.' And be able to ask them those hard questions."

If people want something other than what you have to sell, you have no right to sell them what you've got. The great paradox is this: The less you care about the sale, the more you sell. This is equally true in dealing with your colleagues: The less you care about imposing your ideas (or taking credit), the more you will accomplish.

The challenge, of course, is when legitimate prospects do not know they could benefit from what you represent. In that situation, your task is to educate by asking questions. Your goal always is not to sell per se, but to learn where the product and service fit the customer.

We start with the premise that what you are selling or representing has merit to some portion of the world. We also must believe that whatever value you offer is currently underutilized; not every person or organization that could benefit from what you offer is currently buying it. You are trying to close the gap between your underutilized product and those for whom it would be valuable. As long as a gap exists, you have opportunity.

I know this is not easy. Once you have a sales manager leaning on you, a quota to meet, and calls to make, it is difficult to keep all this in mind—or to believe you should not care primarily about the sale. After all, your commission is based on sales, not relationships. To keep from falling back into a former pattern, your overriding objective has to be clear. We have a problem when we don't focus on what others want, when we focus on what we want.

You must have a deep belief that these ideas will pay off—that the relationship will pay off. You have to be able to leverage the relationships you have with those customers and colleagues.

You are not doing all this work only to make friends. You can't just have these strong business relationships and then not share the uniqueness and value of the products and services you are selling. Because then it is all about you; it is not about them. You are not trying to help them in their jobs, their careers, their successes. You just want to be friends, which is not the point of relationship building.

It's not because of their egos that people miss leveraging their business relationships. They miss the chance because they are more concerned about the relationship they have with the customer than they are with the relationship the customer has with the product or service.

What you do really matters. The way you behave, the questions you ask, and the way you approach customers can be the difference between success and failure. You gain other people's respect through consistent and predictable actions that demonstrate your values.

It all starts with your values: the rules you live your life by, the qualities you and others respect. Your values drive your beliefs, and your beliefs drive your behavior. When your values are solid, when you understand that your motives matter, you will strive to discover what people want and will help them get it.

Most people want to have more than a job. If you have a positive business relationship with customers and colleagues, your job will almost certainly be far more rewarding and much more fun.

And because you do not want to be one of the many who do not know *what* they want—forgetting for a moment whether or not you know what's available to you—you ought to have goals. After all, without goals, how will you know whether you've accomplished what you want?

CHAPTER 11

WRITE CLEAR, SPECIFIC GOALS

Few people have clearly defined and articulated goals, exact statements of desired end results. Most have never said, "I *will* achieve this," whether "this" is a personal or a business accomplishment. Most have never thought through what they truly want to achieve, nor do they know what they could realize if they were to have clear, written goals, which are not simply "to do" items but would be significant achievements.

A 1952 survey of graduating Yale seniors found only 4 percent had clearly defined, written goals. Twenty years later, a survey of the same group found that the 4 percent with goals had a greater net worth than the other 96 percent combined. To learn if this were a fluke, a duplicate study was conducted in 1971 of Harvard graduating seniors. Again, 4 percent had goals, 96 percent didn't. Ten years later, the 4 percent who had goals were on average earning 10 times more a year than the 96 percent who did not have goals. While money is not the only or necessarily the best test of accomplishment, it is relatively easy to measure. But whatever your measure, you can't reach a goal you haven't set.

You first have to establish that whatever you really want, you can have. It has to be within the realm of human possibility; I'll talk about that in a moment. If a blind 17-year-old can learn to race down mountains at 60 miles an hour, you can probably reach your goals, even if at first they seem equally outrageous.

If you want a strong relationship with your biggest customer, you can have it.

If you want a strong relationship with that brusque colleague, you can have it.

If you want a positive relationship with the charge nurse who seems to resent you, you can have it.

UNDERSTAND YOUR GOAL-SEEKING MECHANISM

Ron Willingham, in his book *When Good Isn't Good Enough,* writes: "In the late 1920s after years of practical research with the most successful people in our country, Napoleon Hill produced his first great work, *The Law of Success*. In it he wrote this about the power of goal setting: 'Any definite chief aim that is deliberately fixed in the mind and held there with determination to realize it finally saturates the entire subconscious mind until it automatically influences the body toward the attainment of that purpose.'"[1] So goal-setting—having a chief aim and fixing it in our minds—is a significant element in any success.

I believe that each of us has a built-in goal-seeking mechanism. Dr. Maxwell Maltz, in his book *Psycho-Cybernetics,* points out that every creature on the planet has a goal-seeking mechanism. In plants and animals, the mechanism focuses on two things only: survival and procreation. But in humans it's focused on more: How do we achieve those things that are within our limits and capabilities? How do we achieve those things within our gifts and talents?

This goal-seeking mechanism, says Maltz, is like a heat-seeking missile. But it has to be activated. If we know how to worry, we also know how to activate the goal-seeking mechanism. Worry is the goal-seeking mechanism gone bad. Worry is the visualization or thought of something negative. The positive goal-seeking mechanism visualizes something constructive. I believe that we all do have this goal-seeking mechanism, and if we do two things—first, understand that we have it and activate it, and second, develop a process to reach goals—there are virtually no limits to what we can achieve.[2]

GOALS HAVE FIVE CHARACTERISTICS

Anybody can set goals, but if you don't have some guidelines to reach them, you're not likely to achieve them. As everyone who writes about goals is required to remind you, they should be SMART: Specific, Measurable, Achievable, Realistic, and Time-Sensitive.

Specific: "I want to earn more" and "I want a better job" are not specific goals. They are too vague, too nebulous. How much more? Better in what way? "I want to earn $75,000 this year," "I want to be a branch manager in two years," and "I want to live in a three-bedroom house in the mid-South no more than 30 minutes from the ocean" are specific goals.

Measurable: With measurable goals, you know when you are making progress or have reached the goal. You can look at your cumulative pay stubs to see how you're doing toward an earnings goal. If you get promoted to assistant branch manager, you're on your way to branch manager.

Achievable goals are challenging but attainable. Reaching the goal may take many preliminary steps, but you are able to take them.

Realistic goals are those you can reach within the time frame you decide and with the skills and resources you have. If your goal is to retire at age 45 and you are 44 and have no savings, your goal is neither realistic nor achievable.

Time-sensitive goals have a deadline or an end point: $75,000 this year, branch manager in two years, new house in six months. One might argue that there are no unrealistic goals, only unrealistic time frames. If you are 44, have no savings, and want to retire, age 45 is unrealistic, retiring at age 50 may be a stretch, but retiring comfortably at age 55 is reasonable.

Many goals require hope to override reason. The goals I'm talking about by their nature are subjective and hopeful. Og Mandino, in *The Greatest Salesman in the World*, writes, "It is not given to know how many steps are necessary in order to reach my goal. Failure I may still encounter at the thousandth step, yet success hides just beyond the next bend in the road and never will I know how close it lies unless I turn the corner."[3] Reaching an ambitious goal takes time. You have to believe it will happen. You have to visualize what it will look like when it happens. And you must be willing to pay a price.

You need goals just as a business needs sales and profit targets. Just as goals have five characteristics, I've identified five rules to achieve goals.

1. Have goals and be clear about what you truly want and believe that you can achieve it.
2. Write down your goals.
3. Set goals in line with your gifts and talents.
4. Don't let others talk you out of your goals.
5. Let your goal-seeking mechanism do the work and take the pressure off yourself.

BE CLEAR ABOUT WHAT YOU WANT

The first part of establishing any goal is to create in your mind a vision of what you would like to accomplish and then believing that what you want can actually happen. The vision is important, so you must think it through clearly. That is why I say you have to make the decision. What is it you really want? Most people never decide what they want. Zig Ziglar says most people are wandering generalities rather than meaningful specifics.

Julie Wroblewski began her career selling frozen yogurt to retailers. After four years, she began to feel she was not making the mark on society that she wanted to make, and she set as a goal to migrate into the pharmaceutical or the medical field, to move from consumer products salesperson to pharmaceutical representative.

It took about six months, she says. "I talked with salespeople in the field who worked for many different pharmaceutical companies. Friends of friends, family friends, you name it, I found everyone who was in that business and I sat down and had breakfast with them or spoke with them over the phone. I learned from them what it took to be hired and to be successful in that field."

She scheduled as many informational interviews as she could, learning the qualities that seemed to be most important for a salesperson in the field. She then practiced demonstrating those qualities. "I went on many, many interviews with companies that were interviewing for specific positions. I didn't get offered most of them. I ultimately took one with Dow Hickam Pharmaceuticals because they were willing to take a chance on me."

Once you make your goals absolutely clear, you may find you have contradictory objectives: I want to double my income in three years and I want to spend every night and weekend with my family. Or: I want to become branch manager and I want to take three months off every summer to travel. Or: I want to build strong relationships with my key customers and colleagues and I want to triple the number of contacts I make each week.

Businesses sometimes promulgate contradictory goals: We want to increase customer contact and we want to cut the travel budget. We want to reduce customer service telephone wait time from a seven-minute average to three and we want to eliminate 10 percent of the department. If the goals are clear but contradictory, you have to modify or eliminate one or both. You or the business must set priorities.

When you get clear in your mind what you want and you visualize it, the universe finds a way of bringing it to you. When you have the kind of goal I'm talking about here, you should not stress over how it will happen. You must believe that your subconscious will begin to create ways for you to reach a goal you could never possibly imagine on a conscious level. This may seem supernatural, but it's not. Have you ever decided to buy a new car, camera, or outdoor grill and suddenly discovered ads for the product were everywhere? The ads were always there, but until you actively entered the market you were oblivious to them. You had to become sensitive to the advertising before you could even see it.

Similarly, you have to be sensitive to your goals to be aware of opportunities you can seize to reach them. The most important thing is to have goal clarity, to know with great specificity what it is you want. Because you've come this far in this book, I can assume you want to develop strong, positive relationships with certain people, people that heretofore you thought you might never have relationships with. You now have to say, "My goal is to have a strong, positive relationship with _____."

WRITE DOWN YOUR GOALS

When you make that your goal, write it down, because then it becomes a commitment. You've made a compact with yourself. Words on paper carry a reality different from thoughts in your head. If you not only write down your goals, but announce them publicly—to your spouse, your friends, your colleagues—the likelihood that you will achieve them is much greater than if you keep them to yourself.

In addition to writing down and talking about your goals, you have to think about them and review them. I carry in my pocket a written list of my goals. I have a half dozen short-, medium-, and long-term goals that are important to me. I read them every day and I rewrite them once a month. I regularly think about the things I want to happen.

Goal clarity is important. Visualizing the goal is important. Believing it can happen is important. Taking the pressure off yourself by trying to figure out how to reach a goal is important. At the same time, of course, you must take realistic steps and seize opportunities as they arise to reach the goal. I'm not suggesting you sit quietly and let the goal find you. It doesn't work that way.

If we get too knotted up on a conscious level thinking about ways to reach our goals, we often talk ourselves out of them. If we believe we will reach our goals, we will.

SET GOALS IN LINE WITH YOUR GIFTS

I see three problems: setting impossible and unrealistic goals (thus positioning yourself for failure), setting too many goals, and being unwilling to pay the price.

The goal has to be achievable. I will never become the Pope. Aside from the fact that I'm married, I'm not Catholic. There is often a fine line between a stretch goal and an impossible one. To ensure that you keep at least one foot in reality, you may want two or three people you trust implicitly (they are at the top of your Relationship Pyramid) to give you an objective response to your goal. They can also help you see your potential when you are oblivious.

A boss named Don Cutcliff changed my life. Don and I had been colleagues for a long time, had been successful in sales, and then Don was promoted to become my boss—when I thought I would be the one promoted. The night that he sat down to talk to me as my boss when I thought I would be his, he said, "Jerry, this job of regional manager isn't big enough for you. You need to be running this company."

At the age of 39, I'd never thought of running the company. My whole focus was on being a regional manager. But at that moment Don Cutcliff helped me see that my capabilities, my gifts and talents, were greater than I'd thought. Because I had such faith in Don, it was easy for me to see that he might be right. But the point is that your gifts and talents may not be as obvious to you as they are to others, so surround yourself with people who can help you understand what you have to offer.

My friend Klaudia Birkner and I have talked about unreasonable goals. Klaudia went almost totally blind as a teenager. Her special high school took her class to a ski area in one of several enrichment programs for handicapped teens. After Klaudia's original terror on the bunny slope subsided, she became an enthusiastic skier. She worked with a guide and coach to become a competitive racer.

Her original goal, to race in grand slalom ski events as a virtually blind teenager, might have seemed unattainable. Klaudia separates impracticable goals from goals she really wants to attempt by determining how genuinely serious she is about the goal. What is she willing to do? What is she willing to give up? She gave up the entire summer of her seventeenth year writing 300 letters to companies she hoped would sponsor her. And she found one. "To me, it is not a matter of right and wrong, success and failure," she says. "I want to try, and I want to know I have done everything I can to a level acceptable to me. Not to other people; not to someone else, not to what other people have done—to me."

Klaudia makes an interesting point: "The important thing may not even be the end, the goal itself, but the process you go through to get there, all the stuff you pick up along the way."

Goals should be challenging. They should be a stretch. Sometimes, though, you need somebody to help you think about what it is you can accomplish that you never thought before. (Someone told Klaudia she ought to try ski racing, for example.) This is why it is important to have a support group who can help you see your potential. Often others see in us things we can accomplish before we see them. And many times achieving a significant goal realizes not only our dream, but also someone else's dream for us.

That is why coaches are so important. Coaches believe in us and recognize our potential long before we see it in ourselves. A coach's vision can encourage us to extend ourselves. Setting a goal is not simply a matter of sitting down and asking "What do I want?" It is making sure you have the right people around you who can help you see your potential. You need people who are constantly building you up because they genuinely believe in your talent, in your ability.

Everybody is unique. Your uniqueness as a human being creates your ultimate potential for greatness, and everyone has it. Though we may have similarities, my potential is different from someone else's. It is therefore vital to discover those talents, abilities, and qualities that make us unique.

Another danger is to set too many goals for yourself. People become what I call *goalfused*. Goalfusion will cause you to be unproductive because you are chasing too many balls. Goal clarity enables us to focus on those few that are truly important to our professional and personal success.

The right number of personal and business goals will vary for everyone, but as a rule of thumb I would not have more than three or four personal and three or four professional goals—six or eight max.

DON'T LET OTHERS DISCOURAGE YOU

We must be willing to pay a price to reach our goals, because it is impossible to extend ourselves in any way without doing something different from what we are doing now.

One test should be whether you can pay the price at all. If the price for becoming an Olympic-level figure skater is being a 15-year-old athlete and you are in your mid-40s, the price is beyond reach. If the price to become branch manager is working nights and Saturdays for the next two years, it may be high, but you could pay it if you were willing to make the sacrifice.

By its nature, attaining new goals means new directions for us. It means new behaviors, new activities, new challenges. We must be willing to take on those behaviors, activities, and challenges to achieve the things we want. Otherwise, we stay right where we are. You must be willing to pay the price. In a business context, the usual price is in the form of working longer, or working harder, or facing more adversity.

Although it is valuable to listen to the positive people in your life—the coaches, the mentors, the friends—it is imperative to ignore the negative, the naysayers, the wet blankets.

The person most likely to talk you out of your stretch goal is you. We have a tendency to judge what we can do by what we have done in the past and what we, with our current worldview, believe is possible. Only when we can get outside of that view can we begin to achieve extraordinary things consistent with our gifts and talents.

What happens when we consider our goals is we go through a mental self-assessment of whether it's possible or not. We mentally examine not only the possible, we ask ourselves what others will think. What's my mom going to say? What's my dad going to say? A friend's mother told her to be a secretary; that's the most she could aspire to. So my friend had to overcome that parent-imposed limitation and began to see what she wanted to be, which was a successful businesswoman. For her, it wasn't being an administrative assistant, although there's nothing wrong with that.

The unfortunate reality is that some people don't want you to accomplish your goals, because your achievement makes their mediocrity stand out. They tell you, "You can't do that! You can't do that! You can't do that!" The truth is because most people don't have goals and don't aspire to much of anything, they try to talk you out of your goals.

You have to ignore them and listen to people who know you can achieve your goals. As the Bourbon Street preacher says, "If you think you can, you can. If you think you can't, you can't." Klaudia tells the story of a man who was locked in a walk-in freezer during a robbery. While inside, he started to shiver, and finally was so cold he wrote his last good-byes with his finger on the steel: "I'm freezing; I'm freezing. I'm cold. I love my family." And he died.

But the freezer temperature was not low enough to kill a man in the time he was confined. Apparently he had convinced himself that because he was locked in a freezer he was going to die, says Klaudia, "and so he did. The power of belief is incredibly profound. If you believe in the negative, believe in the positive."

I went to Virginia Military Institute, and every day for four years I walked under the Jackson Arch, on which was inscribed a quotation from General Stonewall Jackson: "You may be whatever you resolve to be." As a young man reading that inscription, I thought he was right. Now, I think the general missed the truth. I believe the inscription should read, "You will be whatever you resolve to be." But most people never resolve to be anything.

TAKE THE PRESSURE OFF YOURSELF

I have also come to believe that the most negative energy you can create is the pressure you put on yourself to achieve any goal. When you put pressure on yourself to achieve something, you create a negative energy that puts a drag on your ability to reach it. How often have you heard a sport commentator say about a quarterback, figure skater, or basketball player, "He's trying too hard"? He's overthrowing receivers, she's flubbing her jumps, he's missing the basket. The principle, I believe, is the same.

You have to have a goal. You have to be incredibly clear about what you want. And you have to believe you can achieve it. Once you do that, you need to forget about putting pressure on yourself to make it happen. You have to believe that if you want the goal badly enough, if you visualize the outcome you desire—as long as it is not insane (my becoming Pope)—it will happen. The laws of the universe will bring it to you. But it will be far more difficult for things to come to you if you are putting pressure on yourself to achieve them. Most of the things we accomplish in life, we accomplish because we have the confidence to do them.

The genuine pursuit of a new goal is, at its core, about accepting the possibility of change. You must believe people can change for the better as well as for the worse. If you accept that for other people, you must believe you can change as well. You must do something different to get what you want that is different. It should be obvious that you can't get what you want that is different if you keep doing the same things you've always done.

Klaudia Birkner tells me she visualized her first apartment when she was 14 years old, an apartment she ultimately achieved. "For me, it is very powerful to visualize my goals. I dream about them; I think about them. Even if they are on the verge of unrealistic, I still do it. I will sometimes wake up in the middle of the night, or I will walk past my dining room table during the day, and some thought will come to my head and I will make myself a note. I am constantly thinking; I am constantly wishing and hoping and thinking and wondering. I cannot imagine waking up every morning and not having a goal."

What are your short-, medium-, and long-term goals? What would you like to accomplish this week, next month, next year, in five years? If you know, write your goals down on the form in Figure 11.1. Make them as SMART as you can. If you don't yet have goals, think about what you want and write it down.

If what you are doing hasn't worked for you in the past, it is safe to say that maybe you should do something different. If you want something beyond what you have or different from what you now have, you must do something different. You don't have to be where you are; you can go farther and you can be more. Success, like

Figure 11.1
What Are Your Goals and When Are They Due?

Long-term goal _____

_____ End point; _____

Long-term goal _____

_____ End point; _____

Long-term goal _____

_____ End point; _____

Medium-term goal _____

_____ End point; _____

Medium-term goal _____

_____ End point; _____

Medium-term goal _____

_____ End point; _____

Short-term goal _____

_____ End point; _____

Short-term goal _____

_____ End point; _____

Short-term goal _____

_____ End point; _____

failure, is about choices you make—or avoid making. You will always hit obstacles, but they are part of success.

Klaudia also points out that success is never final—and neither is failure. "I learned that believing in myself was my strongest asset, because I believed in myself to the point that giving up was not an option, nor was there room for it in my life. Never allowing myself to believe I will fail: That is what drives my goals."

A lot of being successful in building strong relationships with customers and colleagues is understanding that sometimes you are going to ask a question and it will not be received well. Sometimes the reaction is a metaphorical punch in the gut. "It's none of your business what I do when I'm not working . . . or where I went to school . . . or where I grew up." But success usually requires getting knocked down and getting back up.

If you are genuine and sincere and passionate and enthusiastic and determined to get what you want, you can get just about anything you want. Most people never make the decision to be anything more than what they already are. Clear goals tend to separate those people who have extraordinary accomplishments from people who just drift through life. To achieve all that is possible, you must attempt the exceptional. To be as much as you can be, you must dream of being more than you are now.

We can accomplish much more in our lives if we have goals and if we develop the habits, skills, specialized knowledge, and attitude that we need to achieve them. If we *do* develop the habits, skills, knowledge, and attitude that we can achieve incredible things, there's almost no limit to what we can accomplish. Indeed, I can virtually guarantee that if you set your goals and follow the five rules, you will accomplish the extraordinary.

Of course, if you maintain your meaningful relationships, they will make your task dramatically easier – and a lot more fun.

CHAPTER 12

MAINTAIN YOUR MEANINGFUL RELATIONSHIPS

To maintain your meaningful relationships, you need to:

- Understand the lifetime value of a customer.
- Make the time to maintain important relationships.
- Help others succeed.
- Keep in constant contact.

Let's look at each of these.

Exceptional business and personal relationships are relatively rare treasures. They will have a lifetime value if you maintain them properly. Although they are incalculable, I should talk for a moment about calculating customer lifetime value.

The theory of customer lifetime value assumes that it is less expensive to retain customers than to find new ones (almost always true) and that it is possible to estimate how much a customer will be worth over an extended period into the future (less certain). Retaining the right customers should always be a business priority, although some companies obviously have problems doing so.

The Forum Corporation analyzed the customers that 14 major companies had lost for reasons other than leaving the area or going out of business. It found that 15 percent switched to a better product, 15 percent found a cheaper product, and 70 percent left because of poor or little attention from their supplier.[1]

A company that looks at its own churn rate—the number of customers who walk away every year and who have to be replaced just to maintain the same revenue—can calculate how much revenue and profit it is losing by those defections. There may not be much you can do about customers leaving the area or going out of business, but good, positive business relationships should eliminate the major problem—of poor or little attention—and strong relationships may also help with the better-product/cheaper-product challenge.

Critics of the lifetime value theory argue that it is much more difficult to estimate how much revenue and profit a customer will bring to a business in the future because too many imponderables affect any given customer's purchases. As they say in mutual fund advertisements, past performance is no guarantee of future results.

Nevertheless, if you manage, say, a dry cleaning business, and a customer spends $20 a week, you can safely estimate that person will account for $1,000 in annual revenue. Over 10 or 20 years and more, the total revenue becomes significant.

When you think about a relationship and the customer lifetime value, it changes your attitude toward customer complaints, among other things. If your regular cleaning customer says he's missing three buttons off a blazer, you cheerfully replace the buttons even when you know it's not your fault.

Obviously, not every customer is equally valuable to a company. Some customers buy large amounts of high-margin products and rarely have service or other complaints. These customers provide the company significant revenue and profit.

Some customers buy only sale items and want all the special treatment they can wring from suppliers. Their business is not worth very much, and sometimes these customers may actually cost more than they're worth to service. It does not take a Harvard MBA to realize that a firm should have as many of the high-volume/high-profit customers as possible and as few low-volume/low-profit as possible.

For individual salespeople and their managers, this all means they should evaluate every prospect, customer, and client on a number of dimensions, not simply on total sales volume. What does it actually cost to serve the customer, and what is the potential short-term and long-term payback? Is the customer's business growing or dwindling? Is the industry itself growing? What is the customer's relationship with other existing or potential customers?

A customer may be valuable not for his or her own sake but for the help that person can give—or damage he might cause—in relations with other customers. Remember Mike Accardi's experience with the Sunbeam repair shop. Because there is not enough time or resources to have winning relationships with every single prospect, customer, or client, you should have solid business reasons for those with whom you do want to build a relationship.

Granted, you can never know for sure what will happen in the future. (Mike could never have known Sunbeam would move to Memphis.) Going through the exercise of measuring potential customer lifetime value can help you and management decide who are the most likely candidates for your time and attention.

Although all relationships need to be nourished, not every relationship is critical. You need to think about categories. One category contains the relationships critical to your business success. Another has the relationships you want to keep alive because you have been close in the past and may be close again in the future.

Mike Accardi says that in his career his whole focus has been to maintain relationships. "Part of it is just showing up. This past week, I've been to two funerals. In one instance, it was for the father of a person I hardly had much contact with. It was an emotional moment for him, and he was startled when I walked in. I said, 'It was your dad who died, so of course I was going to show up and pay my respects.' "

I believe serious and deep bonding takes place when people are in some sort of trouble or crisis or disappointment in their lives and we step in to be some support. Many acquaintances do not come forward when you are fired, experience a business reverse, or have a death in the family; indeed, they pull away. In some cases, I think they are afraid the misfortune will affect them somehow, and in some cases they simply don't know what to say. There are many reasons to avoid someone else's suffering, but the truth is almost anything you do to sincerely reach out to people in those situations is a humane act and will probably cement a relationship faster than anything else you can do.

As Mike says, "I try to think in terms of what makes me feel good. I found that everybody I deal with, regardless of their color or station, has the same needs. They want their children to be protected and educated; they want their property to gain in value. They want to have a decent life. When you think about it, it is really not hard to relate to everybody, because we are all the same."

But though people may be the same in their aspirations, not all relationships are the same. So how do you make time for them?

CREATE TIME FOR RELATIONSHIPS

In his book *Raising Positive Kids in a Negative World*, Zig Ziglar writes that children spell "love" T-I-M-E.[2] In fact, adults spell "love" and "care" the same way. If you care for people, you give them your time. But where is that time going to come from?

How many people reading this book feel there are enough hours in the day to accomplish everything that needs to be done?

Not many. Most are already stretched to the limit. Indeed, I recognize that reading this book means you have made a substantial investment of time you could have spent on something else, and now I'm asking you to spend time maintaining your relationships. Either something has to give, or you have to manage your time differently.

One approach to solving time management problems is to exploit calendars and to-do lists and follow the rules of time management. Read selectively (newspaper and magazine headlines to decide what articles are worth reading in their entirety); prioritize your tasks; do one important thing at a time, several trivial things simultaneously (sign letters while talking on the phone); divide large projects into manageable bites; learn to say no; don't procrastinate; set deadlines for yourself; reach closure on at least one thing every day.

The rules, calendars, and to-do lists are all valuable. If you don't have them, I think you should acquire some. But valuable as they are, time management tools in themselves are not the way to solve a time management problem. The objective is to spend your time, not necessarily more efficiently, but more effectively. You can spend your time more efficiently on even more of those unimportant tasks. As Stephen Covey has pointed out, spending time effectively means:

- You spend your time on important matters, not just urgent matters.
- You are able to distinguish clearly between what is an important activity for you and what is unimportant.
- Results rather than methods are the focus of time management strategies.
- You have no reason to feel guilty when you must say no.

Important matters are those that produce the result you want. They accomplish a valued end or they achieve a meaningful purpose. When you do them, they help move you closer to your goals.[3]

Urgent activities are those that demand immediate attention. They are associated with a need expressed by somebody else, or they relate to an uncomfortable problem or situation that requires a solution as soon as possible. A customer complaint is urgent and important. A fire in the factory is urgent and important. A ringing telephone is (usually) urgent and unimportant, as is a casual visitor to your office. Building a relationship is important but not urgent. Planning next month's—or next year's—production schedule is important but not urgent. Internet chat is not urgent and not important.

There is not much you can do about urgent and important activities. If a customer has a complaint or the building is on fire, you have to deal with it. If you're right against a significant deadline, you have to work until you meet it. Your goal, however, should be to minimize these urgent and important activities as much as possible so they don't consume you. Managers and employees whose working hours are filled with only urgent and important activities need help—and are rotten managers and soon-to-be-burned-out employees.

With the urgent and unimportant activities, the goal is to delegate and eliminate. Have someone else open the mail and answer the phone. Make it clear that you do not want to be interrupted except for a crisis. If possible, skip meetings at which you cannot make a contribution or will receive no benefit.

Try to eliminate entirely activities that are neither urgent nor important. They are escapes (sometimes from the urgent and important activities). They neither accomplish a valued end nor achieve a meaningful purpose; they waste your time and, finally, your life.

With the important but not urgent activities, your goal should be to spend as much time on them as possible because these are the activities you use to determine your future.

Professors David A. Whetten and Kim S. Cameron write:

> One of the most difficult yet crucially important decisions you must make in managing time effectively is determining what is important and what is urgent. There are no rules for dividing all activities, demands, or opportunities into those neat categories. Problems don't come with an "Important/Nonurgent" tag attached. In fact, every problem or time demand is important to someone. But if you let others determine what is and is not important, you will never effectively manage your time.[4]

But if there are no rules, how do you decide which activities are truly important, if not urgent? Whetten and Cameron say the only answer is "to identify clear and specific personal priorities. It is important for people to be aware of their own core values and establish a set of basic principles to guide their behavior." To help evaluate an activity's importance, Whetten and Cameron suggest asking the following questions:

- What do I stand for? What am I willing to die (or live) for?
- What do I care passionately about?
- What legacy would I like to leave? What do I want to be remembered for?
- What do I want to have accomplished 20 years from now?

- If I could persuade everyone in the world to follow a few basic principles, what would they be?

Careful readers will have noticed that these questions augment the goals I talked about earlier. Between your goals and your answers to these questions, you can usually decide if an activity is important or not. Does it help you reach an important goal?

If you eliminate all the time wasters—the unimportant and not urgent activities, which may include things like television—from your life, and delegate or eliminate as many of the unimportant and urgent activities as possible, you will have made the necessary time to maintain your important relationships.

If the way you connect (or don't) with people sends a message that you have no time for them, they will naturally conclude that they are not important to you.

HELP OTHERS TO SUCCEED

I have suggested throughout this book that creating and maintaining relationships should be a priority in your business and personal life. Strong, positive relationships can help you build whatever legacy you want to leave, accomplish whatever you want to accomplish. Most of the time, building and maintaining relationships are not urgent activities (but they are important), and by the very nature of relationship building, they cannot be hurried along.

In *Love Is the Killer App: How to Win Business and Influence Friends*, Tim Sanders, Yahoo!'s chief solutions officer, writes:

The secret to being a high-impact leader, and the essence of individual corporate success, is to learn as much as you can as quickly as you can and share your knowledge aggressively; expand your network of people who share your values and connect as many of them with each other as possible; and, perhaps most important, be as openly human as you can be and find the courage to express genuine emotion in the harried, pressure-filled world of work. And one last point: Behave this way not because you expect something in return—a quid pro quo—but because it's the right way to behave. The less you expect in return for acts of professional generosity, the more you will receive.[5]

I can hear the cynics in the back of the room muttering at this point: Yeah, right, and just what will this do for me? Five things, says Sanders:

1. You differentiate yourself from others. You become useful, memorable—special.

2. You create an experience. "When you represent knowledge, opportunity, selflessness, and intimacy you are not just a smart colleague; you are fun, interesting, and valuable."[6]

3. You command (or at least can claim) people's attention. This goes back to my point at the very beginning of the book: When you have a good relationship and therefore meaningful dialogue, people listen to what you have to say differently than when you do not have a relationship.

4. You harness the power of positive presumption. As I've said, you want to gain people's trust and respect, to be at the top of their Relationship Pyramids. Once you have their trust, customers and colleagues will believe your arguments hold water, your recommendations are solid, and your referrals are valuable. They will believe you have their best interests at heart, which you do.

5. You receive feedback. "If you are eager to offer people knowledge, they will be eager to give you helpful feedback in return," says Sanders. "They'll tell you which ideas worked out well and which didn't work out so well, which contacts were helpful and which weren't."

KEEP THE DIALOGUE CONTINUAL

To keep a relationship, there must be contact, and it must to be in the course of what I would call "continual dialogue." You should not build the relationship, drop it, then try to pick it up again.

Why risk taking the chance that you will not be able to reignite a relationship?

The trick is to devise some systematic way of keeping track of the people on your relationship map so you can group them in terms of how often you get in touch with them. And you should have some concrete plan to contact them on a routine basis.

The contact can be whatever is appropriate for that person: a telephone call, a text message, an e-mail letter, a handwritten note, a card, a lunch date. This is a key point: You should reach people the way they want to be reached—e-mail, text message, phone call, fax (remember fax?), snail mail, or smoke signals.

I find that as people gravitate toward one or two technologies they become dependent on, it becomes their technology of choice. Learning that early in your relationship is important. Not long ago, two people independently told me that I needed to meet an executive I'll call Bob Rose. One of them went so far as to send an e-mail to us both saying we need to meet. I sent Rose an e-mail saying, "I would like to meet you. It sounds like we have some mutual interests." I never heard back.

A month or so later, I was talking to somebody and he said I really ought to meet Bob Rose. I said that I tried to meet him but he won't respond to my e-mail. "Bob's never going to respond to your e-mail," said my client. "He doesn't read e-mail. He has his administrative assistant read his e-mail. If she doesn't have a clue who you are, my guess is you got passed over. If you really want to reach Bob, you need to either call him on his cell phone or send him a text message."

I said I didn't have his cell number, so the guy gave me the number. I sent Rose a text message. Within an hour he called me. Within a week we had a meeting. He ultimately became a major client. Now I always try to ask early in the relationship, "What is the best way to reach you? If I really need to get in touch with you, is it at work? Is it your cell phone? Is it texting? E-mail?" Almost always they tell me the one or two that they prefer.

Some people are text people, some are e-mail people, and some are phone people. If you learn people's habits that drive their technological preferences, you can increase the likelihood you will be successful with them and can connect with them when you need to. And of course this is a two-way street. When you meet with somebody, mention the best way to get in touch with you. If you are a text person, say this is your communication preference. Depending on the cell phone contract, calls may cost money while texts are free or cheaper. For example, I have only so many calling minutes, but I can send as many text messages as I want. So some people's technology preference might be driven by economics. But learning those preferences and telling other people yours is very important.

Also, at the end of my e-mail notes and on my business card I include my cell phone number and my website address. I want prospects and clients to be able to find me and more information about me easily. I want them to be able to reach me on my cell phone.

Julie Wroblewski says she makes a conscious effort to stay in touch with the people who are important to her. "There are times when I think, oh boy, I haven't talked with so-and-so in a while. I make time for that simple phone call or handwritten note—I am a big firm believer in handwritten notes, even though e-mail is great. There is something to be said for that handwritten note."

Still it is possible to build a strong business relationship with someone and then, through inattention, neglect, or circumstances (one of you is transferred, takes another job, moves to another company), you lose touch. Thanks to social media like LinkedIn, Facebook, and other sites this is becoming less and less common. Indeed, one of the positives of social media is the ability to find people with whom you've lost touch.

You must make a conscious effort to keep in touch. If I haven't talked to somebody for a while, I will call just to say something like, "Hey, I was riding down the road the other day and I was thinking about the fact that I haven't called you in two or three months. I just wanted to say hello and let you know I was thinking about you. I might be in Chicago in December. If I'm going to be there I'll give you a call."

Sometimes circumstances may cause you to lose contact. If the relationship is strong, you can pick it up again. Sometimes someone will renew a relationship with you via an e-mail or a phone call. When you hear from somebody who was important to you, or with whom you had a good relationship, it engenders positive emotions. It makes you smile, it makes you feel great, and it makes your day. If you do that for other people who are important in your life, you make their day. Sometimes it is more powerful to call for no reason than if there is a reason.

You need to develop some sort of system or methodology that works for you to stay in touch with these people because it is in your best interest to continue to do so. The relationships are personally rewarding. They make your life more enjoyable. They are people you enjoy knowing.

To maintain a relationship, I stay in touch. I put a note in my monthly to-do list; it takes two seconds. With e-mail, cell phones, LinkedIn, Facebook, and all the rest there is almost no excuse for not staying in touch with somebody. You can send them a one-line e-mail once a quarter, and you can send the same e-mail to 25 people. The responses may fill your inbox, but what is important here, your inbox or your relationships?

You can maintain your contacts with personal notes, which are probably more effective than phone calls, and they are certainly more effective than e-mail. They are more effective because they take more time and, even if you send the same short note to 25 people, each recipient knows you had to actually write out the note.

About once a quarter, I go through my e-mail and telephone lists, to see who I need to contact because I haven't written or called for a couple months. I know their birthdays, and I call them.

Not long ago, I sent an executive an e-mail. "Tom, I read somewhere in a book, never forget a customer and never let a customer forget you, and it occurred to me we had not talked in a while. I am going to be Pennsylvania in two weeks. I know it is a long shot that you will be there, but just wanted to let you know that if you are around I would like to say hello."

He replied to my e-mail the next day. "It was really great to hear from you—I will be in town, and I want you to stop by because I need to talk to you."

I had no idea what he wanted to talk about. It may be just to reminisce about old times, and that would be fine. It would be better to do some business with the company, but if he never gives me any business, I wouldn't lose any sleep over it. I like the man. I like seeing him and I enjoy talking to him. I admire his business acumen. He is a very impressive executive, thoughtful and intelligent. I always leave his office feeling a little more knowledgeable and a little better about myself because we had a nice chat.

Julie Wroblewski agrees that one cannot generalize about ways to maintain relationships. It depends on the individual and what you know about his or her individual interests. Whenever she comes across an article about something she knows will interest someone, she sends the article to the contact. One customer has told her on more than one occasion, "It's the coolest thing anyone has done. I continue to stay at the front of his mind without being aggressive. It is just a friendly, thought-you-might-be-interested-in-reading-this-article." The articles may be about the company, industry news, or even about a restaurant Julie knows he frequents.

This experience is special for Julie because this customer is a person who, for the most part, does not care for salespeople. What is more, her company and his have not always been in agreement. "So he had some negative feelings about what and who we were," says Julie. "He has said on numerous occasions, 'It's because of you and the business message you provide, as well as following through, that the feeling of I-don't-think-I-want-to-do-business-with-them is gone.' It's the little things along the way they don't forget." As Harvey Mackay noted in *Swim with the Sharks,* little things don't mean a lot, they mean everything.[6]

You can accomplish the same goal by forwarding articles, blog entries, pictures, and other things that you come across on the Web. The challenge here is to be sure that what you forward interests the recipient and that you use good judgment. I suspect we all have acquaintances who seem to have nothing better to do than forward old (and offensive) jokes, softcore porn, and political rants from the right or the left. These do not build relationships.

Bob Holman at Donaldson, Holman & West says that when a client's monthly financial statement crosses his desk for final review, he tries to write a personal note. "I don't type it. I handwrite it, so they know it wasn't something somebody else did that I just signed. It may say things like, 'Terrific month.' Or, 'Your ratios look good, your sales are up by 20 percent over last year, your costs are right in line with last year—looks like you are on a good year.' Or, 'What happened to your costs this month?' Clients seem to appreciate that I have taken the time to actually note some of the things I want them to look at rather than just passing the report on to them."

That is the point you would like to reach in your strong business relationships. When you are at the top of their Relationship Pyramid, you know they would do anything within reason for you because you would do anything for them.

MAKE CONTACT WHEN YOU DON'T NEED HELP

You need to make contact when you do not need the people or their help. If you get in touch with them only when you need a favor, a name, an introduction, they soon understand you are simply using them—and that diminishes your relationship instead of building it.

Bob Holman says that he had a client he would see only between the middle of August and the end of September, when the firm was preparing financial statements, and on one day in March when the client brought his tax return into the office. Other than that, they had no contact at all.

Bob called him one day on the spur of the moment to invite him to lunch. "We didn't talk about business at all. I told him that up front. And I found out that he and I both enjoyed some of the same authors. I had found a new author who was similar to some of the authors we both read and had some of those books at home that I was about to give away to Goodwill. I brought them to the office, wrapped them up, and mailed them to him." Another example of an inexpensive, unexpected, and thoughtful act.

Bob says that he and the client are now talking once a month about authors and other topics. "I have gotten a lot more business from him because we have been talking more frequently," although that was not the goal of the original lunch.

Greg Genova had a very difficult time winning over some of the key engineers to the Kennametal products at one prospective company. In one office, Greg found a photograph of several lobsters the engineer had caught while diving and he learned that this engineer treasured diving. He and Greg talked diving, and Greg says, "He has actually become one of my key dive buddies. We typically dive once or twice a month now. I was never the first call, but that relationship has grown to where now I am the first call for all their tooling questions."

John Fitzgerald, the financial advisor in Phoenix, says he tries to mail something personal to his clients once a quarter in addition to a weekly newsletter. This is not sales information, he notes, "but just contact information. It may not even be about the market. If I see a newspaper article that relates to one of my clients and I think they might be interested—it might be something about their business—I will send it to them. Magazine articles, some type of thing. I try to call people on their birthdays. I also send birthday cards, but I am getting to the point where I think a phone call is better than a birthday card, because it is a more human contact. I call these phone calls touches—just to reach out and let them know I am here."

If you do maintain contact through e-mail (which makes staying in touch inexcusably simple), phone calls, text messages, notes, cards, faxes, and anything else you can devise, when you finally meet after five years you can almost pick up where you left off.

There is probably such a thing as relationship equity. You build equity in relationships, and the longer the relationship continues and deepens, the greater the equity. But you have to make deposits before you can make withdrawals. The deposits are in the form of making sure that people know you are thinking about them and that you care about them even if in ever so slight ways.

Again, relationship building cannot be self-serving. A self-serving relationship is exploitive, manipulative, and dishonest. I try to be careful when I talk about relationship building from a proactive point of view because it does not require a great leap to make much of what I prescribe sound self-centered. But when you build your relationships in the right way and for the right reasons, there is as much in it for the other person as there is for you.

We have all had associates who are users, people who take and never give. They may be pleasant colleagues or significant customers, but they never reciprocate except in the most cold-blooded way – with a purchase order, which is not the real basis of a relationship.

If people are users, they are not going to have good relationships with very many people. As I said earlier about customers who can be bought, they are not worth having. Their motives are not pure, so they will always go to the highest bidder. It is the same thing with users. Users will use you until you are used up. Just as it is sometimes appropriate to fire a customer, so it is sometimes appropriate to end a relationship.

Strong positive relationships are about give and take. If you contact people over and over when you don't need them, they are more likely to help you when you do need them. If you contact people regularly—"How you doing?" "What's going on?" "Just saying hello," "Going to be in town, thought we'd have lunch"—and occasionally you do need their help, they will not mind because you've built some equity into the relationship over time.

The best relationships are those in which people give proportionately: You give 50 percent and they give 50 percent. It seldom balances so precisely—and you're not keeping score anyway—but you would like to maintain a rough balance. It has to be generally equal, because if you are the one doing all the giving, the other person may see you as no more than an easy touch and not value the relationship.

You can make a difference—sometimes major, sometimes minute—in the lives of the people you touch. The critical question becomes: Is the difference positive or negative? If you hope to make a positive difference, you most likely need to be skilled in dealing with people. You should also understand that no matter how good you are, you can be better.

If you ignore the relationships you have built, it is like allowing a lovely garden go to seed. It is a waste that diminishes your life and reduces your potential. You can't establish relationships and then take them for granted. They have to be nourished and treated as the precious things they are.

When you have good relationships, it is possible to have meaningful dialogues. It is possible to learn what customers and colleagues truly believe and what they treasure because they trust and respect you. When you know what people treasure, you can help them obtain it. By helping other people achieve what they want, they will help you achieve what you want.

CHAPTER 13

USE SOCIAL MEDIA TO BUILD RELATIONSHIPS

I've talked throughout this book about social media and the use of technology, and up to this point it's been about how to use technology to stay in touch or to find people. What about using it to be found? How does being involved with social media help you build a positive business relationship? We know social media sites can be a giant waste of time, but what good are they?

I'm talking primarily about sites like LinkedIn, Twitter, Facebook, YouTube, and your blog and your website. Sales consultant Jeffrey Gitomer argues they should be called "*business* social media" to distinguish what you do on them from what teenagers write on Facebook, MySpace, and other social media sites.

I am going to assume that you know what they are and what they do. If you don't, stop reading and check out the sites that tell you how to use them.[1]

As I said earlier, while you cannot build a positive business relationship with social technology alone, it can prepare the ground for a relationship. People who find you via social media have already moved up your Relationship Pyramid at least one level—they know your name. They may also have advanced another level—they may like you based on what you've posted. Once someone has found you, you have an opportunity to build a relationship and create a customer.

Valerie Sokolosky, who heads Valerie & Company, tells me she's signed two clients who found her from her LinkedIn profile. "They were looking for my area of expertise and they chose to call me. I might have been one of several companies they called; I don't know. But I got those clients because they found me on LinkedIn."

One was a client she'd worked with in corporate America years ago and with whom Valerie had lost touch. The client thought of Valerie for a project, wondered if she was on LinkedIn, perhaps the best social media site for professional businesspeople, and after a minute's search found her. So that was a situation where someone already knew Valerie's name but had lost track of her.

The second client was a man who was looking for executive coaching. He found Valerie's name when he searched that topic, and when he saw personal branding among her areas of expertise he called her. At that point she tells me she did what she does in any business development sales call. She asked him to tell her how he found her. "And then I went from there into, how can I meet your needs? What are you looking for? What are your goals and objectives? Where do you live? What are you looking for in a coaching relationship? I interviewed him and he liked what he heard and said he wanted to hire me."

Two points: Putting your profile on a social media site is a little like putting up a billboard or speaking into a live microphone; you don't know who you're going to reach. Also, while social media can be the start of a relationship, to build a positive relationship you must still go through the process: Have the right mind-set, gather information, and take inexpensive, unexpected, and thoughtful actions.

THE GOAL IS TO OFFER VALUE

Many senior executives are afraid of social media because, I believe, they do not understand it or its business potential. They see it as a giant time-suck: "Why are you Twittering when you should be selling?" They have also read the horror stories of business people posting inappropriate messages. A Vodafone customer service representative sent the following tweet to the company's 8,824 Twitter followers: "VodafoneUK is fed up of dirty homo's and is going after beaver." The rep was suspended and Vodafone apologized. Virgin Atlantic fired 13 cabin crew members when they called passengers "chavs" (a derogatory British term for young people) on Facebook and claimed the airline's planes were full of cockroaches.[2]

It *does* take time to use social media, but so does cold calling, and a case can be made that social media are a better source of leads than most traditional methods. The issue is not that consulting social media takes time, but that if used well it can save time elsewhere. If social media do not help you sell more efficiently or more effectively, then I agree—don't use them.

Also it's always possible in a moment of irritation or thoughtlessness to post something inappropriate, just as it was always possible to send an intemperate, offensive letter. The big difference is that social media allow you to reach many more people simultaneously and, like a letter, it is difficult (or impossible) to recall or destroy your thoughtless text, comment, or tweet. This means only that people have to be trained to think before they post. Is this something you want your boss or your most able competitor to read? They're going to see it. The issue is not the medium, it's the message-writer.

Your goal with social media should be to connect with customers and prospects, to offer value, insights, information, and more. If you do not offer value *in the customers' terms*, you are wasting their time and yours. So the first question you must always ask yourself about any comment, blog post, or tweet is: Does this offer value? Tweeting "Just had oatmeal and a slice of whole wheat for breakfast" does not offer value. "How Philips is using LinkedIn to make health professionals into brand advocates," which includes the link http://tinyurl.com/2wm838r, does.

The more value you offer, the more valuable you become. In the best of all possible situations, you begin a blog (it's free), set up a Twitter account (it's free), join relevant LinkedIn groups (free), set up a Facebook page for business friends (free), and begin recording short videos that you post on YouTube (free). When you post something significant to your blog or add a video to YouTube, you tweet about it to alert the people who are following you on Twitter. You make sagacious, useful comments in your LinkedIn groups. If others find what you post valuable, they tell their contacts and ripples spread ever outward.

Rod Kirby, the editor-in-chief of The Success Center, writes in his blog, "Remember the Biblical principle of Sowing and Reaping? That applies to relationship building as well. Sow good seeds (information, how-to's, links, articles, resources, etc.) into good ground (other bloggers, your followers, your fans, colleagues, etc.) and you'll reap a harvest (donations, sales, endorsements, resources, tools, etc.)." Kirby's point is that you have to plant a lot of seeds to have a crop, and you never know which specific seeds are going to sprout.

Kirby adds, "I find that Facebook is great for cultivating relationships since it really brings things to a personal level. I enjoy chatting with you all there as well as other bloggers that I follow and it really brings people together. Note: I especially enjoy the business chat at my Fan Page as well."[3]

(I should point out in passing that in doing research for this book, I found Kirby's blog. I thought it offered enough value to quote here. I am sure that Kirby's followers also found it valuable and told others about it, and I would not be surprised to learn that some of my readers look up Kirby's complete post. Offer value and your words live on.)

FORM A NETWORK OF RELATIONSHIPS

I asked Portland, Oregon, software developer and author Thomas Duff why relationships are important to him and how he uses social media. He pointed out that a software developer tries to develop solutions for people. "You may be technically great at developing those solutions, but if the people who you are working with don't trust you to deliver the solutions or to do what you say, it becomes problematic whether you will be able to work with these people in a close, one-on-one basis. So, on top of being able to deliver good solutions, I think the relationship is critical."

Tom says that social media sites are his life. He actively blogs and tweets. These activities help establish your reputation and let people—prospective clients, customers, and employers—know you exist, he says. "Depending on whether or not you decide to share personal aspects or you decide to keep it professional, it can also add color as to who you are as a person."

As an example of what he means by that, Tom says that he has always included personal material on his blog along with the technical information. Five years or so ago, he shared with his readers that he was dealing with depression and that he took medication for it. He feels that for some people—especially men—mentioning this is a major taboo. To some, it may suggest personal weakness. "You're depressed? Just shake it off! Work yourself out of it!"

But Tom's sharing his situation with his blog's readers caused people to come forward and to comment on what he'd shared. They wrote things like, "You know, I thought I was the only one. . . ." "I thought I was alone in this. . . ." "I am so glad to see that somebody else is dealing with this, too. . . ." Tom believes his post helped make him a real person to people he had never met. "Because I was willing to step out there in the social media world and say, you know, I'm not perfect; I'm struggling, it made me much more approachable."

It means, says Tom, that when he goes to a conference to meet people he has known only online through blogging or tweeting or whatever, they can start conversations—that is, building relationships—as if they've known each other for years, which, in a sense, they may have. He says that he was speaking at a major conference not long ago, presenting in one of the sessions with someone he'd never met in person before. "We *had* known each other through blogging, through Twitter, and online chats and stuff like that, so the running joke at the conference was, 'Oh, Tom, have you met Kathy? She's your co-speaker.' Without social media, I would never had had the chance to develop the relationship with her and be able to suggest to her that because we're both interested in a subject we could do a presentation on it."

Tom says that blogging, tweeting, sharing online, writing articles, and books (he's an active Amazon book reviewer) and more are all critical in forming a large network of people who say, "Oh, I know what he's good at. I know what he does. I feel like I know him as a person." Tom feels he can say he's very good friends with some of the people he's built a relationship with online, although they never have met in person. "It's all because of that online presence. Social media make you more than just a picture on a Web page or a one-liner on somebody's conference listing. People can go back and see who you are, and what kind of things you do, what kind of things you're interested in. And it helps establish that opening, if it's not there already, for those who you do work with and deal with on a regular basis. It helps deepen the relationship because you are always able to share without actually being able to be face-to-face."

DON'T FRIEND OR LINK TO EVERYONE

George C.D. Griffith at ConneXion360 tells me that "when I think about social media, there are two primary players: Facebook and LinkedIn. I really consider Facebook something just for your friends and LinkedIn a place to do business."

George says he does not even have a wall on his Facebook site, the place where people can post words and pictures. While it can give someone a window into your personal world, it does nothing for your professional image to see one of your fraternity brothers talking about Saturday at College Homecoming. "My opinion is that having a wall on a Facebook page only adds up to trouble at the end of the day."

He says he warns his sales team: Don't Friend your clients after the first meeting. "It's like asking a girl to marry you on the first date. You shouldn't be friending someone that you just had a meeting with or you went out to dinner with. You met them two or three times and it may seem like a friendly relationship, but I think friending someone on Facebook can be advancing the relationship a little too fast."

George does have a few very close business friends on Facebook, but doesn't rush to add folks to this social network unless he is positive that he has earned the right to do so.

Rather, George regards LinkedIn as a true business selling asset. It enables you to connect through other people—the idea being that we are only six degrees of separation away from anyone on earth. LinkedIn, he remarks, is like an online dinner party where you can get introduced to a person through a friend that they find to be credible and that, in many ways, enhances your opportunity to obtain an appointment. "If I am looking to break into a certain company, I can search by brand managers, pull up their contact information, cold-call them. Or there is a certain formula to the e-mails of every company and, once you know it, you can e-mail them. Or you can see how you might connect to that person via someone you know and ask your friend to introduce you that way."

When we spoke, his company, ConneXion360, was debating the merits of launching a Twitter campaign. He'd gone round and round with questions like: How could we best utilize this? How can it help the company the most? Who will be responsible for tweeting? You don't want to tweet once then wait four months before you tweet again. Someone has to think about Twitter and tweets that offer value regularly.

George does say that he uses Twitter as a resource to help him gain knowledge and education as a salesperson and business owner. He follows everything from *Harvard Business Review* (a recent tweet. "RT @TiffanyPR: Six Keys to Being Excellent at Anything - Harvard Business Review http://bit.ly/9hWNw1") relevant articles to other sales professionals. Twitter gives you the ability to follow and listen to all sorts of people and participate in the conversation. The "RT" at the beginning of the tweet quoted above means that the tweeter is forwarding—retweeting—someone else's message, which means you do not even have to write your own 140-character-or-less notes. Of course, if you retweet too much or retweet too many tweets that do not interest your followers, you are going to lose them.

Valerie Sokolosky says that she tweets about any resources she finds that she believes are valuable. "I try to be a resource tweeter. I never tweet about going to lunch, for example. I use it for business." She tries to stay alert to possibilities for tweets. "I might even tweet that I was just interviewed for Jerry Acuff's new book . . . stay tuned."

Valerie points out that your messages on Twitter can either be public—anyone can read what you've said—or private and directed to a specific person. She routinely sends tweets to people she wants to follow. "Therefore we then have that connection. Also I always look at who's following me."

She, like every professional who uses social media, stresses that she always has a business motive behind anything she does. "I do not use any of it for friends—even Facebook. I am on Facebook, but Facebook 'friends' are business associates who usually invite me. I don't use Facebook for just anybody who wants to get to know me." For example, she recently received an invitation to become a Facebook friend. She emailed back, "How do I know you?" The correspondent responded, "I don't know. I might have met you here, there or yon." Valerie hit the "Ignore" button.

I asked Valerie why she thought it was worth all the time she had to invest in social media—she writes a blog as well (http://www.valerieandcompany.com/blog). Why take the time? Her reply: "To get visibility and credibility, and to up my Google Quotient." A site's GQ is a measure of how digitally distinct it stands out on the Web. "On my Web page and my blog page you will see a little Digitally Distinct logo, which means I have got to a point where I have enough visibility on the Web that I have a distinctive online identity. That's what you work toward."

SIX TIPS FOR BETTER SOCIAL MEDIA RELATIONSHIPS

While social media are still new and evolving, which makes it difficult to lay down any hard and fast rules, certain principles seem to make sense. Some of these, of course, are merely extensions of sales fundamentals that have been around for years. Chris Conrey, who maintains the blog Conrey is for Closers,[4] has written that salespeople should have one basic rule for employing social media: Don't sell anything on them.

"Don't sell anything," he writes. Don't start publicly bidding on things, don't throw prices around, don't brag about your product, don't ask for business. These things will get you labeled as a spammer, or desperate, or a loser or some combination of all three.

To be successful on social media, says Conrey, all you have to do is be visible and authentic. "Be in the conversation. Answer questions. Ask questions. Be helpful. Pay attention to the conversation about markets or things that are relevant to your selling. Answer questions honestly and fairly—even if they don't directly make your product look better. Be available when people are complaining or questioning about what you're selling. Be a part of the online community—and use it to be a part of your local community and your business community."[5] Again, offer value. The more value you offer, the more valuable you become to customers, prospects, co-workers, and your organization.

Brett Borders, who edits the website Social Media Rockstar, offers six tips for creating "sticky" social relationships, actions that tend to encourage people to return to your blog, LinkedIn group, Facebook page, or to follow you on Twitter.

1. *Send a quick personal note* every time you follow/fan/friend someone. Borders suggests that you don't mechanically add people to your LinkedIn profile without interacting with them. And don't send automatic direct messages or boilerplate notes. Sending a quick, personalized request that says something like, "We met last week at the Social Media Meetup, enjoyed discussing design with you. Let's keep in touch?" Or "Just checked out your Flickr photos. Amazing mountain shots!" is enough to make a strong personal impression. With your personal note, most people will take a moment to check you out or take your request seriously.

2. *Leave a quick comment on friends' blogs* every time you stop by. As Borders points out, "If you're already wasting two minutes to check out a blog post, why not go all the way and take another 30 seconds to leave a quick comment? This will transform you from an anonymous nobody to a friend and supporter who is a valuable and unforgettable part of their online social community. This isn't just altruism; it quickly builds up your own

reputation and social karma card." He adds a technical tip: The easyComment plugin for Firefox makes entering your name and e-mail address into comment sections quick and painless.

3. *Retweet, link to, and talk about other views.* Once again: The goal here is to add value. One way to add value is to either augment what someone else has said or modify it with other evidence. If someone has tweeted something you feel is worth sharing or endorsing, retweet it. Whenever possible, link to what other sites have said; links in this context serve as electronic footnotes taking readers to the original sources. Neglecting to do this, says Borders, is "the online equivalent of going to a cocktail party and launching into an endless monologue about yourself."

4. *Respond to everyone who reaches out.* The more active you become on social media, the more "requests" will start to show up in your inbox, in direct messages, and @replies. People are usually reaching out to ask for something, says Jeremiah Owyang, a partner at The Altimeter Group. Try to get back to everyone who sends you a personal request . . . but don't be afraid to say no or be very brief in your response.

5. *Never pitch people without getting to know them.* This, of course, is the thread running through this book. Don't try to sell someone something unless or until you've established that what you have to sell—a product, service, idea, advice—is something the prospect can actually use or benefit from. Borders says, "It's tacky and rude to request something of a blogger or power user without knowing their name and what they do. Don't think of pitching/requests as a one-time hustle—think of it as building the recognition and trust from someone who can help you over the long- term. You never know when you're gonna need their help again—so first impressions are huge."

6. *Be grateful and explicitly thank people.* We call it common courtesy, but in my experience it's not that common to thank people when they've done something for you, like promoting your content or links to you. As Borders notes, a little recognition and gratitude creates an inducement for more positive action.

"It goes a long way toward making sure that person doesn't forget you."[6]

One more very small thing (but then, as someone said, life is in the small print), be sensitive to e-mail signatures. Dave Johnson, writing on Bnet, observes that "Sent from my iPhone" or "Sent from my BlackBerry" can sound snobbish, the e-mail equivalent of "My other car is a Lexus." Johnson says that it's easy to interpret the signature as an attempt to broadcast a status symbol, whether you intended it that way or not. It can also sound like an excuse for typos and being curt. If a response is truly necessary, take the time to compose a thoughtful, correctly spelled one. If you are pressed for time and the response can wait, let it wait until you can compose an effective one—even if it's no more than a sentence.

Johnson added that a formula e-mail signature can also poison business relationships. "A friend mentioned to me the other day that he just bought an iPad and sent his first e-mail with it. He sent it to his boss, and then discovered, to his horror, that the iPad defaults to attaching the 'Sent from my iPad' signature to all messages." Dave's friend works for a company that has an adversarial relationship with Apple. Unless you know the business relationship all of your partners have, broadcasting the technology you use may not be the way to build a positive business relationship. Unless, he says, "you think it's cool to park a Toyota in a Ford factory parking lot."[7]

CHAPTER 14

AND WHAT IF YOU'RE THE BOSS?

The process I've presented in the first 13 chapters should help virtually anybody build better business relationships and thereby be more effective (and happier) at work. But what if you are the boss? How does a manager incorporate these ideas into the organization's fabric to improve the effectiveness of the organization's relationship-building?

I talk about sales managers throughout this chapter, but clearly the issues affect more than the sales department. This process is especially relevant for customer service departments, law practices, management consultants, accountants, matrix organizations—any business or job function where relationships play a large role in success.

I will talk about the six drivers of business success, the problems I see with much sales training, what a manager must do to implement relationship-building within the organization, and conclude with a guide to coaching relationship development.

All of this begins, of course, with the manager's mind-set. If managers do not truly believe that building strong business relationships is a valuable skill, they will have a difficult time convincing others. They can go through the motions, even say the right things, but without their own conviction the message comes across as just another management fad. Experienced employees will know that if they keep their heads down, it'll pass like a bad cold.

With the Link 20 questions, managers now have a tool by which they can measure their people's progress toward relationship development with key customers or colleagues: "Where did your key customers go to school? What do they like to do on vacation? What are the biggest challenges they face in their business?" The answers, as I said earlier, are means, not ends.

Managers must also ask, "What have you done with this information? What unexpected, inexpensive, and thoughtful acts have you performed to build your relationship? Where are you on the Relationship Pyramid with your key customers and prospects? How do you plan to move up to the next level?"

Managers should help their people identify the specific prospects, customers, and clients to be targeted. The organization should develop guidelines to identify the customers with which the staff should have meaningful relationships, given that there are not enough resources to have close relationships with everyone.

For that matter, if you want to manage your career more effectively, it is also a sensible idea to target the people in your company with whom you need a better relationship to facilitate better teamwork, get promoted, or obtain vital information from various gatekeepers within the organization. This is neither brown-nosing nor corporate politicking; done correctly, it is improving the organization's effectiveness.

THE SIX DRIVERS OF BUSINESS SUCCESS

In my experience and from my reading, I've found that six factors drive business success. True, one could argue that business success depends on many other factors—product innovation, financial and other controls, efficient marketing, and much more. And I would agree.

I am perhaps oversimplifying to make my points clear. Nevertheless, I would also argue that, as important as other factors may be, a business cannot sustain success without talent, climate, relationships, coaching, effectiveness, and recognition.

Let's talk about each of these in some detail.

Talent

The first job of anybody in a supervisory role is to ensure that the organization has talented and productive people and to replace those who are not. I maintain that the right people not only have the right skills for the job but also know how to build positive relationships. It's the manager's job to retain top talent and to dismiss people who don't do the job.

You are better off having no employee in a given position than an inferior one. When the position is empty, you tend to look for a replacement while other people cover the vacancy. When you carry an inferior employee, the person causes new messes the organization has to clean up.

David Snow is executive director, commercial operations, AstraZeneca LP, and responsible for a $1.3 billion business of hypertension/heart failure brands. He points out that a manager "can spend an inordinate amount of time with the problem children, because you are always going to have them. You are always going to have challenges. If you have a fairly large group of people"—David has had as many as 85 people on his team—"you have a bell curve, and there are going to be some people at the tail who are going to be a problem."

A manager can spend an enormous amount of energy trying to improve their productivity, to bring them up to average. Alternatively, the manager can invest time in the top 10 or 25 percent. Those people, says David, "with a little more help might contribute another 50 to 75 percent and make an astounding difference in the business's performance. I think you have to be careful not to try to become a miracle worker, trying to correct the 10 to 15 percent at the bottom, while ignoring the people at the top."

David says he does his best to help the people who are the most effective to find ways they can be more productive. "It is easy to help people who just can't get enough, who want to develop, who have a sense they are good, but they are not good enough. They want to continue to evolve and develop. That is great stuff. It is easy to help those folks."

Ewell Hopkins at Sapient points out that some salespeople can sell only to certain profiles and to certain types of people. "I have seen sales organizations created with a distinct personality because the guys who run the sales organization hired clones of themselves."

This may not necessarily be a bad thing. "Most people hire and do business with people they feel comfortable with," says Ewell. "If you are selling Mary Kay Cosmetics, getting a bunch of construction workers out there representing your product may not be a good idea, even if they are great salespeople for construction equipment."

Other firms need a diverse sales force because the target market is so diverse. Ewell says, "I have seen business relationships with good old boys work very well, but they can't sell to anybody else. There are some people who don't want to buy anything unless the person selling is over 50. You have to understand we are not all open, receptive, seeking spirits here. A lot of us are pretty closed-minded and have some pretty strong opinions about what is right and wrong."

Climate

Every work environment should include three things:

1. Fun
2. Unity and community
3. Continuous learning

It is the leader's responsibility to create the environment. To create the unity and community, the manager should help people get to know one another within the group. It is hard to have fun with people you don't like, and it is easier to create unity and community when people know one another. That's why it's important for people to create some sort of identity about their group or their department that is bigger than themselves. It gives them something to be proud of. If people are continuously learning—and recognized and rewarded for doing so—an organization, department, or group grows more effective almost by definition. Certainly, it makes fewer mistakes and becomes more efficient.

Relationship-building as an intracompany value may be as important as building relationships outside the company, and, in some situations, it may even be more important. Ray Ozzie, when he was CEO of Groove Networks, a software company, said that when he was building the company, he held biweekly sessions with the entire staff in which somebody from the organization gave a presentation of what they did or what was happening in their part of the world. He did it, he says, "because marketing people often have a negative attitude toward software development people, development people have an attitude toward the finance people, and nobody knows what consulting people do." Getting people to recognize that others in the organization had valid job functions and to see how they contributed to the success of the company was invaluable.

Julie Wroblewski recalls a manager who did this exceptionally well in one of her previous jobs. At the time, Julie and nine others were recent appointees to new, stressful positions around the country. The company brought the group to Atlanta once a quarter, and on one of those nights Julie's manager "invited us into her home. We were able to get together, just the small group of us. She not only had us in her home, she cooked for us. She loved to cook and to entertain."

The experience created such a bond that, although Julie left that job several years ago, the group still keeps in touch. "I never worked harder than I did in that particular position, because I really didn't want to let her down," says Julie. "There was such a bond with the unselfish time she devoted to us. Even though we were stressed out, strapped for time, all the stuff we are even today, it was important for her to get to know the individual and to really let us know how much she cared about us as individuals. She was really a breath of fresh air to work for."

I have invited my staff to our home, and it was rewarding and fruitful in building relationships with the people I worked with. Certainly Julie's manager wanted to share her love of cooking, but whether you have the event catered or do a simple cookout, the results will be much the same. Both cooking and opening your home make a different dynamic from dinner in a restaurant's private room.

The climate is fundamental because, as Dr. Herb True said on an audiotape I heard years ago (*Are You an Amateur or Professional in Selling?*), how people feel determines their behavior more than what they know. We can teach people everything they need to know, but if they don't feel good about their situation, about their work environment, about the people they're working with, about the things they're trying to accomplish, or about all of the above, the likelihood they will be successful drops precipitously.

Relationships

The manager is responsible for a positive relationship with the employee and the employee's positive relationship with the company. If I am running a company, I want to know that my managers have good relationships with their employees rooted in meaningful dialogue.

Meaningful dialogue, you recall, is speaking the truth; it is talking about what is real, important, and factual. You can truly work with people and help them be more productive only when you have meaningful dialogue and they understand you want to help them succeed. In a perfect world, they would want to tell you their issues and real challenges and have more than a surface association.

Because meaningful dialogue comes only with strong, positive relationships, it is another reason why the ability to build relationships is so important for managers. How often have you seen managers crash and burn because they had poor relationships and, therefore, no meaningful dialogue with key people?

David Snow gives an example of how important a good relationship can be with an associate: "I had a guy in finance who was working with me. I was traveling overseas and was in a hotel asleep when he called me. He said, 'I see there's a deadline for some information here and I noticed you are accountable for providing it and we're right up on the deadline. I don't know if you got it in, but I wanted to make sure you got it done.' I could have hugged him. The call saved me an enormous headache, because we were able to talk through the data. He helped me make sure I had the right information and we met the deadline."

If you don't have good relationships with your people, says David, "you can't get where you want to go." A manager needs good relationships "if you want to take people to a higher level and to move beyond a baseline attitude."

He says having an open door policy and managing by walking around has worked well for him, adding, "I really don't want to get voice mail messages. I get a lot of e-mail messages, and while that is good and bad, that is not the way I want to manage. I want to manage by looking people in the eye and getting the context for what they're feeling and for the challenges they're facing, and to interact with them. So, I frequently get up and go to them."

David does hold brief, routine meetings in his office, but more often he is out of his office to see what is going on. "I think I get more out of that, and we get a lot more accomplished that way because we knock down questions and challenges and just move on. We don't have to have formal meetings to make a decision."

He holds everybody to a professional standard. He expects his people to carry themselves in a professional manner and to do the right thing. "By doing so, I think people respond. If they make a decision that might not have been the decision I would have made, and they come and talk to me about it, we look at it and discuss it. There are a lot of different ways to skin the horse. I don't go in saying my idea is the only one that will get you where you want to go. I hold people accountable for good decision-making. If a bad outcome results from a bad decision—that's a problem. But if a bad outcome results from a reasonable decision, then that's business, and it could happen to anyone."

At the risk of being redundant, let me say once again: Business relationships are not the same as friendships. This is particularly true for a manager who may have to dismiss an associate. I once asked the exceptionally successful CEO of a $2 billion corporation what elements of his job were the most stressful. He said that nothing matched having to let go someone with whom he had worked for years, but who, through alcohol, dishonesty, or some other serious issue, was no longer an effective executive. "You've been to their home, you know their children, but you can't let your compassionate feelings for the individual jeopardize the organization."

In a perfect world, your good relationship would have helped turn the situation around before it became a threat to the organization or the individual's career. This is not a perfect world, however, and the effective manager walks a line between callous disregard for human weakness ("Drunk at the Christmas party? You're fired!") and misguided pity ("You wrecked the seventh company car? You poor thing!").

Building strong, positive relationships with employees where meaningful dialogue is the rule and not the exception greatly improves the likelihood you will perform exceptionally as a leader. Among the worst managers are those who surround themselves with toadies and sycophants. You cannot have a strong relationship with someone you do not respect, and someone you respect and who respects you will, on occasion, tell you you're wrong.

Use what you learn here to build a successful work environment in which meaningful dialogue thrives.

Coaching

The manager must be able to coach, to teach staff how to be more effective. Essentially, the manager's job is to work with the employee to figure out the next best thing to do to be more effective. In many cases, that may be relationship-building.

In other cases, it may be finding a mentor. Both Lance Perkins at General Electric Medical Systems and Ewell Hopkins offer the same advice, "Get a sales mentor." Says Ewell, "Have somebody who you can bounce ideas off of—it is the best thing in the world. Find out what works in your industry and what people have done and what is going on. It makes a difference. Don't try to do it alone."

Lance feels he was successful in pharmaceutical sales because of his mentor. A representative sharing the same territory, selling different products, had a brain abscess and seizures and could not drive. "It was a perfect fit, because I had a chance to drive him around for three months. This guy had been in pharmaceutical sales for twenty-five years, and one of the things he taught me, in just watching how he dealt with physicians, was you have to sell doctors the way they want to be sold. You can't just have one-size-fits-all."

Keep in mind, however, that coaching is rarely effective if the relationship isn't strong. For coaching to work, the coach must be good at coaching, but the coached must also have a keen desire to listen, to learn, and to do what is suggested. Coaching doesn't work unless it's a two-way street. The manager should be good at coaching, but people have to want to learn.

If the relationship isn't strong, it makes coaching much more difficult. If the relationship is strong, it is more likely people will want to learn. When athletes, students, or employees trust, admire, and respect their coaches, they want to listen when the coaches counsel them.

The best coaching builds on people's strengths. As Phil Jackson once said, "You don't build people up by tearing them down." The best coaches know the strengths of their charges and build on them.

Effectiveness

The manager is responsible for the representative's effectiveness. Sales effectiveness is the function of two things: the ability to build meaningful, positive business relationships and the ability to make compelling sales calls that provoke thought and engender meaningful dialogue with customers and prospects.

The leader is responsible for accountability. The problem with relationship-building in the past has been its subjectivity. Formerly, a manager might encourage salespeople to build relationships with key customers, but had no objective way to determine whether they were making progress or not.

By using the process this book describes—and the fact that it is a process—a manager is able to hold people more accountable. Granted, where someone stands on the Relationship Pyramid (or says he or she stands with his key customers) is still not perfectly objective, but it is a beginning step in the relationship-building process. The process will still open the eyes of those representatives who in the past may not honestly have had the best rapport with their customers.

Lance Perkins notes that consultants, academics, and business books all say that business success rests on customers. No customers, no business. The problem, he also notes, is that it is too easy to lose focus, to forget what you're there to do—to teach the value of your product and services while understanding the way the customer wants to be sold. Too many sales representatives do not understand how to bend and flex and adapt their style to the hodgepodge of all the different customer styles.

A manager who has trained his or her staff in this relationship-building process has the right not only to ask, but also to expect people to get the answers to at least the 20 questions. The manager has a right to expect that once the salespeople obtain the answers to those 20 questions with their key customers, they will do things that are unexpected, inexpensive, and thoughtful. The manager can also act as a clearinghouse for ideas so that the less inspired members of the team can be helped by the more inspired to come up with unexpected, inexpensive, and thoughtful acts.

Recognition

Recognition is both formal and informal; it is for the individual and for the team. Many books have been written on recognition, so I am not going to spend space on it here.[1] If you have a strong relationship with the person you want to recognize, you should know how he or she wants to be recognized. Some people don't want any sort of formal display; others crave formal attention. You don't buy a bottle of wine for somebody who doesn't drink or take somebody who doesn't eat Indian food to an Indian restaurant. The key question for you as a leader is: Are you providing enough recognition and the right kind of recognition for your key employees? Many times a simple congratulations or thank-you card does wonders for morale.

I should also note that these six drivers for success are intertwined. Each depends on the other five; none is independent. Fortunately, if you are able to attract and retain people with the right skills who are able to build relationships, they tend to create an enjoyable working environment, engender a sense of unity and community, encourage continuous learning, and coach and reward. Each element supports and promotes the others.

Nevertheless, some managers feel all this is not hardheaded enough; they look at the Army (or the Marines) for their management model. Few military officers worry about creating a climate of fun. They believe in command and control.

PROBLEMS WITH COMMAND AND CONTROL

Many executives still feel the only way to manage is with many rules and reports. They say, "You can't manage what you can't measure," which is true, but then they often measure the wrong things—the number of calls per day, the timeliness of call reports, or customer satisfaction scores—surrogates for what the company really wants.

Operationally excellent and fundamentally sound companies do much better in any economy than companies that are not operationally excellent. What makes companies different is the people they employ. The truth is organizations don't perform; people do. Therefore, an organization's ability to manage the right activity is absolutely key. It does not make sense to demand reports for the sake of the report. This is the "rearranging deck chairs on the Titanic" syndrome.

I know that many companies are activity oriented, not achievement oriented. But ultimately, if you are managing a sales territory, your success is far less a function of the instructions you take from headquarters than the actions you take in the field every single day. If the instructions you receive conflict with the actions you know are necessary to be successful—to build relationships, to make sales—I suggest you focus on what it takes to be successful. In this situation, perhaps you should develop the relationship with your superior so it is possible to have a meaningful dialogue about what needs to be done or what changes should occur. This could well be the first relationship on which you focus.

Managements install rules and procedures and reporting systems because they believe there is a direct relationship or link between activity and achievement. They believe that if salespeople make 10 . . . or 15 . . . or 20 . . . or some arbitrary number of calls a day, every day, the activity will result in more sales. They even have consultants with computer models built by very smart people (who may never have made a sales call) to tell them exactly how many calls it will take for success.

Ultimately, however, the salesperson who breaks sales records while averaging, for example, five calls—but the right five calls—a day will be rewarded handsomely; the salesperson who makes the prescribed number of calls but never sells much has a bleak future. Sooner or later the activities will become less important than the accomplishment. For the individual salesperson or manager, the accomplishment is always more important than the activity. And if it isn't for management, it certainly is for the shareholders.

Salespeople who manage to meet with prospects or customers must decide the next thing to do to move those people closer to buying. That is the fundamental decision. The situation should always be a combination of what the salespeople do to build the relationship, what they do to understand what that customer desires, and trying to determine how a product or service can meet the need. Salespeople should not focus on the relationship exclusively, nor should they focus on only the product or service.

In my experience, the salespeople who can give attention to both the relationship and the business need are the most successful. The point is to create productive professional relationships. Many times, these can become personal relationships, although very few will become lasting deep personal friendships. Nonetheless, productive professional relationships are enjoyable, and they make your life more fun and your career more productive.

The salesperson's goal, always, is to help clients understand that the organization's product or service is worthwhile. (If it truly is not, they should not be trying to build a relationship—at least not with these prospects.) It is much easier to convey that worth when there is a good relationship. Remember that where trust and rapport are strong, selling pressure will seem weak. When buyers believe sellers truly have their best interests at heart, they listen with an open mind.

Organizations spend a great deal of time and money trying to motivate employees. But I believe that all motivation is self-motivation. What organizations and leaders need to do is create the climate in which people want to motivate themselves.

JOB SATISFACTION AND DISSATISFACTION

If you're a manager, building relationships with and among your associates is related to Frederick Herzberg's work on job satisfaction. I would argue that workers who have many strong, positive relationships with customers and colleagues are more satisfied with their jobs than those who have few positive relationships.

More than 40 years ago, Herzberg developed his two-factor theory of motivation.[2] He asked 200 accountants and engineers to recall times when they had been satisfied and motivated and times when they were dissatisfied and unmotivated. He found that different kinds of factors were associated with satisfaction and with dissatisfaction. A person, for example, might cite "low pay" as a cause for dissatisfaction, but would not necessarily cite "high pay" as a cause for satisfaction. Indeed, these interviewees mentioned different factors such as recognition and accomplishment as a cause for satisfaction and motivation. In fact, contrary to what common sense might suggest, most studies have found that recognition is more powerful than money in encouraging job satisfaction.

The traditional view of job satisfaction had held that satisfaction and dissatisfaction were at opposite ends of a continuum. An employee might be satisfied, dissatisfied, or somewhere in between. Herzberg's interviews identified two different dimensions, one ranging from satisfaction to no satisfaction, the other ranging from dissatisfaction to no dissatisfaction, which is not the same as satisfaction.

Factors associated with the satisfaction dimension—the so-called motivation factors—include achievement, recognition, the work itself, responsibility, and advancement and growth. These are all related to the work content.

Factors associated with the dissatisfaction dimension—the so-called hygiene factors—include supervisors, working conditions, interpersonal relations, pay and security, and company policies and administration. These are all related to the work environment.

Herzberg's research suggests that a manager who uses only one dimension or the other—for example, only good working conditions and above-average pay—to encourage employees to do their best probably will not be successful. To encourage employees (reduce turnover and absenteeism, improve customer satisfaction, and all the other good things that come with enthusiastic employees) and produce a high level of satisfaction, managers must also offer responsibility and the opportunity to advance.

Once you decide it is important for your people to build relationships, you have to make sure they have the right targets and hold them accountable for those targets. You must regularly inspect the activities and the information gathering and recognize and reward those who are doing a good job. If you do those things, you will dramatically increase the likelihood that you will be successful.

It would not hurt if you targeted your own key business contacts with whom to build relationships. Ideally, every level of management would have some of its own internal as well as external customers to target. If I were the president of Dial, my target would be somebody at Walmart. If I were the president of a pharmaceutical company, the target might be the most influential cardiologist in the country or the Mayo Clinic. If I were the president of Philips Lighting, it might be Home Depot. If I were the head of marketing, it would be the head of sales. Ideally, organizations would think about relationships and hold people accountable for relationship development at different levels.

PROBLEMS WITH SALES TRAINING

Why doesn't most sales training work as well as we hoped it would when we delivered it?

Because most companies never clearly define what selling is to their salespeople and, therefore, the training addresses peripheral or irrelevant issues. Because the training often does not connect with the real and immediate concerns of the salespeople, they tend to regard it lightly. Salespeople tend to apply very little of what they hear—only those things that seem most immediately relevant to their situation.

Organizations do not usually build in the accountability necessary to ensure that the sales training takes effect. Accountability is first a function of inspecting. Effective managers let their people know that they will be paying attention to something (whatever the "something" may be) and provide recognition and reward to those who respond. It does not have to be part of performance appraisal or salary evaluation, though if you can make it so, much the better.

When I listen to some of the things people say they learn in my seminars—such as "I am going to listen better" or "I am going to ask more probing questions"—it sounds positive, but none of that is actionable. How does a manager hold people accountable for "listening better" or "probing questions"?

Unfortunately for sales trainers, 96 percent of everything people learn is forgotten in 30 days. Studies have found that people forget about 30 percent of what they learn within the first hour. By the end of two weeks, they've forgotten 74 percent. Salespeople (and others) simply don't remember much of what they hear in training.

When managers give sales representatives (or others) very specific questions or information they should obtain about prospects and customers, they can hold them accountable for the acquisition of that information. When managers give representatives specific ideas of what they can do with the information—ideas for unexpected, inexpensive, and unselfish acts—they can hold people accountable for performing those acts.

I do not believe managers can do it with large numbers of people; there are not enough hours in the day. If managers are going to inspect, they have to inspect a reasonable number of people; exactly how many will vary by the organization and the manager's personality. Hold representatives responsible for five key customers, not 25.

In addition to the lack of accountability, salespeople by and large have a negative view of what they do for a living. I've heard Ron Willingham say in his training sessions dozens of times that if you play word association games with salespeople, more than 90 percent of the responses will be negative when you say "sales." Even salespeople have disapproving attitudes toward other salespeople.

So even among many people who sell for a living, "sales" can carry a negative connotation. Salespeople often wind up with a cognitive dissonance—they are asked to do something they are against doing at their very core. They do it because they want to feed their families.

To overcome this disconnect, we ask them to put pressure on customers or prospects, we give orders, we teach negotiating skills to overcome sales resistance, we explain how to cope with price resistance, and we teach closing techniques. We try to put across all these hard things. But most people are not hard; most are soft. Many salespeople do these things as directed by their organizations, but they feel uncomfortable doing them.

SELLING IS LEARNING AND TEACHING

Managers can overcome the cognitive dissonance by teaching people a different definition of selling. Selling is two things: learning and teaching.

Selling is learning what people want and helping them get it. As I've said before, people often don't know what they want because they have no concept of what is available. It is the job of the account executive and the salesperson to know enough about the customers' and the competitors' businesses to be able to ask the right questions, to uncover what people are truly looking for.

(Again, I use salesperson for convenience. The principle is the same for anyone who wants to persuade a colleague or a client to follow a course of action.)

When you ask questions as part of a meaningful dialogue, it is a lot easier to discover what someone needs or wants, which is one reason that building strong relationships is important. You should spend time thinking about what questions you need answered to learn whether your product or service fits that prospect. If you ask the right questions, for the right reasons, prospects will decide themselves whether they are prospects or not and the salespeople will not have forced the issue.

Selling is also teaching. In every successful sale, some education takes place. Customers learn something they did not know before, and that knowledge causes them to want to buy. But if selling is teaching, it means salespeople must be teachers. And what makes a good teacher?

Think back to the teachers who were most effective in your life. If they were like mine, they were not the ones who lectured the entire time. Few people—high school and college students, spouses and children, customers and colleagues—enjoy being lectured to. They may need the information, but they don't want to learn it in a lecture, which is the way representatives generally perform during a sales call.

The most effective teachers were the ones who encouraged mean-ingful dialogue. They got you involved, forced you to do one thing that rarely happens in sales calls today: to think. Salespeople cannot change behavior if they do not get prospects to think.

Two points: Since people often don't know what they want, sales-people have to help them see what they want; and if people want what the company does not have, salespeople have no right to sell them what they do have.

When most sales representatives hear that—if someone wants what we do not have, we have no right to sell them what we do have—the game changes dramatically. Salespeople feel an incredible freedom to be customer-focused, to help customers solve their problems, and to be focused no longer on what the company is trying to push.

That realization may encourage bright people to work only for companies that have a reasonable value premise, which is probably not a bad thing. But if your sales representatives understand this concept and can practice it, it is incredibly liberating because they stop caring about the sale. As I said earlier, the less you care about the sale, the more you sell. Caring about trying to find out what is right for the customer is what works.

Zig Ziglar says in his book *See You at the Top* that selling is transference of feeling.[3] People cannot transfer feelings they don't have. If managers try to get salespeople to transfer a feeling they don't have, they are not going to be very effective at it. At some subconscious level, customers will sense the sales representative's manipulation. When sales representatives do not feel good about asking customers to do (or not do) something, they communicate that feeling.

Last, selling is about making sure that people understand what it is you are trying to get them to do.

WHAT MANAGERS SHOULD BE DOING

Sales managers should be helping their salespeople identify the key prospects, customers, and clients the organization should target. There should be some organizational imperative/mandate/guidelines/direction about the kinds of customers with whom the firm wants to have relationships. This should be limited because there is only so much time and only so much inspecting any manager can do.

At the same time, I believe that if a manager can focus his or her staff on building strong business relationships with a small number of people, the staff will begin to build relationships naturally in everything that they do. The spillover effect will be huge.

Typically, regional managers have a number of district managers reporting to them, who in turn have a number of sales representatives in the field. Regional managers should identify the critical customers in their region, regardless of the district, and they must ensure that the company maintains excellent relationships. District managers should have their own lists. Who are the key customers in the district? In addition, the sales representatives should have their lists.

Everybody in the chain needs to think about the key contacts with whom they need to develop relationships. If a representative leaves (it can happen) and the district manager has not developed a relationship with one or more key customers, the manager may be in jeopardy. If a district manager leaves and the regional manager has not developed relationships with key customers, the regional manager faces a crisis. What information about the key customers and what they treasure can we share with the new representative?

A COACHING PROCESS FOR RELATIONSHIP DEVELOPMENT

The fundamental objective of all coaching is to help another succeed. I believe that every sales call should be planned carefully with the goal of moving the customer closer to buying the company's product or service. This requires that sales representatives always be seeking the next best thing to do. The representative's call plan should answer one question: "What is the next best thing to do to advance the customer toward the sale?" The answer to that question should also make call planning simple (especially if the representative has kept good sales call records).

The coach needs to help the sales representatives determine the next best thing to do, which is central to relationship development of targeted customers. This coaching process has four steps:

1. What is the situation?
2. What do you think must be done to make the sale or move the customer forward?
3. What can you suggest to do next?
4. What do we agree you will do next?

Here are some suggested approaches to flesh out this coaching process.

What Is the Situation?

Before making any suggestions about what the sales representative should do next, the manager should obtain as much information as possible about the situation. The following questions should get you the information you need:

- Where would you say [this targeted prospect or customer] sees you on the Relationship Pyramid right now, and why do you say that?
- Talk to me about the relationship development process as it relates to this targeted prospect. What do you think of __ [the prospect]?
- What do you think the prospect thinks about you?
- Will your current mind-set about __ [the prospect] get you the relationship we need? If not, how do you suggest we deal with this?
- What specific questions from the 20 in Chapter 4 have you asked? Tell me everything you know that is important to and absolutely true for this prospect—especially what the person has told you.
- Based on what you have learned about __ [the prospect], what specific actions (unexpected, inexpensive, and thoughtful) have you taken that demonstrate you care, that you are unselfish, and that you are genuinely interested in them?
- What other relationships do you have that might help you with __ [the prospect]?

What Does the Representative Think Should Be Done?

Once you have a grasp of all that the representative knows and has done so far to build the relationship, the next step is to ask the representative for his or her ideas for the next best thing to do. Good questions to ask include:

- Based on all you have learned so far, what question or questions from the list of 20 should you ask the next time you see __ [the prospect]?
- Based on what you know right now, what actions (unexpected, inexpensive, thoughtful) could you take that would

245

demonstrate your care/concern about what's important to __ [the prospect]?

- What thoughts do you have about what I, or someone else here at the company, might do to assist your efforts to build a meaningful relationship with __ [the prospect]?

What Can You Suggest?

As a manager and experienced industry veteran, it is likely you will have ideas about the next best thing to do. Think about several things as you are contemplating what you would suggest to do next.

- Who do you know who might be able to assist in this process of relationship development?
- What other areas of common interest should the representative be exploring with the targeted customer?
- Think about other representatives in similar situations and brainstorm some next steps.

Never forget that what must be uncovered and acted on is what is important to the targeted customer. Think through additional ways to learn what is important and half the battle is won.

What Do You and the Representative Agree Should Be Done?

At this point, the coaching process should move from fact-finding and idea-generation to accountability. Get representatives to agree on the specific actions they will take over the next two or three months to build the relationships that are crucial to their success.

Specific action plans should be ongoing with the representatives' entire targeted list, and your biweekly conversation should simply be updates of the agreed-to plans.

Figure 14.1 suggests the competency toward which salespeople (and others) should be working, with ten behavioral examples that define the competency.

Figure 14.1
What Is Relationship-Building Competency?

Relationship-building competency establishes and maintains effective relationships with customers and colleagues and gains their trust and respect.

When Does Someone Have It?

1. Develops relationships with key customers through deep knowledge of the customer's business and organization and provides breakthrough insights that customers value.

2. Demonstrates a caring, sensitive, and sincere nature to get closer to customers.

3. Routinely seeks to learn from customers what they "treasure" professionally and personally.

4. Uses knowledge of what customers treasure to plan relationship-building conversations in addition to presenting products and their potential benefits.

5. Uses knowledge of what customers treasure to do inexpensive, unexpected, and thoughtful actions.

6. Employs relationships to gain routine access and make sales calls characterized by meaningful dialogue.

7. Leverages the excellent relationships they have to make connections and gain access to other important but difficult-to-reach customers.

8. Consistently demonstrates the ability to understand the customer's perspective and not appear biased in the customer's eyes through actions, language, and probing.

9. Demonstrates a balance between the caring dimension necessary for building relationships and the assertive dimension necessary to create results.

10. Demonstrates a long-term view of relationships and their importance and not a short-term view of relationships as a means to quick sales results.

BUILD RELATIONSHIPS ROUTINELY, CONSCIOUSLY, DELIBERATELY

I truly believe that if managers incorporate relationship-building into the fabric of their organizations, their people will be more effective and happier in their jobs. As I said at the beginning of this book, virtually everyone knows how to build strong relationships; they just don't know how to do it routinely, consciously, and deliberately.

Because most people have built relationships, the process is less alien to them than many traditional sales techniques—the trial close, for example. When your associates see the value of improving their relationships with key prospects, customers, clients, and colleagues, they will, I suspect, embrace the process and enjoy the benefits of the Relationship Edge.

Management is still responsible for finding talented employees, creating a conducive climate, building its own winning relationships, coaching the staff, promoting effectiveness, and providing recognition and reward. Note that these imperatives apply to virtually any organization, not only sales. They are as important for a nonprofit as for a retail store, as important for a manufacturer as for a research laboratory.

I also believe that organizations should clearly understand what selling is—learning and teaching—and with that understanding improve their sales training. With continuous reinforcement and accountability by management, an organization can absorb relationship-building into the fabric of the business.

I know that what I've described in this book is easier to say than to do. But I also know that readers who fill out the forms in the book, who deliberately and routinely ask the 20 questions, and who act on the answers build many strong, positive business relationships. Perhaps you will not build them with every single customer or colleague, but you will build them with enough people that your life—business and personal—will be richer, more rewarding, and a lot more fun.

I wish you every success.

NOTES

Chapter 1 Relationships Are Everything

1. Adapted from Ron Willingham, *Integrity Selling: How to Succeed in Selling in the Competitive Years Ahead* (New York: Doubleday, 1989), 50.

Chapter 3 How to Build a Relationship

1. "Study Sheds Light on What Makes People Shy," reported at www.livescience.com/health/shy-brain-process-information-differently-100405.html.

2. Harvey Mackay, *Swim with the Sharks without Being Eaten Alive* (New York: William Morrow & Co., 1989), 27.

3. Zig Ziglar, *See You at the Top* (Gretna, LA: Pelican Publishing, 1982).

4. "Social Media at Deloitte," May 2010, 5.

5. Robert B. Cialdini, *Influence: Science and Practice* (Boston: Allyn & Bacon, 2001), 167.

Chapter 4 Ask the Twenty Questions

1. Dale Carnegie, *How to Win Friends and Influence People* (New York: Pocket Books, 1982), 54.

Chapter 5 Ask the Questions Properly

1. Robert B. Cialdini, *Influence: Science and Practice* (Boston: Allyn & Bacon, 2001), 150.

Chapter 6 Probe for Small World Connections

1. John Maxwell, *Becoming a Person of Influence* (Thomas Nelson Publishers, 1997), 43.

2. David Lewis, "Making It Work," *Fairfield Country Business Journal* (June 4, 2001): 11.

3. Ann Field, "Networks Open Doors for Small Companies," *New York Times*, June 8, 2003, section 3, 12.

4. Zig Ziglar, *Secrets of Closing the Sale* (Old Tappan, NJ: Fleming H. Revell Co., 1984), 18.

Chapter 7 Build Relationships on Actions

1. Dennis Murray, "Gifts: What's All the Fuss About?" *Medical Economics* (October 11, 2002): 119.

2. Melinda Ligos, "Gimme, Gimme, Gimme!" *Sales & Marketing Management* (March 2002): 33.

3. Linda, Richardson, *Stop Telling, Start Selling: How to Use Customer-Focused Dialogue to Close Sales* (New York: McGraw Hill, 1998).

Chapter 8 Map Your Key Relationships

1. Brian Uzzi and Shannon Dunlap, "How to Build Your Network," *Harvard Business Review* (December 2005): 53.

2. You can find these at www.yammer.com/; www.jivesoftware.com/about; and www.salesforce.com/chatter/.

3. Brian, Dumaine, "Buffett's Mr. Fix-it." *Fortune*, August 16, 2010, 86.

Chapter 9 Hop from One Pyramid to Another

1. For a look as the scope and variety of these sites, check out the Wikipedia listing at http://en.wikipedia.org/wiki/Social_networking_websites.

2. Brian Uzzi and Shannon Dunlap, "How to Build Your Network," *Harvard Business Review* (December 2005): 54.

Chapter 10 Gain Respect Thirteen Ways

1. Les Giblin, *How to Have Confidence and Power in Dealing with People* (Englewood Cliffs, NJ: Prentice-Hall, 1956), 3.

Chapter 11 Write Clear, Specific Goals

1. Ron Willingham, *When Good Isn't Good Enough* (New York, Doubleday, 1988).

2. Maxwell Maltz, *Psycho-Cybernetics* (New York, Pocket Books, 1989).

3. Og Mandino, *The Greatest Salesman in the World* (New York, Frederick Fell Publishers, 1968), 68.

Chapter 12 Maintain Your Meaningful Relationships

1. Frederick F. Reichheld, "Learning from Customer Defections," *Harvard Business Review* (March/April 1996): 56–69.

2. Zig Ziglar, *Raising Positive Kids in a Negative World* (New York: Ballantine Books, 1996).

3. Stephen R. Covey, *The 7 Habits of Highly Effective People* (New York: Simon & Schuster, 1989), 150.

4. David A. Whetten and Kim S. Cameron, *Developing Management Skills* (Upper Saddle River, NJ: Prentice Hall, 2002), 115.

5. Tim Sanders, *Love Is the Killer App: How to Win Business and Influence Friends* (New York: Crown Business, 2002), 37–55.

6. Harvey Mackay, *Swim with the Sharks without Being Eaten Alive* (New York: William Morrow & Co., 1989).

Chapter 13   Use Social Media to Build Relationships

1. You can find a good introduction to LinkedIn at: http://learn.linkedin.com/; http://linkedintelligence.com/smart-ways-to-use-linkedin/; and http://blog.guykawasaki.com/2007/01/ten_ways_to_use.html#axzz0wz9JIcvh.
   To Twitter at: www.mahalo.com/how-to-use-twitter; and www.doshdosh.com/ways-you-can-use-twitter/.
   To Facebook at: www.mahalo.com/how-to-use-facebook and www.readwriteweb.com/archives/how_to_use_facebook_5_tips_for_better_social_networking.php.
   To YouTube at: www.mahalo.com/how-to-use-youtube-like-a-pro and www.youtube.com/t/ngo_tips.

2. Richard Wray and Charles Arthur, "Vodafone suspends employee after obscene tweet," www.guardian.co.uk/technology/2010/feb/05/vodafone-twitter-obscene-tweet.

3. Rod Kirby, "The Used Car Salesman's Guide to Social Media Marketing," November 23, 2009, www.rodkirby.com/archives/1833.

4. www.chrisconrey.com/social-media-sales/.

5. Chris Conrey, "The First and Only Rule of Social Media for Salesmen," *Conrey Is for Closers,* December 9, 2009, www.chrisconrey.com/social-media-sales/.

6. Brett Borders, "6 Tips for Creating 'Sticky' Social Relationships," *Social Media Rockstar,* August 24, 2009, http://socialmediarockstar.com/5-tips-for-creating-sticky-social-relationships.

7. Dave Johnson, "Why Mobile E-mail Signatures Can Hurt Your Business Relationships," July 9, 2009, www.bnet.com/blog/businesstips/why-mobile-e-mail-signatures-can-hurt-your-business-relationships/8083.

Chapter 14   And What If You're the Boss?

1. You may want to look at *Encouraging the Heart: A Leader's Guide to Rewarding and Recognizing Others* by James M. Kouzes and Barry Z. Posner (San Francisco, Jossey-Bass, 2003); or *Sales Rewards and Incentives* by John E. Fisher (Hoboken: John Wiley & Sons, 2003).

2. Frederick Herzberg, Bernard Mausner, and Barbara Snyderman, *The Motivation to Work* (New York: John Wiley & Sons, 1959).

3. Zig Ziglar, *See You at the Top* (Gretna, LA: Pelican Publishing, 1982).

INDEX

INDEX

INDEX